get ready to smile

The beloved cupcake gets my nod for food of the year—make that any year. It's chic and elegant, cozy, comforting, and cute. Cupcakes are easy to prepare and taste of all flavors of the rainbow. A cupcake is a sweet handful that needs no knife, no fork. You just peel back the paper and eat. My cupcake world is one of great pleasure, and I'd like to welcome you to it.

KEY LIME PIE CUPCAKES PAGE 75

ORANGE MARMALADE RICOTTA CUPCAKES PAGE 70

CHOCOLATE ALMOND CUPCAKES PAGE 41

HOT FUDGE SPUMONI ICE CREAM CAKES PAGE 47

No one outgrows cupcakes. Just because you're all grown up doesn't mean you can't indulge. In fact, cupcakes—from decadent chocolate to mouth-puckering Key lime— are all about indulgence. And they're the perfect ending to your next dinner party or casual buffet.

cupcakes

Shower them with coconut. Slather them with whipped cream. Fill them with surprises. Cupcakes are a class act.

RED VELVET CUPCAKES PAGE 36

COCONUT SNOWBALLS PAGE 66

with class

MINI LEMON CURD CUPCAKES PAGE 63

WARM
CHOCOLATE
CUPCAKES
WITH MOLTEN
CENTERS
PAGE 29

cupcakes for kids

When you're a child, cupcakes look larger than life. And when they take on extra personality, they're even more fun than any birthday party game. Who wouldn't be charmed by these whimsical butterflies, monkeys, caramel apples, ice cream sundaes, and groovy tie-dyed cupcakes? To kids, the cupcake is saying, "Let's get this party started!"

BUTTERFLY CUPCAKES PAGE 97

MONSTER MONKEYS PAGE 109

TIE-DYE CUPCAKES PAGE 155

PRETTY IN PINK CUPCAKES PAGE 106

THE BEST BIRTHDAY CUPCAKES PAGE 138

PLUM GOOD CUPCAKES PAGE 152

LEMONADE ANGEL CAKES PAGE 101

NEOPOLITAN SUNDAE CUPCAKES PAGE 158

CARAMEL
SPICED
APPLE
CUPCAKES
PAGE 144

celebration cupcakes

Should you need a reason to bake cupcakes, just check your calendar. The months are filled with special days and holidays, all deserving of a festive treat. Bake sprinkle-covered, sweet-faced chocolate groundhogs or Easter baskets topped with coconut grass.

EASTER BASKET CUPCAKES PAGE 191

GROUNDHOG DAY CUPCAKES PAGE 176

FIREWORKS CONFETTI CUPCAKES PAGE 200

KISS ME CAKES PAGE 179

Surprise your valentine with a chocolate heart topped with raspberries or a delicate Strawberry Rose Cake. Dazzle everyone with Fireworks Confetti Cupcakes on the Fourth of July.

STRAWBERRY ROSE CAKES PAGE 182

celebrate some more

As the year moves into autumn, cupcakes can take on the guise of pumpkins, spooky spiders, dapper snowmen, even festively wrapped holiday presents. Buy shiny foil liners for more razzle-dazzle.

HOLIDAY GIFT CUPCAKES PAGE 216

HALLOWEEN SPIDER CUPCAKES

PAGE 203

SNOWMAN
CUPCAKES
PAGE 213

Stock up on orange and red sugar sprinkles, and try your hand at building an easy marshmallow-topped cupcake snowman. Let the children and grandchildren help assemble these recipes, sip hot cocoa together, and share memories from your childhood.

muffins:
breakfast cupcakes

MINI PEACH MUFFINS AND FRUIT KEBABS PAGE 270

For those of you who like to start the day with a home-baked muffin, here are some moist, fresh recipes to help you rise and shine. Crunchy toppings and lots of fruit replace the sweet icings of their cakey counterparts. And do they ever smell and taste good first thing in the morning.

PUMPKIN MUFFINS WITH CHOCOLATE CHIPS PAGE 252

DOUBLE LEMON POPPY SEED CHEESECAKE MUFFINS PAGE 244

SWEET
POTATO
CASSEROLE
MUFFINS
PAGE 250

BANANA MUFFINS WITH BIG BLACKBERRIES & SUGAR CRUST PAGE 226

CARROT CAKE MUFFINS WITH
A CREAM CHEESE
SURPRISE
PAGE 254

BLUEBERRY YOGURT STREUSEL MUFFINS AND PINEAPPLE MUFFINS WITH COCONUT CRUMBLE PAGE 222

cupcake cousins

With a cupcake pan and a collection of easy recipes, you'll turn out restaurant-style desserts made from ingredients in your pantry and freezer.

FROZEN ICE CREAM CUPCAKES PAGE 282

PEACH COBBLER CUPCAKES PAGE 292

These aren't traditional cupcakes—although they probably wish they were—but they are cupcake size and just right for single portions.

MINI STRAWBERRY TRIFLES PAGE 277

FRESH RASPBERRY CREAM CAKES PAGE 284

LITTLE CHOCOLATE BAR CAKES PAGE 288

cupcake creations

By chance, do you play with your food? Your children's Legos? Then you may be a cupcake architect, someone who needs to arrange cupcakes just so, like using them to spell out a name or something visual. This chapter will help you turn ordinary cupcakes into masterpieces that set the tone for your next birthday celebration, bridal shower, or holiday party.

**ICE CREAM
CONE CAKES
PAGE 312**

All the instructions are here to help you make cupcake cones, wreaths, bouquets, purses, and more.

CUPCAKE BOUQUET
PAGE 303

CUPCAKE PURSE
PAGE 309

Anne

CUPCAKE WREATH
PAGE 301

a cupcake wedding cake

Cloaked in sumptuous frosting, bedecked with gold dragées, and decorated with roses and other favorite flowers, cupcakes come together easily and elegantly to form a new kind of wedding cake. How can anyone not smile and say, "I do" to cupcakes!

CUPCAKE
WEDDING CAKE
PAGE 314

CUPCAKES

FROM THE

CakeDoctor
mix

CUPCAKES

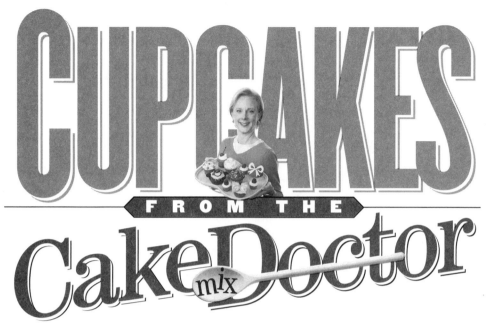

FROM THE

Cake mix Doctor

by ANNE BYRN

Photographs by Susan Goldman

WORKMAN PUBLISHING · NEW YORK

▲▲▲

This book is for my sisters, Ginger and Susan, remembering the birthdays, bake sales, and cupcakes of our childhood

▼▼▼

Library of Congress Cataloging-in-Publication Data
Byrn, Anne
Cupcakes from the cake mix doctor / by Anne Byrn.
p. cm.
ISBN-13: 978-0-7611-3548-7; ISBN-10: 0-7611-3548-0 (alk. paper)
ISBN-13: 978-0-7611-3819-8; ISBN-10: 0-7611-3819-6 (hardcover)
1. Cake I. Title
TX771.B985 2005
641.8'653—dc22   2004066423

Cover design: Paul Hanson
Book design: Lisa Hollander and Lori S. Malkin
Photography: Susan Goldman
Food and prop stylist: Karen J. M. Tack

Workman books are available at special discounts when purchased in bulk
for premiums and sales promotions as well as for fund raising or educational use.
Special editions or book excerpts can be created to specification.
For details, contact the Special Sales Director at the address below.

Workman Publishing Company, Inc.
708 Broadway
New York, NY 10003-9555
www.workman.com
www.cakemixdoctor.com

The Cake Mix Doctor is a registered trademark of Anne Byrn.

Printed in U.S.A.
First printing: March 2005
10 9 8 7 6 5 4 3 2 1

Acknowledgments

❖ ❖ ❖

When I think back over the past six years, I know I never would have been able to write four books had it not been for my family and friends. Thanks go, again, to my husband, John, for being patient and putting up with my stress as a deadline approached. And I thank my children, Kathleen, Litton, and John, for their humor, enthusiasm, and resourcefulness in managing things on their own while I finished up *Cupcakes*. Their friends may think it's enviable to have your mother be the Cake Mix Doctor. And they may think our kitchen counters are always lined with cupcakes (they are from time to time), but in reality this mother is like all working moms, short on time and appreciative of help from everyone around the house!

Thanks go to Martha Bowden, my right arm, a true friend and a gifted baker who has helped me meet deadlines time and again. Her creative energy was invaluable to this book, especially when it came to putting together the kids' and celebration chapters. To Lucille Osborn, my friend in Pennsylvania who is a wonderful food stylist, thank you for your help in planning those holiday cupcakes, even if it was via the telephone! Lucille helped me visualize many of these cupcakes before I set out to make them doable for you.

To my friend Mindy Merrell in Nashville, thank you for your wit and help with the muffins. To my agent

Nancy Crossman, I cannot imagine these projects without you there in the wings. To Anne Hathaway in Atlanta, thank you for your cupcake ideas. Thanks also to Amy Baron, who, when this book is published, will be studying in college. Amy was my intern for a month during this project, washing dishes, shopping, planning recipes, baking cupcakes, typing recipes, and offering her two cents. You're a real foodie, and I hope you pursue a food career. And to Augusta Cole, another high school student who helped me with typing recipes at the eleventh hour, I thank you for your dedication in getting the instructions just right.

For keeping our home life running smoothly, thanks go to Diane Hooper and Allison Schaffner, who looked after my children and me! Thanks, too, to Julie Bulger and the St. Luke's Community House meals program for accepting my cupcakes and muffins to share with the less fortunate in the neighborhood. To the Harpeth Hall School Class of 2008 and to the many employees of AmSouth Bank in downtown Nashville, I offer my heartfelt thanks for gobbling these cupcakes and offering your constructive feedback. And to my friend Nashville author John Egerton, I must say thank you for something you mentioned to me as I wrote the first Cake Mix Doctor book. You said to tell stories that people want to read. I took that advice to heart and have enjoyed choosing stories to share through the headnotes I write with each recipe.

But I wouldn't have been writing any of these recipe stories had not James Wehrle, a sales manager at Workman Publishing, arrived slightly late to a meeting while I was in New York, found a seat, then blurted out that I needed to write "The Cupcake Doctor." Thank you, James.

Thank you also to my editor Suzanne Rafer, who had been nudging me in the direction of fun, family-friendly cakes, and thank you to her kind assistants Beth Doty and Robyn Schwartz. Thanks to Peter and Carolan Workman for their continued creative vision and support; to Katie Workman for her delightful stories, energy, and lunches in New York; to Pat Upton for her diligence and patience as we begin new projects; to Jenny Mandel for being your positive self (you can talk me into just about anything); and to David Schiller, Amy Lewis, and Justin Nisbet, who manage the busy Web site cakemixdoctor.com. Thanks to Ann ffolliott, who carefully copyedited this book; to production editor Anne Cherry; to Paul Hanson, Lisa Hollander, and Lori S. Malkin in the art department, who packaged the book like one big adorable cupcake; to typesetter Barbara Peragine; and to photographer Susan Goldman and food stylist Karen Tack, who made the recipes look so good, I am still hungry for cupcakes! And a special thanks to models Bleue and Phoenix Silkensen, whose pleasure in eating the cupcakes is reflected in their joyous smiles.

Thanks to Kate Tyler and all in publicity who must get the word out that we authors have new books. It isn't an easy job, and I appreciate all that you do. Thanks to Kim Upton of the *Los Angeles Times* syndicate (which carries the Dinner Doctor column), and Dana Cowin and Kate Krader of *Food & Wine* magazine, who loved my chocolate cupcakes and featured them in a story. Even gourmet cooks appreciate a few tasty shortcuts!

Thanks last, and most of all, to the readers who have baked the cakes in my books and have spread the word that you can really bake a terrific cake (and cupcakes) in your own kitchen. Enjoy!

Contents

❀   ❀   ❀

Cupcakes 101
PAGE 4

Mastering the art of the cupcake, from mixing the batter to frosting and decorating. The pans, the pantry, and all you need to know to tote cupcakes to school functions, potlucks, and family reunions.

Cupcakes with Class
PAGE 22

No one outgrows the love of cupcakes. Rich in sophisticated flavors, these are the desserts to serve at your most elegant dinner party: Warm Chocolate Cupcakes with Molten Centers, Cherry Cheesecake Cupcakes, Fresh Pear and Gingerbread Cupcakes with a Creamy Lemon Frosting, and Coconut Snowballs.

Cupcakes for Kids

PAGE 94

Loaded with kid appeal, these cupcakes are irresistible no matter what your age is. Try Butterfly Cupcakes with Pastel Frostings, Pineapple Banana Smoothie Cupcakes, Buried Treasure Cakes, Peanut Butter Surprises, and A Cupcake Zoo, or one of the many other treats in this chapter.

Celebration Cupcakes

PAGE 170

Special occasions deserve the most festive cupcakes. Make Strawberry Rose Cakes for Valentine's Day, Fireworks Confetti Cupcakes for the Fourth of July, Pilgrims' Hats for Thanksgiving, and adorable Snowman Cupcakes for the winter holiday season.

Muffins: Breakfast Cupcakes

PAGE 220

Freshly baked, warm muffins make a delicious start to the day, and this chapter has plenty of favorites, both sweet and savory: Blueberry Yogurt Streusel Muffins, Butter Pecan Banana Muffins, Easy Granola Muffins, and Green Chile and Corn Mini Muffins, to name a few.

Cupcake Cousins

PAGE 272

Desserts with cupcake aspirations: Mini Strawberry Trifles, Fresh Raspberry Cream Cakes, Little Chocolate Bar Cakes, and Mini Crème Brûlées—all made in a cupcake pan.

Cupcake Creations

PAGE 296

When is a cupcake not a cupcake? When it becomes part of a wreath or a wedding cake or an artist's palette or a bouquet. With the right decorations, cupcakes can be used to form a magical centerpiece for any party.

Frostings and Glazes

PAGE 316

A cupcake just isn't a cupcake without that final touch—a pretty swirl of homemade frosting or glaze. There are twenty-five to choose from, including Chocolate and Malted Milk Buttercreams, Creamy Lemonade, Butterscotch Maple, and Caramel Pan Frostings. And an easy Basic Chocolate Ganache. What could be better?

GREAT THINGS
COME IN SMALL PACKAGES

• • • • •

What I love about baking is that it brings me closer to my family and friends, especially my three children. With their love of creating and enjoying fun food in the kitchen, they have been the heart and soul of the *Cake Mix Doctor* books and the subsequent *Dinner Doctor*. For them and for all the children of the world, ages 1 to 101, here is *Cupcakes from the Cake Mix Doctor.*

Just say the word "cupcake," and you've got to smile. To me, cupcakes conjure up cozy, comforting, celebratory memories of parties past when I carefully peeled back the paper liner and then put gentility aside and dove face first into the crunchy decoration, the smooth and creamy frosting, the soft cake—I ate them all at once. I remember some boys being able to inhale a cupcake in one bite. I always marveled at that because it took me three or four. But now I can appreciate the time it takes to savor a cupcake. I'm not in a hurry.

When I was growing up, I would frequently spend Friday nights with friends or with my sisters in our mother's kitchen (because she didn't mind the mess), baking cupcakes for fun. We licked the beaters, too, even though you weren't supposed to do that. And we baked cupcakes for others—for school bake sales and teenage service projects. I remember cramming many chocolate cupcakes into many cardboard shirt boxes lined with waxed paper.

These are just a few of my cupcake memories, and I am sure you have yours. It's no surprise that cupcakes appeal to all of us, no matter our age. This single serving of cake has "mine" written all over it. It was *not* meant to be shared. And we will never outgrow the ease and convenience of baking cupcakes, especially when the batter begins with a cake mix and is simply doctored to make it extraordinary.

Recently, cupcakes have developed even greater panache. Like home-baked meat loaf and real mashed potatoes, they are terribly chic. Walk into an upscale bakery in New York, Chicago, or Los Angeles and you will see great gilded cupcakes literally put up on pedestals (stainless steel cake stands lined with paper doilies). They are often coated in fudge or caramel and might have a candied violet or white chocolate shavings on top. And they might cost you $5 a pop.

However chic the cupcake is, don't worry that all this will go to its head. It can still be made at home, still be decorated with what you have on hand, and still be crammed into a shirt box. Inside this book I share 135 recipes for children and grown-ups, for every day and for special days. Most are for cupcakes and frostings, but I have included muffin recipes, too, which are baked in cupcake pans, though less sweet than cupcakes. They make great breakfasts on the go. And I have included a chapter of ideas for cupcake party presentations, such as a cupcake Christmas tree or wedding-style cake. Granted, they will never make the Lego catalog, but you'd be surprised how much fun it is to stack up cupcakes in attractive and whimsical ways.

Because I am often asked at book signings and cooking classes which are my favorite recipes, I've decided to list some of the ones I love today (I may, however, think of an entirely different group by tomorrow!): Red Velvet Cupcakes with White Chocolate Peppermint Cream Cheese Frosting (page 36), Warm Chocolate Cupcakes with Molten Centers (page 29), Fresh Pear and Gingerbread Cupcakes (page 59), Coconut Snowballs (page 66), Orange Marmalade Ricotta Cupcakes (page 70), White Russian Cupcakes (page 85), Blueberry Yogurt Streusel Muffins (page 222), Sweet Potato Casserole Muffins (page 250), and Green Chile and Corn Mini Muffins (page 238). My children would say that their favorites are Butterfly Cupcakes with Pastel Frosting (page 97), Jelly Doughnut Cupcakes (page 115), Milk Chocolate Rocky Road Cupcakes (page 131), Banana Pudding Cupcakes, (page 147) and Tie-Dye Cupcakes with Psychedelic Buttercream (page 155). And I haven't mentioned any holiday cupcakes, so here are a few I love: Kiss Me Cakes (page 179) and Strawberry Rose Cakes (page 182) for Valentine's; Easter Basket Cupcakes (page 191); and the Stars and Stripes Cupcakes (page 197).

And because I am frequently asked where leftover cake from recipe testing goes, I will tell you that of the 7,500 cupcakes and muffins that emerged from my kitchen, some went to family and friends, some to a variety of local schools, some to my husband's office, and many to the Mobile Meals program for needy seniors at St. Luke's Community House in Nashville.

As in the other *Cake Mix Doctor* books, I have included a how-to section. Cupcake 101 is a list of what to keep on hand in the Cupcake Pantry. As in the other books, there are plenty of sidebars on decorating, baking ahead, planning parties, you name it. And at the end of every recipe I have included at least one additional tip so that you'll be assured of success with each batch of cupcakes. I hope that you enjoy this newest member of the family as much as I have enjoyed working on it. I have grown to love cupcakes even more than I did when I was young. Great things come in small packages, right?

Cupcakes 101

❀ ❀ ❀

You may wonder how something as uncomplicated as a cupcake could need a chapter on construction. Isn't the joy of the cupcake or muffin its sheer simplicity? Possibly. The best recipes are often the simplest. Yet I have learned that the trick in pulling off any recipe—making it work, presenting it well, and enjoying it thoroughly—is to understand it completely. With this book, I want you to be able to pull off cupcakes and muffins with ease, bake them often, tote them to friends, and above all, enjoy them. So I want you to understand cupcakes down to their tiniest crumb.

It's no secret that my chief baking shortcut up until now has been a box of cake mix and a few ingredients from my kitchen cupboard. That doesn't change with this book, and you'll find that these smaller cakes—adorable cupcakes and muffins—can be made in the same fast fashion.

As a busy mother of three, I have learned to rely on a box of good cake mix—and muffin mix, brownie mix, and self-rising flour—to jump-start recipes and allow me to bake even on a hectic schedule. In the old days I might have said, "No!" when asked the night before a bake sale or party to bring in two dozen cupcakes, but now I answer, "What flavor?"

Before working on this book, I'd have thought I baked a pretty decent cupcake. But what is it they say about practice making perfect? With the practice of testing recipe after recipe, my cupcakes got better, and I experienced a few epiphanies about cupcake making that I share on the following pages—you know, those "aha!" moments when you race to record a great idea before you forget it.

Even when a recipe was stellar, I found myself tweaking it, as I did with Chocolate Almond Cupcakes (page 41). After the third batch, I realized I didn't need to layer the almond paste filling between layers of batter for it to settle perfectly in the center. It was so heavy it could be dolloped on top right before the cupcakes went in the oven and would sink to the center while baking. The chocolate glaze was nice, but on the second go-around I noticed it needed a little something. A tad of almond extract, maybe? And right after I bit into the perfected cupcake, I wondered out loud, "What about a blond version, with a bit of orange?" It's no wonder my children call me obsessed about cake, and that my cookbook manuscripts arrive late! I did become a bit obsessed with cupcakes, but I think that is part of the natural process of research.

This book has turned out to be not only a labor of love but also an expression of creativity. Left alone, cupcakes baked by the package directions might be boring, but when you add a little of this and that, bake them big and beautiful, moist and magnificent, and top them with something irresistible—possibly finishing with a sprinkling of decorations—cupcakes aren't just food, they are art. People will gravitate to them and savor them and then search for a piece of paper on which to scribble the recipe.

Enough babble. On to baking. Here are my tricks, tips, and how-to's for everything from shopping for ingredients, to selecting the right equipment, to assembling, baking, and then storing your home-baked cupcakes and muffins.

INGREDIENTS TO HAVE ON HAND

Here are the basic ingredients I nearly always have on hand so I can bake cupcakes and muffins. For a complete list of my cupcake baking cupboard, see The Cupcake Doctor Pantry (pages 20 to 21).

In the refrigerator, I have lightly salted butter for frostings and batters and unsalted butter for recipes using self-rising flour and for brownie mix. I also have reduced-fat sour cream and cream cheese, yogurt (for when I want to slim down the sour cream recipes a bit), buttermilk, and always milk. For frostings and some cupcake recipes I prefer whole milk, and if the recipe needs it I will call for it specifically. But in most cases, any milk you have on hand will do. Keep a dozen large eggs ready for baking, too.

In the freezer I keep nuts of all sorts and frozen grated coconut, should I find it in the market, which has a more pronounced coconut flavor. And in the cupboard, I always keep a variety of cake mixes, instant pudding mixes, flavored gelatin, chocolate, sugar, flavorings, food colorings, and spices. I also keep canned goods and sweetened flaked coconut there.

EQUIPMENT TO HAVE ON HAND

I had so many assorted muffin pans that I didn't need to run out and buy a lot of new pans to write this cookbook. And I think that will be true for many of you when you bake. Muffin or cupcake pans tend to last a long time if you take care of them. Mine once

What if I Don't Want to Make Cupcakes . . .

▼ ▼ ▼

Yes, you can turn most of these cupcake recipes into layer cakes and Bundt cakes. As a rule, layer cakes need three eggs, and most Bundts do best with four eggs. Add the extra egg as needed. Don't forget to oil and flour the pans before filling them with batter. Bake the layers from 25 to 30 minutes and the Bundts for 45 to 55 minutes. But these are just estimates. Look for signs of doneness—a golden brown color (on a yellow cake), the cake beginning to come away from the sides of the pan, and the top of the cake feeling firm and springing back when pressed with the tip of your finger.

belonged to my mother, and that makes them more special to me.

PANS: Two or three shiny metal pans that hold one dozen regular-size (2½-inch) cupcakes or muffins is plenty to begin cupcake or muffin baking. It's nice to have a pan that holds 24 miniature muffins, those measuring up to 2 inches across. I like shiny pans because they don't cause the light batters to bake dark, which is what can happen with some of the darker pans. For easiest cleanup, use paper liners in the cupcake pans, but, as you will learn in the muffin chapter, this isn't always possible or preferable. So if you have a heavily soiled muffin pan on your hands, place it in warm, soapy water to soak overnight, then clean with a stiff brush.

Silicone pans may appear to be a better solution, but these flexible pans that can withstand high baking temperatures are costly. They must be placed on a sturdy metal baking pan, not directly on the oven rack. And the muffins or cupcakes must cool completely in them before removing. They should not be placed in the dishwasher.

Although silicone pans need no prepping with vegetable oil or flour and need no paper liners, I found they were cumbersome to clean with soap, warm water, and a sponge.

If you're in the market for specialty pans, you will have fun looking. There are cupcake-style pans that bake the cakes into serving-size roses, other flowers, and heart shapes, as well as square muffin pans, even muffin-top pans—shallow pans in which just an inch of batter bakes up into a domed, crunchy muffin top.

LINERS: Perhaps you love paper cupcake liners, perhaps you don't. If you love them, you are possibly drawn to that nostalgic look and feel about them—the way you peel them back from a warm cupcake, which reminds you of childhood. If you detest liners, it might be because the liner grabs a good portion of your cupcake as you peel it back. And the sides of the cupcake don't develop a nice sturdy crust.

As a matter of sheer practicality, cupcakes need liners and muffins do not. Nearly all cupcake recipes in this book call for paper liners, and you can use the handy pastel liners found in nearly every supermarket. Or, you can order seasonal patterned liners from Wilton, or find pristine white liners at

10 Steps to Sensational Cupcakes

1. Buy an oven thermometer and check to see if your oven is baking at the correct temperature. Or call your appliance serviceman for a more accurate digital test.

2. Place the oven rack in the center position.

3. Preheat the oven for 10 to 15 minutes before baking.

4. Read the recipe before beginning. Make sure you've got the right pan size. Regular cupcakes and muffins go in 2½- to 2¾-inch cups.

5. Find paper liners that fit your pan snugly. For muffins, mist the bottom of the cups with vegetable oil spray.

6. Measure ingredients correctly. Dry ingredients go into measuring spoons and cups and should be leveled off with a straight edge. Brown sugar needs to be packed lightly into the cup. Liquid ingredients, on the other hand, go into liquid measuring cups and you need to check the measurement at eye level (unless you have the new liquid measuring cup that you can read from above).

7. Blend the batter for the amount of time the recipe specifies. Use a hand or stand mixer for cupcakes and a wooden spoon for most muffins.

8. Spoon or scoop batter into the prepared cups, filling them two thirds (¼ cup batter) or three quarters (⅓ cup batter) full, depending on the recipe instructions.

9. Check the cupcakes for doneness, looking for browning in light-colored cupcakes or pressing the top to see if it springs back.

10. Allow up to 5 minutes for cupcakes to cool in the pan before transferring them to a rack to cool completely. Then frost or glaze as desired.

baking and craft shops. You can even find pretty brown paper baking molds (mini panettone molds) into which you pour the batter and don't need a pan at all. These molds can be found in many fine baking shops nationwide, or by mail order (see Cupcake Mail-Order Supplies, page 19).

In the supermarket you'll also find small liners that fit the 1¾- to 2-inch miniature-cup pans, and there are mini foil liners strong enough to hold baking batter without the aid of a muffin pan. Like the panettone molds, you just line them up on a baking sheet, spoon in the batter, and bake.

The 2½-inch cupcake liners are just the right size for regular pans that measure anywhere from 2½ to 2¾ inches across the top of each cup and are between 1 and 1½ inches deep. But I could not find cupcake liners to fit cups measuring 3 to 4 inches across. You'll need to lightly mist the bottom of the cups with vegetable oil spray or use a silicone pan.

MIXING BOWLS: Just use what you have, whether they are stainless steel, plastic, glass, or ceramic. Should you need to purchase mixing bowls, buy stainless steel. And check prices, because discount stores and restaurant supply stores are often less expensive. I love stainless steel bowls because they don't trap flavors the way plastic does, are lightweight when compared to glass, won't chip, can take hot and cold mixtures, and can be cleaned in the dishwasher. I have an assortment of these bowls, from small to large, and they nest beautifully together in a large kitchen drawer.

ELECTRIC MIXER: You'll need an electric mixer to prepare cupcake batter and frostings, but please, don't overmix these recipes. The times suggested will pull the ingredients together and incorporate air, without making the cake tough, which can happen if you overbeat. I like a small seven-speed hand mixer for this task. For most muffin recipes, simply use a wooden spoon.

SCOOPS: The ice cream scoop has changed my cupcake baking forever. I used to measure out ⅓ cup in a dry

Do the Cupcake Math

How many cupcakes will a recipe make? How long will they need to bake?

✿ Regular: Batter from an 18.25-ounce box of cake mix yields 20 to 24 of the 2½-inch cupcakes. They need to bake for 18 to 25 minutes.

✿ Mini-cupcakes: Batter from an 18.25-ounce box of cake mix yields 36 of the 2-inch cupcakes. They need to bake for 13 to 18 minutes.

✿ Jumbo cupcakes: Batter from an 18.25-ounce box of cake mix yields 12 of the 3- to 4-inch cupcakes. They need to bake for 25 to 30 minutes.

How much batter goes into each cupcake pan?

✿ To fill the cups of a regular pan two thirds full, use ¼ cup batter. The cupcakes will bake up domed and even with the top of the pan.

✿ To fill the cups of a regular pan three quarters full, use ⅓ cup batter. The cupcakes will bake above the top of the pan, appear oversize, and may spread out to form a muffin-like top.

✿ To fill the cups of a jumbo pan three quarters full, use ½ cup batter. This makes an extremely large, 3- to 4-inch cupcake.

✿ And to fill the cups of a miniature pan two thirds to three quarters full, use 1½ to 2 tablespoons batter. These cupcakes will dome above the top of the pan.

measuring cup, then with a small plastic spatula try to scrape the batter into the cupcake pan. I wound up with more batter on me and the spatula than in the

pan. Now, using a large ice cream scoop (that holds about ⅓ cup) with a spring-action lever that sweeps across and removes the batter, I can scoop the batter straight from the bowl into the pan. And with a slightly smaller scoop, one a little larger than a melon ball scoop, I can scoop the 1½ to 2 tablespoons needed for a miniature muffin pan. Experiment with the ice cream scoop you already own. Pay attention to how full the pans need to be for the particular recipe. I specify not only how much batter should go into the pan but also how full the cup should appear.

SPATULAS: You can't have too many spatulas, both rubber spatulas for scraping bowls of batter and frostings and for cleanups, and also flexible metal spatulas for frosting cupcakes. Look for a short metal spatula called a cupcake spatula. You can run it around the edge of the cupcake or muffin to release it from the pan, then frost the cupcake easily. What's really nice is that this size spatula fits perfectly in a child's hand.

VEGETABLE OIL MISTER: Unlike the commercial vegetable oil sprays that contain propellants and cause the outside of your cakes and cupcakes to darken, this mister is an empty pump that you fill with fresh vegetable oil. Pump it eight or nine times and it's ready to spray oil into the bottom of muffin cups.

MIXING THE BATTER AND FILLING THE PANS

The method for mixing most of the cupcakes in this book is the same as I have used in my *Cake Mix Doctor* books. Use the ingredients in the order they are listed, and follow the recipe instructions. Blend first with an electric mixer on low to incorporate the ingredients, then on medium for the batter to smooth and lighten. You can also prepare these cupcakes with a wooden spoon, using about 150 strokes.

For the muffins, however, the methods change a bit. If the batter calls for soft butter, place it in a mixing bowl with the sugar and cream it by blending with an electric mixer on low speed until the two ingredients come together and are creamy. You then add the egg (or eggs), blending it in with the electric mixer as well. Once the wet ingredients are blended together, the dry ingredients, like the muffin mix or the self-rising flour, should be folded into them with

Sometimes It Just Depends on the Batter . . .

▼ ▼ ▼

If you are working with a thinner batter, it is best to underfill the cupcake cups because the cupcakes will spread as they rise and can make a mess on the top of the pan. Thicker batters will bake up tall and are less likely to spread, so you can be more generous when filling the cups. It's logical that four-egg batters will rise more than those with fewer eggs. And it makes sense that batters with a lot of added ingredients will yield more cupcakes than those batters that have nothing added to the cake mix except eggs, water, and oil.

a wooden spoon or rubber spatula so the flour is only lightly beaten and the batter does not toughen.

For muffin batters in which oil is the fat, you begin by placing the dry ingredients, like the muffin mix, self-rising flour, sugar, and spices, in a large bowl and making a well in the center.

You fold in the combined wet ingredients or you dump the egg and other wet ingredients into this well, depending on what the recipe suggests. Muffin batters only need 20 strokes of a wooden spoon to come together. The batter should still appear lumpy; these lumps will disappear in the oven and the resulting muffins will be moist.

HOW MUCH BATTER SHOULD GO IN THE PAN?

Follow the recipe, looking both for how much batter to use and how full the cups should look before the pan goes into the oven. Use an ice cream scoop—or a smaller scoop for smaller pans—or a large spoon to scoop or spoon the batter into the cups. See Do the Cupcake Math (page 10) to better understand cupcake yields.

LET'S BAKE

Your oven needs to be preheated before baking, and all the recipes will direct you to do this. Depending on the oven, the preheating process takes from 10 to 20 minutes. Make sure an oven rack is placed in the center position.

Cupcakes bake best at 350°F, which is a moderate and all-purpose temperature for baking. The exceptions are those recipes in which the batter needs to bake up quickly to encase a filling, and these recipes call for temperatures of up to 400°F. Muffins, on the other hand, need the higher heat to rise and set and to form a crust around the edges. Bake them all at 400°F.

If your oven is wide enough, place two pans side by side, allowing a bit of space between the pans, and the sides of the pans and the oven. If not, place one pan on the center rack and the second pan on the rack above. Rotate the pans midway through the recipe.

Cupcakes and muffins are done when the top springs back when you lightly press them with a finger. To determine this, open the oven door, carefully reach in, and, with one finger, press the top of the closest cupcake. If they are not yet done, close the oven door and continue cooking for a few more minutes.

I like to keep the oven light on while baking so I can see if light-colored muffins and cupcakes are browning, another sign of doneness. Yellow and white batters will bake up golden or lightly golden when done. And you should always refer to the recipe and the suggested baking times. Begin checking for doneness at the earliest doneness time.

COOLING CUPCAKES

Remove the pans from the oven carefully and place them on a heat-resistant spot to cool, preferably one with ventilation underneath, like the burners of your range or a wire rack. Let the cupcakes and muffins cool for about 5 minutes in the pan, then transfer them to a rack to cool completely. For muffins and cupcakes without liners, this initial cooling period allows the steam to help the muffins or cupcakes release from the pan. Leave cupcake liners on until serving time. They keep the cupcakes moist and neat.

If you are not going to frost the cupcakes within an hour, drape a clean, light kitchen towel (linen and cotton are best) over the cupcakes so they don't dry out.

STORING CUPCAKES AND MUFFINS

Each of the recipes includes storage information, so you can bake ahead of time. When recipes contain whipped cream or whipped topping, it's best to store the cupcakes in the refrigerator, but remember that the refrigerator dries out baked goods. For optimum flavor, bake these as close to serving time as possible. Other cupcakes and muffins, such as those flavored with spices or those that contain pumpkin, fruit, carrots, or zucchini, actually improve while they sit. Bake them a day

ahead of serving and leave covered on the kitchen counter.

Thinking ahead, you can bake cupcakes up to three months in advance and freeze them, unfrosted, in sturdy plastic containers or, if freezer space is tight, flash freeze them on baking sheets and store them in plastic freezer bags. Open the bag of cupcakes to let moisture out, then thaw the cupcakes on the kitchen counter before frosting.

FROSTING CUPCAKES

Compared to layer cakes, frosting cupcakes is a stress-free experience. It's really a lot of fun! A batch of cupcakes needs slightly less frosting than a layer cake. You can make your favorite layer-cake frosting recipe, but you'll have some left over. From 2½ to 3 cups confectioners' sugar is the right amount for frosting 24 cupcakes. And I have found that for every 1 cup sugar used, you need 1 tablespoon liquid.

Plop frosting by the heaping tablespoon onto cupcakes using a tablespoon or one of those neat short metal cupcake spatulas (see Spatulas, page 11). My favorite frosting trick is to cover the tops completely but to let a tiny bit of cake show around the edges (where the cake meets the liner) if there is a color contrast between the cake and the frosting.

YOU GOTTA GARNISH

You do not, and I repeat, *do not*, need a cake-decorating degree to garnish the cupcakes in this book. It is totally fine to sprinkle them with confectioners' sugar and add a chocolate curl, one toasted pecan, or nothing at all. (See 5 Ways to Decorate a Cupcake Effortlessly, on this page).

If you want to frost and garnish, remember the garnish should have something in common with the cupcake. Lemon cupcakes call for lemon zest or lemon candy. Strawberry cupcakes beg for a slice of strawberry. Chocolate cupcakes want chocolate sprinkles or curls or crushed coffee candies or fresh mint leaves or mint candies. The exception is weddings and showers and festive occasions where you might place fresh (untreated, nonpoisonous) flowers or candied violets on cupcakes for the

5 Ways to Decorate a Cupcake Effortlessly

▼ ▼ ▼

1. Chocolate curls

2. Shiny gold or silver dragées

3. Toasted pecans

4. Lemon or orange zest strips

5. Edible flowers

sheer beauty of it. Should you want to go beyond frosting and sugar sprinkles, here are some ways to branch out, be creative, and yet not spend a weekend or a fortune in the process.

DECORATING STENCILS: Buy a set of plastic stencils (from Kaiser Bakeware, found at Williams-Sonoma). These sets are designed for cakes, but many of the designs are small enough to be placed on top of a cupcake, including the leaf, flower, horse, and so forth. Dust confectioners' sugar, cocoa powder, or spices over the stencil openings and remove the stencil carefully. Wash the stencil in warm water and dry it before storing.

INTERESTING FOOD COLORINGS:
Shop the supermarket for classic primary colors, but should you want to go a step further into buttercup yellow or teal blue, Wilton, the cake-decorating supplier, has lovely specialty sets that contain more subtle shades. The Wilton colors are pastes, so you need less and can easily increase the color intensity by adding a bit more. You can dye your favorite buttercream frosting and coarse decorating sugar to match, which is a really elegant touch.

DECORATING PENS: Available from Williams-Sonoma and other on-line outlets, these are pen-like tubes filled with white chocolate decorating frosting in luscious colors like lavender, orange, and sage green, as well as white. Use these to write names or make faces on cupcakes after they are frosted. You immerse the frosting-filled pens in hot tap water for 5 minutes, then snip off the top and pipe away. The beauty of these pens is that the frosting hardens and you can tote the decorated cupcakes without smudging the writing. Gel frosting pens are found in grocery stores, but the consistency of the frosting is, not surprisingly, more gel-like and not quite as nice.

CHOCOLATE CURLS: All you need to make luscious curls is a swivel-headed vegetable peeler and a bar of chocolate, white or dark, at room temperature. The larger the surface on which to drag the peeler, the larger the curl, and the warmer the chocolate, the larger the curl. Small squares of cold chocolate will yield chocolate shavings. And these, too, are pretty, piled up in the center of a frosted cupcake.

INSTANT DECORATIONS: My friend Lucille Osborn, a cake decorating expert, creates just about any design to top a cupcake by first drawing a pattern, then placing it under parchment paper (the pattern is dark enough to be seen through the parchment). She melts chocolate or colored confectionery coating wafers (Wilton calls them Candy

Melts), found at baking stores or online, and places the resulting goo in a pastry bag. Then she pipes the warm melted wafers between the lines of the pattern, right onto the parchment paper. Once the pattern is filled, she carefully slides it to a clear spot under the parchment and pipes again. You can do this all over a sheet of parchment and turn out enough decorations for a batch of cupcakes. Let the designs harden on the parchment. Lucille makes letters, musical notes, even fan-shaped tails for little turkey cupcakes.

PRESENTING CUPCAKES

Cupcakes really need no dramatic presentation, because they are head-turners on their own. But I do think they are stunning all lined up on over size flat platters, interspersed with fresh flowers. And they look whimsical and garden-party ready when you stack them on a selection of cake stands. Place one smaller stand on a medium stand, and the medium on a large stand, and you create a tiered, wedding-cake effect like the one in the color section of the book. Place cupcakes on the stands, add flowers, berries, cherries, and ribbons, and let the party begin!

HAVE CUPCAKES, WILL TRAVEL

Unless the gathering is taking place at your house or unless you are planning to stock your freezer, there's a good chance you'll be toting those cupcakes and muffins to the office, school, or a party.

I used to pack cupcakes in cardboard shirt boxes that had been lined with waxed paper, but then, that was in the dark ages before plastic carrying cases and pans with matching lids! I have learned that some cupcakes are better travelers than others. Choose frostings or glazes that harden, not those creamy, buttery frostings that are delicious but seem to smear on just about anything. If you must travel with cupcakes with creamy frostings, pack a plastic knife for repairing smudges once you get to the party. And bring along extra toppings and garnishes to sprinkle on top.

Here are some useful ways to transport your little cakes:

A plastic 13- by 9-inch carrying case with matching, locking lid. Tupperware makes one of these with a handle. One side is flat for a sheet cake, and the other side has indentations to keep cupcakes from sliding.

A 13- by 9-inch brownie pan. Certainly not as spiffy as the carrying case, but it works if the pan is deep and you cover it with sealing plastic wrap or, even better, if it has a matching plastic snap-on lid.

A 13- by 9-inch disposable aluminum pan with plastic lid. You'll find these in the supermarket, and they work well because the lid is raised and won't rub off the frosting. These can be reused several times if you bring them home, rinse, and store.

A plastic cake carrier with a pie stand. These carriers are meant to carry one pie on the bottom and one on top, but you can fit cupcakes on both levels.

A plain plastic cake carrier. You can fit nearly a dozen cupcakes on one level in these carriers with snap-on lids.

A 1-cup plastic container. Rubbermaid makes these small containers with snap-on lids that are perfect for toting single cupcakes in lunch bags or boxes.

A serving plate. Arrange the cupcakes or muffins on a serving plate. Place four or five toothpicks in cupcakes, like columns, placing one toothpick in the center cupcake and one in each of four outer cupcakes. Drape plastic wrap over the cupcakes and secure it on the bottom of the plate. If desired, you can place miniature marshmallows on top of the toothpicks so they don't tear the plastic wrap. You can repair the frosting holes with a plastic knife on site after you remove the toothpicks.

When all else fails? A clean cardboard shirt box. Line it with waxed paper and pack the cupcakes side by side. Drape plastic wrap or aluminum foil over the top, or use the top of the shirt box.

CUPCAKE MAIL-ORDER SUPPLIES

You really don't need to go beyond your local supermarket to purchase the supplies needed to make stellar cupcakes. You'll find ingredients for terrific batters and frostings as well as food colorings, sugar sprinkles, and easy garnishes right there. But should you want to take cupcake making a step further and decorate them in an out-of-the-ordinary fashion, bake them in an unusual pan, or present them on some fancy tiered stand, then you might want to browse these catalogs and on-line sources. I have ordered from all of them, and the items arrived in good shape and on time. No doubt this is just a handful, and many more may pop up over time, but it is a solid start.

❀ **Beryl's Cake Decoration and Pastry Supplies.** www.beryls.com. 800-488-2749. Not only the hard-to-find brown paper cupcake molds (panettone cups), but also an incredible selection of food colorings, sugar sprinkles, and silver, gold, pearl, and pink dragées await you.

❀ **King Arthur.** www.kingarthurflour.com. 800-827-6836. Out-of-the-ordinary bakeware like silicone pans, muffin-top pans, and paper mini panettone molds.

❀ **N.Y. Cake & Baking Distributors.** www.nycake.com. 212-675-2253. Extensive selection of baking pans and equipment, including edible decorating icing pens, edible decorations, food colorings, and chocolate supplies.

❀ **Sweet Celebrations.** www.sweetc.com. 800-328-6722. (Formerly Maid of Scandinavia.) Look for white, pastel, and novelty paper cupcake liners as well as nice cupcake pans.

❀ **Williams-Sonoma.** www.williamssonoma.com. 877-812-6235. Parchment paper, cupcake and muffin pans, spatulas, tiered stands for presenting, decorating sugars and icing.

❀ **Wilton.** www.wilton.com. 800-794-5866. A dazzling selection of seasonal and novelty paper cupcake liners, decorating sugars, and food colorings. Nice pans, too.

The Cupcake Doctor Pantry

If you bake a couple times a week, you'll want to keep the following basics in your kitchen.

Baking Basics

✿ Assorted cake mixes, such as plain yellow, white, lemon, orange, German chocolate, and devil's food, as well as angel food, butter recipe golden and fudge, butterscotch, gingerbread, and white, chocolate, and butter pecan mixes with pudding, and brownie mix

✿ Muffin mixes: blueberry, lemon–poppy seed, cinnamon swirl, cinnamon streusel, chocolate chip, bran, and chocolate

✿ All-purpose and self-rising flour

✿ Sugar: confectioners' for frostings, both granulated and brown sugars for batters, coarse sugars for decorating.

✿ Instant pudding mixes: I like vanilla, chocolate, and pistachio. Use these to increase the volume of plain cake mix and to make batters moist.

✿ Vegetable oil: Select light, flavorless oils such as canola, corn, and safflower.

✿ Chocolate: unsweetened cocoa powder and semisweet chocolate chips.

✿ Extracts and spices: Choose pure vanilla, almond, and peppermint extracts and maple and coconut flavorings. Ground cinnamon, nutmeg, ginger, pumpkin pie spice, and poppy seeds are my favorite spices to have on hand.

✿ Milk: Unless I specify whole milk, use 2 percent, skim, or whatever is in your refrigerator.

✿ Butter: Choose lightly salted unless the recipe calls for unsalted.

✿ Reduced-fat sour cream and cream cheese

✿ Low-fat yogurt: Use plain (instead of sour cream) and, if they complement the cupcake batter, flavors like lemon, blueberry, and chocolate.

✿ Large eggs: Keep a dozen in the refrigerator.

✿ Citrus fruit: I love the flavors of fresh lemons and oranges in cupcakes and muffins. Store them in the drawer of your refrigerator for zest and juice.

✿ Assorted nuts: Keep chopped pecans and walnuts and sliced almonds at their freshest in the freezer. Lightly toast them or add them to the batter or topping while still frozen.

The Extended Pantry

The selection of optional ingredients is up to you. Here is an extended pantry, including the ingredients needed to prepare most any of the recipes in this book.

REFRIGERATOR:

- Orange juice
- Key lime juice (bottled)
- Buttermilk or buttermilk powder
- Heavy cream
- Ricotta cheese
- Pie crusts
- Cheddar cheese
- Carrots
- Zucchini

FREEZER:

- Frozen grated coconut, if available
- Whipped topping
- Sweetened raspberries and strawberries
- Sliced peaches
- Chopped rhubarb
- Lemonade concentrate
- Frozen chocolate chip cookie dough

CUPBOARD:

- Vanilla and chocolate cook-and-serve pudding mixes
- Fruit-flavored gelatins, such as strawberry
- Food coloring, both liquid and paste, and decorating pens
- Instant coffee powder or espresso powder

- Sweetened condensed milk
- Evaporated milk
- Canned fruits and vegetables: crushed pineapple, strained plums (baby food variety), pumpkin, cherry pie filling, unsweetened applesauce, cream-style corn, chopped green chiles, sweet potatoes, spiced apple rings
- Sweetened flaked coconut
- Marshmallow creme
- Chocolate syrup
- White chocolate and milk chocolate chips
- German's sweet chocolate
- Bran cereal, old-fashioned oats, and granola
- Smooth and chunky peanut butter
- Orange marmalade and blueberry and strawberry preserves
- Lemon curd
- Almond paste
- Vanilla wafers, chocolate wafers, Oreo cookies, gingersnaps, animal crackers, graham crackers
- Dried fruit, such as tart cherries and raisins
- Unsalted peanuts
- M&M's, Hershey's Kisses, Reese's Peanut Butter Cups, caramels
- Sugar sprinkles of all colors
- Liqueurs and spirits for flavoring: bourbon, vodka, Galliano (anise-flavored), crème de cacao, and Kahlúa

Cupcakes with Class

✿ ✿ ✿

Who says cupcakes are just for kids? These mighty miniature cakes—slathered in chocolate, or dripping with lemon glaze, or crowned with a spoonful of cinnamon crème anglaise—are tempting for grown-ups, too. It's impossible to outgrow the pleasure of peeling back the paper liner and releasing that vanilla scent, then opening wide and taking a bite big enough to include plenty of chocolate frosting. Getting older doesn't mean forgetting how to savor a cupcake.

And the beauty of cupcakes is that no matter the reason or the season, you can find one that's suitable. On certain days you *deserve* a Red Velvet Cupcake with White Chocolate Peppermint Cream Cheese Frosting, or a White Russian Cupcake topped with Kahlúa-flavored whipped cream, or a Fresh Pear and Gingerbread Cupcake slathered in Creamy Lemon Frosting. On other days, well, there are a multitude of reasons to enjoy a Triple Butterscotch Cupcake. You might be celebrating a birthday, an anniversary, the arrival of a new pet, the first spring daffodil in bloom, or other similarly important occasions.

Cappuccino Chip Cupcakes, with their Mocha Buttercream, are delicious in the late afternoon. Rhubarb Crumble Cupcakes can be eaten for breakfast. Prune Spice Cupcakes taste good morning, noon, or night, whereas those sinful, dark chocolate cupcakes—like Warm Chocolate Cupcakes with Molten Centers and Brooklyn Blackout Cupcakes—are best shared with friends after dinner, accompanied by a cup of really impressive coffee.

We may have graduated from sugar sprinkles into the intoxicatingly delicious realm of dark chocolate, toasted almond, orange, and coconut. We may shiver in anticipation of tart lemon and get a kick out of whipping up a batch of Harvey Wallbanger Cupcakes with Galliano and vodka or Orange Marmalade Ricotta Cupcakes with a chunky but creamy Marmalade Buttercream. But despite our sophisticated palates, when it comes to size, grown-ups are just big kids. We fall for luscious little cakes. All we need fits right in the palm of our hand. And just one bite returns us to childhood, when times were simpler, less complex, and as warm as our mother's embrace.

BROOKLYN BLACKOUT CUPCAKES

• • • • •

A Brooklyn, New York, bakery called Ebinger's was famous for its intense chocolate cake, called Brooklyn Blackout, packaged in a signature blue box. The bakery closed in the early 1970s, but the buzz about these cakes lives on. I have received recipes for all kinds of variations on this chocolate cake cloaked in cake crumbs, and have adapted the version I like best as cupcakes.

✿ **MAKES 20 CUPCAKES (2½ INCHES EACH)**
✿ **PREPARATION TIME: 50 MINUTES**
✿ **BAKING TIME: 17 TO 20 MINUTES**
✿ **ASSEMBLY TIME: 15 MINUTES**

FILLING AND FROSTING:

1 package (3.4 ounces) "cook and serve" chocolate pudding mix
2 cups whole milk
½ cup semisweet chocolate chips
2 tablespoons butter
1 teaspoon pure vanilla extract

CUPCAKES:

24 paper liners for cupcake pans (2½-inch size)
1 package (18.25 ounces) plain devil's food cake mix
3 tablespoons Dutch process unsweetened cocoa powder (see "the Cupcake Doctor says")
1½ cups buttermilk
½ cup vegetable oil
3 large eggs
1 teaspoon pure vanilla extract

1. Prepare the filling and frosting: Place the pudding mix and milk in a 2-quart

5 Ways to Fill a Cupcake

▼ ▼ ▼

Cupcakes are never boring, but if you want, you can easily put a surprise filling inside.

1. Spoon 1 tablespoon of your favorite fruit jam on the cupcake before baking. It will sink into the batter, and the cake will rise up around it as it bakes.

2. Place a chocolate truffle or unwrapped Hershey's Kiss on top before baking.

3. Place a large raspberry or blackberry on top before baking.

4. Use a pastry bag to squirt 1 tablespoon of pudding into the center of the cupcake after it's baked.

5. Insert a fortune before baking. Write on strips of parchment paper and wrap them in aluminum foil before pressing them into the batter.

---

saucepan over medium-high heat. Whisk constantly until the mixture comes to a boil and thickens, 4 to 5 minutes. Turn off the heat. Add the chocolate chips, butter, and vanilla and stir until the butter and chocolate chips melt, 2 minutes. Remove the pan from the heat and cover the pudding with plastic wrap placed right on its surface. Let it cool for 45 minutes at room temperature.

2. Place a rack in the center of the oven and preheat the oven to 350°F.

3. Prepare the cupcake batter: Line 24 cupcake cups with paper liners. Set the pans aside. Place the cake mix, cocoa powder, buttermilk, oil, eggs, and vanilla

in a large mixing bowl. Blend with an electric mixer on low speed for 30 seconds. Stop the machine and scrape down the sides of the bowl with a rubber spatula. Increase the mixer speed to medium and

the Cupcake Doctor says...

Dutch process cocoa powder is intensely flavored and darker in color than regular cocoa. It will darken the already dark color of the devil's food mix and contribute to the "blackout" appearance, as well as intensify the flavor of these cupcakes.

beat 2 minutes more, scraping down the sides again if needed. The batter should look thick and well combined. Spoon or scoop a heaping ¼ cup batter into each lined cup, filling it two thirds of the way full. (You will get 24 cupcakes.) Place the pans in the oven.

4. Bake the cupcakes until they spring back when lightly pressed with your finger, 17 to 20 minutes. Remove the pans from the oven and place them on wire racks to cool for 5 minutes. Remove 4 cupcakes from the pan and crumble them into a bowl to make coarse crumbs. Run a dinner knife around the edges of the remaining cupcake liners, lift the cupcakes up from the bottoms of the cups using the end of the knife, and pick them out of the cups carefully with your fingertips. Place them on a wire rack to cool for 15 minutes before filling.

5. Divide the filling and frosting into two portions. Fit a pastry bag with a large round tip and spoon 1 cup of the filling portion into the bag. Gently push the tip into the center of each cupcake and squirt a generous amount of pudding inside. Refill the bag as needed and repeat for all 20 cupcakes.

Big, Big Cupcakes
▼ ▼ ▼

If you want to make bigger cupcakes in a 3½-inch cupcake cup, spoon or scoop ½ cup batter into the prepared pans. They will take about 25 minutes to bake, and the yield will be 16 to 18 big cupcakes.

6. Place a heaping tablespoon of the remaining pudding portion on each cupcake and spread it out with the back of a spoon, taking care to cover the tops completely. Top the frosting with a sprinkling of cupcake crumbs, pressing them down so they stick. The cupcakes are ready to serve.

✿ *Store these cupcakes, in a cake saver, in the refrigerator for up to 5 days. Or freeze them, wrapped in aluminum foil or in a cake saver, for up to 6 months. Thaw the cupcakes overnight in the refrigerator before serving.*

GERMAN CHOCOLATE CUPCAKES

WITH CHOCOLATE SHAVINGS

• • • • •

There is something so homey and at the same time so intoxicating about German chocolate cake done right. These cupcakes stem from that classic cake. The batter is enriched with sour cream and streaked with slivers of grated German's sweet chocolate. On top, what else? The traditional coconut and pecan frosting. Tote these to the potluck and wait for the oohs and the aahs.

✿ **MAKES 22 TO 24 CUPCAKES (2½ INCHES EACH)**
✿ **PREPARATION TIME: 30 MINUTES**
✿ **BAKING TIME: 19 TO 22 MINUTES**
✿ **ASSEMBLY TIME: 5 MINUTES**

24 paper liners for cupcake pans
  (2½-inch size)
1 bar (4 ounces) German's sweet chocolate
1 package (18.25 ounces) plain
  German chocolate cake mix
  (see "the Cupcake Doctor says")
1 package (3.4 ounces) vanilla instant
  pudding mix
1 cup sour cream
½ cup water
½ cup vegetable oil
4 large eggs
Coconut Pecan Frosting (page 346)

1. Place a rack in the center of the oven and preheat the oven to 350°F. Line 24 cupcake cups with paper liners. Set the pans aside.

2. To grate the chocolate, break the bar into pieces and drop them, one at a time, through the feed tube of a food processor while it is running. Or, carefully rub the

~~~~~~~~~~~~~~~~~~~~~~~~

the Cupcake Doctor says...

I find German chocolate cake mixes to be a bit bland, so they benefit from added ingredients, especially the grated chocolate. True to its name, German's sweet chocolate is a pale, sweet chocolate that makes a stellar cake. You could just as easily fold in grated semisweet chocolate or 1 cup miniature chocolate chips if that's what you have on hand. If the plain German cake mix is hard to find, substitute the one with pudding in the mix, but don't add more pudding mix.

~~~~~~~~~~~~~~~~~~~~~~~~

chocolate bar with a hand-held coarse cheese grater, such as a Microplane. Set the grated chocolate aside.

3. Place the cake mix, pudding mix, sour cream, water, oil, eggs, and the grated chocolate in a large mixing bowl. Blend with an electric mixer on low speed for 30 seconds. Stop the machine and scrape down the sides of the bowl with a rubber spatula. Increase the mixer speed to medium and beat 2 minutes more, scraping down the sides again if needed. The batter should look thick and well com-

bined. Spoon or scoop ⅓ cup batter into each lined cup, filling it three quarters of the way full. (You will get between 22 and 24 cupcakes; remove the empty liners, if any.) Place the pans in the oven.

4. Bake the cupcakes until they spring back when lightly pressed with your finger, 19 to 22 minutes. Remove the pans from the oven and place them on wire racks to cool for 5 minutes. Run a dinner knife around the edges of the cupcake liners, lift the cupcakes up from the bottoms of the cups using the end of the knife, and pick them out of the cups carefully with your fingertips. Place them on a wire rack to cool for 15 minutes before frosting.

5. Prepare the Coconut Pecan Frosting.

6. Place a heaping tablespoon of frosting on each cupcake and spread it out with a short metal spatula or a spoon, taking care to cover the tops completely. The cupcakes are ready to serve.

✿ *Store these cupcakes, in a cake saver or under a glass dome, at room temperature for up to 3 days or in the refrigerator for up to 1 week. Or freeze them, wrapped in aluminum foil or in a cake saver, for up to 6 months. Thaw the cupcakes overnight in the refrigerator before serving.*

WARM CHOCOLATE CUPCAKES

WITH MOLTEN CENTERS AND CINNAMON CREME ANGLAISE

• • • • •

It was chef Jean-Georges Vongerichten of New York City who put little chocolate cakes with warm, melting centers on the map. The method he uses is to bake a rich chocolate batter with very little flour at a high heat until the sides of the cake set but the centers are still runny. This method works in a restaurant kitchen, but there is a more practical method for the home cook. This one uses a chocolate cupcake batter with a center of chocolate ganache—that luxurious mixture of semisweet chocolate and hot cream, stirred until smooth, and allowed to cool. The ganache sinks into the batter as the cupcake bakes, creating a creamy molten center. Serve these *tout de suite,* as the French would say, and have ready to go the dessert plates, forks, sauce, and sugar for sifting.

✿ **MAKES 22 TO 24 CUPCAKES (2½ INCHES EACH)**
✿ **PREPARATION TIME: 20 MINUTES**
✿ **BAKING TIME: 12 TO 14 MINUTES**
✿ **ASSEMBLY TIME: 5 MINUTES**

Basic Chocolate Ganache (page 332),

    chilled at least 1 hour

    (see "the Cupcake Doctor says")

Cinnamon Crème Anglaise (page 354)

Vegetable oil spray for misting the pans

All-purpose flour for dusting the pans

1 package (18.25 ounces) plain devil's

    food cake mix

1 cup water

½ cup vegetable oil

3 large eggs

1 teaspoon pure vanilla extract

½ teaspoon ground cinnamon

¼ cup confectioners' sugar, for dusting

1. Prepare the Basic Chocolate Ganache, cover it with plastic wrap, and place it in the refrigerator to chill. Prepare the Cinnamon Crème Anglaise, cover it with plastic wrap placed right on the surface, and place it in the refrigerator to chill.

2. Place a rack in the center of the oven and preheat the oven to 400°F. Lightly mist 24 cupcake cups with vegetable oil spray and dust them with flour. Shake out the excess flour. Set the pans aside.

3. Place the cake mix, water, oil, eggs, vanilla, and cinnamon in a large mixing bowl. Blend with an electric mixer on low speed for 30 seconds. Stop the machine

and scrape down the sides of the bowl with a rubber spatula. Increase the mixer speed to medium and blend 1½ to 2 minutes more, scraping down the sides again if needed. The batter should look well combined and thickened. Spoon or scoop ⅓ cup batter into each prepared cup, filling it three quarters of the way full. (You will get between 22 and 24 cupcakes.) Drop a heaping teaspoonful of ganache onto the top of the batter in each cup. Place the pans in the oven.

the Cupcake Doctor says...

You will most likely prepare these special cupcakes for company, and I would recommend them heartily! Make the ganache the day or night before, cover with plastic wrap, and chill. For a bigger, bolder flavor prepare it with Ghirardelli double chocolate baking chips, a bit less sweet than typical semisweet chips. You can add 1 tablespoon crème de cacao to the ganache to make it special, but this is easily omitted. Flavor these as you desire, by adding almond extract instead of vanilla, for example.

5 Places to Savor a Cupcake

▼ ▼ ▼

Cupcakes can be enjoyed anytime, anywhere. Here are some of my favorite places.

1. At the kitchen table, alone, late at night or in the morning, with a cup of coffee or tea

2. On an airplane. Cupcakes are totable!

3. At a picnic in the park

4. At a bridal shower, wedding, or baby shower. Cupcakes look gorgeous in white.

5. At a friend's potluck. After umpteen casseroles, one delicious cupcake is all you need.

4. Bake the cupcakes until the cake bakes up around the ganache, the tops are domed, and the cupcakes spring back when lightly pressed with your finger, 12 to 14 minutes. Remove the pans from the oven and place them on wire racks for 1 minute. Run a dinner knife around the edges of the cupcake cups, lift the cupcakes up from the bottoms of the cups using the end of the knife, and pick them out of the cups carefully with your fingertips. Place them on dessert plates, sift confectioners' sugar over the top, spoon the crème anglaise in a pool around each cupcake, and serve warm.

✿ *Store these cupcakes, in a cake saver or under a glass dome, at room temperature for up to 1 day. To reheat so the centers are molten once again, place the cupcakes on a microwave-safe plate and cover with paper towels. Heat on high power for 10 seconds, carefully remove, and serve.*

Your Cupcake "Horoscope"

You might be surprised how the signs of the zodiac align with your taste in cupcakes. It's in the stars!

AQUARIUS *(January 21 to February 19):* An opinionated Aquarius knows what he or she likes and tends to have a hearty appetite for worldly flavors. See Hot Fudge Spumoni Ice Cream Cakes (page 47) or Prune Spice Cupcakes with Butterscotch Maple Cream Cheese Frosting (page 81).

PISCES *(February 20 to March 20):* Mystical Pisces prefers flavors entwined with dreamy fantasies. Best to hand over the frosting, shimmering sugars, and sprinkles and let Pisces design their own cupcakes. See Lemon Chiffon Cupcakes with a Frosty Lemon Glaze (page 61) or the Cherry Cheesecake Cupcakes (page 53).

ARIES *(March 21 to April 20):* Energetic, mentally quick Aries needs a cupcake to match a competitive attitude. No plain yellow cakes with chocolate frosting for them. Go exotic and rich with exciting flavor combinations they've never had before, such as Fresh Pear and Gingerbread Cupcakes with a Creamy Lemon Frosting (page 59) or Cappuccino Chip Cupcakes with Mocha Buttercream (page 39).

TAURUS *(April 21 to May 21):* Classic elegance attracts your down-to-earth Taurus. Forgo crazy colors and sprinkles. Taurus prefers rich earth-toned goodies, such as German Chocolate Cupcakes with Chocolate Shavings (page 27) or Triple Butterscotch Cupcakes (page 83).

GEMINI *(May 22 to June 21):* The sharp, clever Gemini appreciates a cupcake appealing to his or her dual sides—the creative and slightly decadent and the quiet and simple. Try Chocolate Cream Cheese Cupcakes with a Creamy Chocolate Blender Ganache (page 34) or Pineapple Upside-Down Cupcakes (page 79)—or better yet, serve them both.

CANCER *(June 22 to July 23):* Moody Cancer craves comfort and purity. So go with an all-white cupcake to coax the cautious crab out from under the rock. Try Coconut Snowballs (page 66) or Bobbye's Italian Cream Cupcakes (page 68).

LEO *(July 24 to August 24):* Center-of-attention Leo demands strong flavors and cupcakes with humor. Brooklyn Blackout Cupcakes (page 24) and Inside-Out Peanut Butter Cupcakes (page 50) will cause the lion to roar with laughter.

VIRGO *(August 24 to September 23):* Health-conscious Virgo won't be tempted by sinfully rich triple chocolate anything. He or she will lean towards delicate fruit flavors and more healthy cupcakes like Mini Lemon Curd Cupcakes with a Lemony Cream (page 63) or Rhubarb Crumble Cupcakes (page 73).

LIBRA *(September 24 to October 23):* A bohemian at heart, Libra likes artistic cupcakes, like Key Lime Pie Cupcakes with a Coconut Meringue (page 75) or Warm Chocolate Cupcakes with Molten Centers and Cinnamon Crème Anglaise (page 29). Libra loves cupcakes you can talk about and savor as a group.

SCORPIO *(October 24 to November 22):* Scorpio is drawn to dark, rich flavors like chocolate-raspberry and anything topped with luscious whipped cream. Try Chocolate Almond Cupcakes with the crumbled almond paste inside (page 41), as well as White Russian Cupcakes (page 85) with the Kahlúa-scented whipped cream on top.

SAGITTARIUS *(November 23 to December 21):* Energetic, sporty, gregarious Sagittarius requires nonconformist cupcakes like Red Velvet Cupcakes with White Chocolate Peppermint Cream Cheese Frosting (page 36) or Orange Marmalade Ricotta Cupcakes with Marmalade Buttercream (page 70).

CAPRICORN *(December 22 to January 20):* Quiet, dignified Capricorn is uncomfortable with conspicuous consumption, so stick to the tried-and-true cupcakes, like Butter Pecan Cheesecake Cupcakes (page 56) or the Peach Cobbler Cupcakes (page 288).

CHOCOLATE CREAM CHEESE CUPCAKES

WITH A CREAMY CHOCOLATE BLENDER GANACHE

• • • • •

If no-nonsense, deep chocolate cupcakes appeal to you, try this recipe with a twist. Slivers of milk chocolate are folded in for fun little bites of contrasting flavor and color. I borrowed the idea for the frosting from baker and author Judy Rosenberg, but my version, using semisweet chocolate chips, is simpler to make. These cupcakes taste best fresh, the day they are made.

✿ **MAKES 22 TO 24 CUPCAKES (2½ INCHES EACH)**
✿ **PREPARATION TIME: 20 MINUTES**
✿ **BAKING TIME: 20 TO 23 MINUTES**
✿ **ASSEMBLY TIME: 5 MINUTES**

24 paper liners for cupcake pans
(2½-inch size)
2 milk chocolate bars (1.55 ounces each)
1 package (18.5 ounces) plain butter recipe
fudge cake mix
1 package (8 ounces) cream
cheese, at room temperature
(see "the Cupcake Doctor says")
½ cup warm water
½ cup vegetable oil
4 large eggs
2 teaspoons pure vanilla extract
Creamy Chocolate Blender Ganache
(page 334)

1. Place a rack in the center of the oven and preheat the oven to 350°F. Line 24 cupcake cups with paper liners. Set the pans aside.

2. Break the chocolate bars into quarters, stack them on top of each other, and slice down the short end of the stack with a sharp knife. You will have about 1 cup of ¼-inch shavings. Set them aside.

3. Place the cake mix, cream cheese, water, oil, eggs, and vanilla in a large mixing bowl. Blend with an electric mixer on low speed for 30 seconds. Stop the machine and scrape down the sides of the bowl with a rubber spatula. Increase the mixer speed to medium and blend for 2 minutes more, scraping down the sides again if needed. The batter should look thickened and smooth. Spoon or scoop ⅓ cup batter into each lined cup, filling it three quarters of the way full. (You will get between 22 and 24 cupcakes; remove the empty liners, if any.) Place the pans in the oven.

4. Bake the cupcakes until they spring back when lightly pressed with your finger, 20 to 23 minutes. Remove the pans from the oven and place them on wire racks to cool for 5 minutes. Run a dinner knife around the edges of the cupcake liners, lift the cupcakes up from the bottoms of the cups using the end of the knife, and pick them out of the cups carefully with your fingertips. Place them on a wire rack to cool for 15 minutes before frosting.

5. Meanwhile, prepare the Creamy Chocolate Blender Ganache.

the Cupcake Doctor says...

It's important to soften the cream cheese thoroughly before beginning this recipe. If the cream cheese is cold, it will lump up in the batter, and no matter how much you blend, you won't be able to rid the batter of those white lumps. Either remove the cream cheese from the refrigerator an hour before baking, or unwrap it and place it in the microwave for 10 to 20 seconds on high power.

Use whatever milk chocolate you like, but I prefer the old-fashioned Hershey milk chocolate bar.

6. Place a heaping tablespoon of frosting on each cupcake and spread it out with the back of the spoon, taking care to cover the tops completely. The cupcakes are ready to serve.

✿ *Store these cupcakes, in a cake saver or under a glass dome, at room temperature for up to 3 days or in the refrigerator for up to 1 week. Or freeze them, wrapped in aluminum foil or in a cake saver, for up to 6 months. Thaw the cupcakes overnight in the refrigerator before serving.*

RED VELVET CUPCAKES

WITH WHITE CHOCOLATE PEPPERMINT CREAM CHEESE FROSTING

• • • • •

Red velvet cupcakes take a beloved traditional recipe and make it even more flavorful. Yes the cupcakes are the *de rigueur* red, but they are filled with mini chocolate chips to bring out the chocolate flavor. To complement the color and the flavor, I've paired them with a white chocolate frosting, delicately seasoned with peppermint.

24 paper liners for cupcake pans (2½-inch size)

1 package (18.25 ounces) plain German chocolate cake mix

1 package (3.4 ounces) vanilla instant pudding mix

1 cup sour cream (see "the Cupcake Doctor says")

½ cup water

½ cup vegetable oil

1 bottle (1 ounce) red food coloring

3 large eggs

1 cup miniature semisweet chocolate chips

White Chocolate Peppermint Cream Cheese Frosting (page 343)

✿ **MAKES 22 TO 24 CUPCAKES (2½ INCHES EACH)**

✿ **PREPARATION TIME: 10 MINUTES**

✿ **BAKING TIME: 18 TO 20 MINUTES**

✿ **ASSEMBLY TIME: 5 MINUTES**

1. Place a rack in the center of the oven and preheat the oven to 350°F. Line 24 cupcake cups with paper liners. Set the pans aside.

2. Place the cake mix, pudding mix, sour cream, water, oil, food coloring, and eggs in a large mixing bowl. Blend with an electric mixer on low speed for 30 seconds. Stop the machine and scrape down the sides of the bowl with a rubber spatula. Increase the mixer speed to medium and beat 2 minutes more, scraping down the sides again if needed. The batter should look thick and well combined. Fold in the

the Cupcake Doctor says...

Use reduced-fat sour cream, and you'll sacrifice only fat and calories, not flavor. If you can't find plain German chocolate cake mix, buy the pudding in the mix version and forgo the added pudding. For more chocolate flavor, use chocolate pudding mix instead of the vanilla, but the cake won't be as red in color.

5 Ways to Top Red Velvet Cupcakes
▼ ▼ ▼

1. Place a valentine heart stencil on top of the cupcake and shake red sugar sprinkles over it. Repeat with the remaining cupcakes.

2. Sprinkle with white or dark chocolate curls (page 16).

3. Crushed peppermint candies

4. Miniature semisweet chocolate chips

5. York Peppermint Pattie Swoops

chocolate chips. Spoon or scoop ⅓ cup batter into each lined cupcake cup, filling it three quarters of the way full. (You will get between 22 and 24 cupcakes; remove the empty liners, if any.) Place the pans in the oven.

3. Bake the cupcakes until they spring back when lightly pressed with your finger, 18 to 20 minutes. Remove the pans from the oven and place them on wire racks to cool for 5 minutes. Run a dinner knife around the edges of the cupcake liners, lift the cupcakes up from the bottoms of the cups using the end of the knife, and pick them out of the cups carefully with your fingertips. Place them on a wire rack to cool for 15 minutes before frosting.

4. Meanwhile, prepare the White Chocolate Peppermint Cream Cheese Frosting.

5. Place a heaping tablespoon of frosting on each cupcake and swirl to spread with a short metal spatula or a spoon, taking care to cover the tops completely. Place these cupcakes, uncovered or in a cake server, in the refrigerator until the frosting sets, 20 minutes. The cupcakes are ready to serve.

✿ *Store the cupcakes, in a cake saver or under a glass dome, at room temperature for up to 3 days or in the refrigerator for up to 1 week. Or freeze them, wrapped in aluminum foil or in a cake saver, for up to 6 months. Thaw the cupcakes overnight in the refrigerator before serving.*

CAPPUCCINO CHIP CUPCAKES

WITH MOCHA BUTTERCREAM

• • • • •

A chapter of grown-up cupcake recipes wouldn't be complete without a recipe combining the flavors of chocolate and coffee. They go beautifully together in this handsome cupcake, which bakes up tall and is crowned with a sublime coffee and chocolate frosting. Whether you wash them down with a cup of joe or a glass of cold milk, these cupcakes are delicious any time of the day.

✿ MAKES 22 TO 24 CUPCAKES (2½ INCHES EACH)
✿ PREPARATION TIME: 20 MINUTES
✿ BAKING TIME: 18 TO 20 MINUTES
✿ ASSEMBLY TIME: 10 MINUTES

24 paper liners for cupcake pans
    (2½-inch size)
⅓ cup water
4 teaspoons instant coffee granules
1 package (18.25 ounces) plain yellow
    cake mix
1 package (3.4 ounces) vanilla instant
    pudding mix
¾ cup whole milk
¾ cup vegetable oil
4 large eggs
1 cup miniature semisweet chocolate chips,
    plus Mocha Buttercream (page 323)
⅓ cup miniature semisweet chocolate chips
    or cracked roasted cocoa beans,
    for garnish (see "the Cupcake
    Doctor says")

1. Place a rack in the center of the oven and preheat the oven to 350°F. Line 24 cupcake cups with paper liners. Set the pans aside.

the Cupcake Doctor says...

By adding more or fewer coffee granules to the water, you can vary the intensity of the coffee flavor in these cupcakes. For a Mexican twist on this recipe, add 1 teaspoon ground cinnamon to the batter. Roasted, cracked cocoa beans are a fun and crunchy garnish. You can find them in specialty food stores. The pudding mix helps suspend the chocolate chips— and you thought it was just to make these cupcakes moist!

2. Place the water and instant coffee in a small glass liquid measuring cup and microwave on high power for 40 seconds. Remove and stir until the coffee is dissolved. Set it aside to cool for 5 minutes.

3. Place the cake mix, pudding mix, milk, oil, eggs, and coffee in a large mixing bowl. Blend with an electric mixer on low for 30 seconds. Stop the machine and scrape down the sides of the bowl with a rubber spatula. Increase the mixer speed to medium and beat 2 minutes more, scraping down the sides again if needed. The batter should look thick and well combined. Fold in 1 cup of the chocolate chips. Spoon or scoop ⅓ cup batter into each

lined cupcake cup, filling it three quarters of the way full. (You will get between 22 and 24 cupcakes; remove the empty liners, if any.) Place the pans in the oven.

4. Bake the cupcakes until they spring back when lightly pressed with your finger, 18 to 20 minutes. Remove the pans from the oven and place them on wire racks to cool for 5 minutes. Run a dinner knife around the edges of the cupcake liners, lift the cupcakes up from the bottoms of the cups using the end of the knife, and pick them out of the cups carefully with your fingertips. Place them on a wire rack to cool for 15 minutes before frosting.

5. Meanwhile, prepare the Mocha Buttercream Frosting.

6. Place a heaping tablespoon of frosting on each cupcake and swirl to spread it out with a short metal spatula or the back of the spoon, taking care to cover the tops completely. Garnish with the remaining ⅓ cup chocolate chips or roasted cracked cocoa beans. The cupcakes are ready to serve.

✿ *Store these cupcakes, in a cake saver or under a glass dome, at room temperature for up to 3 days or in the refrigerator for up to 1 week. Or freeze them, wrapped in aluminum foil or in a cake saver, for up to 6 months. Thaw the cupcakes overnight in the refrigerator before serving.*

CHOCOLATE ALMOND CUPCAKES

· · · · ·

I dream about these big, luscious, chocolate-coated, almond-packed cupcakes. They are as delicious to eat as they are delicious to the eye, with the almond–scented chocolate glaze dripping down the side. But the secret inside isn't visible—you have to bite in to find the treasure of soft almond paste mixed with sliced almonds. It's an almond island encased by deep chocolate cake, and that's pretty dreamy stuff.

✿ **MAKES 18 TO 20 CUPCAKES (2½ INCHES EACH)**
✿ **PREPARATION TIME: 25 MINUTES**
✿ **BAKING TIME: 20 TO 25 MINUTES**
✿ **ASSEMBLY TIME: 5 MINUTES**

20 paper liners for cupcake pans
　　(2½-inch size)

ALMOND FILLING:
½ cup almond paste (half of a 7-ounce tube;
　　see "the Cupcake Doctor says")
1 bag (2.25 ounces) sliced almonds

CUPCAKES:
1 package (18.25 ounces) plain devil's
　　food cake mix
2 tablespoons unsweetened cocoa powder
1½ cups buttermilk
½ cup vegetable oil
3 large eggs
1 teaspoon pure almond extract

CHOCOLATE ALMOND GLAZE:
1 cup semisweet chocolate chips
3 tablespoons butter
2 tablespoons light corn syrup
½ teaspoon pure almond or
　　vanilla extract

1. Place a rack in the center of the oven and preheat the oven to 350°F. Line 20 cupcake cups with paper liners. Set the pans aside.

2. Prepare the filling: With clean hands, crumble the almond paste into a medium-size mixing bowl. Reserve 1 tablespoon of the almonds for garnish and add the rest to the almond paste. Toss the mixture together with your hands and set it aside.

3. Prepare the cupcake batter: Place the cake mix, cocoa powder, buttermilk, oil, eggs, and almond extract in a large mixing bowl. Blend with an electric mixer on low speed until the ingredients just come

the Cupcake Doctor says...

Almond paste is a combination of blanched ground almonds and sugar, with glycerine or another liquid to hold it together. It is sold in a slender log in the baking aisle of many supermarkets. It needs to stay moist, so seal leftover almond paste in a zipper-lock bag in the refrigerator, where it will keep for a month. Add ½ cup to the batter of any baked good and it will provide a lot of pure almond flavor.

together, 30 seconds. Stop the machine and scrape down the bowl with a rubber spatula. Increase the mixer to medium and beat 1½ to 2 minutes more, scraping down the sides again if needed. The batter is smooth and thickened. Remove ¾ cup of the batter and stir this into the almond paste mixture. Set it aside.

4. Spoon or scoop ⅓ cup of the remaining batter into each lined cupcake cup, filling it three quarters of the way full. (You will get between 18 to 20 cupcakes; remove the empty liners, if any.) Dollop a heaping teaspoonful of almond paste mixture, centered, on the top of each cupcake. Place the pans in the oven.

5. Bake the cupcakes until they spring back when lightly pressed with your finger, 20 to 25 minutes. The almond filling will sink into the center of the cupcakes as they bake, and may create an attractive mottled appearance on the tops. Remove the pans from the oven and place them on wire racks to cool for 5 minutes. Run a dinner knife around the edges of the cupcake liners, lift the cupcakes up from the bottoms of the cups using the end of the knife, and pick them out of the cups carefully with your fingertips. Place them on a wire rack

in a small saucepan over low heat and stir until the chocolate melts and the glaze comes together, 2 to 3 minutes. Remove the pan from the heat and stir in the almond extract.

7. With a soup spoon drizzle glaze over each cupcake in crosswise lines, then switch direction and drizzle in crosswise lines again to create a crosshatch pattern. While the glaze is still warm, gently press a few reserved sliced almonds onto the top of each cupcake so that they stick to the glaze. The cupcakes are ready to serve.

✿ *Store these cupcakes, in a cake saver or under a glass dome, at room temperature for up to 3 days or in the refrigerator for up to 1 week. Or freeze them, wrapped in aluminum foil or in a cake saver, for up to 6 months. Thaw the cupcakes overnight in the refrigerator before serving.*

5 Things to Drink with Cupcakes

▼ ▼ ▼

Honestly, anything goes well with cupcakes—even a glass of cola—but these are classic. Or should be.

1. Hot tea

2. Hot coffee or cocoa

3. Sparkling wine

4. Lemonade

5. Cold milk

to cool for 15 minutes before glazing.

6. Meanwhile, prepare the glaze: Place the chocolate chips, butter, and corn syrup

ORANGE-ALMOND CUPCAKES

• • • • •

*U*nable to leave well enough alone, I had to try a blond version of the Chocolate-Almond Cupcake on page 41. Don't believe the blond jokes, for this is one very together cupcake with an irresistible orange flavor.

20 paper liners for cupcake pans
(2½-inch size)

ALMOND FILLING:
½ cup almond paste (half of a 7-ounce tube,
see "the Cupcake Doctor says,"
page 42)
1 bag sliced almonds

✿ **MAKES 18 TO 20 CUPCAKES (2½ INCHES EACH)**
✿ **PREPARATION TIME: 25 MINUTES**
✿ **BAKING TIME: 20 TO 25 MINUTES**
✿ **ASSEMBLY TIME: 5 MINUTES**

CUPCAKES:
1 package (18.25 ounces) plain yellow
cake mix
1 package (3.4 ounces) vanilla instant
pudding mix
1¼ cups orange juice, purchased or fresh
¾ cup vegetable oil
4 large eggs
1 teaspoon pure vanilla extract
1 teaspoon pure almond extract

GLAZE:
1½ cups sifted confectioners' sugar
1 generous teaspoon fresh orange zest
2 to 4 tablespoons orange juice,
commercial or fresh

I. Place a rack in the center of the oven and preheat the oven to 350°F. Line 20 cupcake cups with paper liners. Set the pans aside.

2. Prepare the filling: With clean hands, crumble the almond paste into a medium-size mixing bowl. Reserve 1 tablespoon of the almonds for garnish and add the rest to the almond paste. Toss the mixture together with your hands and set it aside.

3. Prepare the cupcake batter: Place the cake mix, pudding mix, orange juice, oil, eggs, and vanilla and almond extracts in a large mixing bowl. Blend with an electric mixer on low speed until the ingredients just come together, 30 seconds. Stop the machine and scrape down the sides of the bowl with a rubber spatula. Increase the mixer to medium and beat 1½ minutes more, scraping down the sides again if needed. The batter will look smooth and thickened. Remove ¾ cup of the batter and stir this into the almond paste mixture. Set it aside.

4. Spoon or scoop ⅓ cup of the remaining batter into each lined cupcake cup, filling it three quarters of the way full. (You will get between 18 to 20 cupcakes; remove the empty liners, if any.) Dollop a heaping teaspoonful of almond paste mixture, centered, on top of each cupcake.

5. Bake the cupcakes until they look golden and spring back when

the Cupcake Doctor says...

Use whatever orange juice you have on hand. Freshly squeezed is delicious, unreconstituted from the carton is fine, and even reconstituted frozen O.J. makes a delicious cupcake.

lightly pressed with your finger, 20 to 25 minutes. The almond filling will sink into the center of the cupcakes as they bake, and may create an attractive mottled appearance on the tops. Remove the pans from the oven and place them on wire racks to cool for 5 minutes. Run a dinner knife around the edges of the cupcake liners, lift the cupcakes up from the bottoms of the cups using the end of the knife, and pick them out of the cups carefully with your fingertips. Place them on a wire rack to cool for 15 minutes before glazing.

6. Meanwhile, prepare the glaze: Place the sugar in a small mixing bowl. Stir in the orange zest until well incorporated. Add 3 tablespoons of the orange juice and stir to make a glaze thin enough to drop from a spoon, but firm enough to harden on the cupcake as it cools. If it seems too thick, add up to 1 tablespoon more of the juice.

7. With a soupspoon, drizzle glaze over each cupcake in crosswise lines, then switch direction and drizzle in crosswise lines again to create a crosshatch pattern. While the glaze is still warm, gently press a few of the reserved sliced almonds onto the top of each cupcake so that they stick to the glaze. The cupcakes are ready to serve.

✿ *Store these cupcakes, in a cake saver or under a glass dome, at room temperature for up to 3 days or in the refrigerator for up to 1 week. Or freeze them, wrapped in aluminum foil or in a cake saver, for up to 6 months. Thaw the cupcakes overnight in the refrigerator before serving.*

HOT FUDGE SPUMONI ICE CREAM CAKES

· · · · ·

I can't decide what I like best about these cupcakes—their eye appeal (pale green pistachio cake), their mouth appeal (hot fudge sauce cloaking cold cherry and chocolate ice cream), or their friendliness factor (squirt of whipped cream and a cherry on top). These cupcakes are a perfect party do-ahead because you can bake and fill them with ice cream, then keep the cupcakes in the freezer until serving time.

✿ **MAKES 20 TO 22 CUPCAKES (2½ INCHES EACH)**
✿ **PREPARATION TIME: 15 MINUTES**
✿ **BAKING TIME: 20 TO 25 MINUTES**
✿ **ASSEMBLY TIME: 10 MINUTES**

22 paper liners for cupcake pans
  (2½-inch size)

CUPCAKES:
1 package (18.25 ounces) plain white
  cake mix
1 package (3.4 ounces) pistachio
  instant pudding mix
1 cup Sprite or ginger ale
¾ cup vegetable oil
3 large eggs
¼ teaspoon pure almond extract
  (optional)

TOPPING:
Easy Hot Fudge Sauce (page 356)
1 can (7 ounces) light whipped cream
20 to 22 maraschino cherries
½ cup dry-roasted salted pistachios
  (optional)

2 pints Ben & Jerry's Cherry Garcia ice
  cream (see "the Cupcake Doctor says")

1. Place a rack in the center of the oven and preheat the oven to 350°F. Line 22 cupcake cups with paper liners. Set the pans aside.

2. Prepare the cupcake batter: Place the cake mix, pudding mix, Sprite, oil, eggs, and almond extract, if desired, in a large mixing bowl. Blend with an electric mixer on low speed until ingredients just come together, about 30 seconds. Stop the machine and scrape down the sides of the bowl. Increase the mixer speed to medium and beat 2 minutes more, scraping down the sides again if needed. The batter should look smooth and thickened. Spoon or scoop ¼ cup batter into each lined cupcake cup, filling it two thirds of the way full. (You will get between 20 and 22 cupcakes; remove the empty liners, if any. Don't overfill these cupcakes. When baked, they should just reach over the top of the pan.) Place the pans in the oven.

3. Bake the cupcakes until they are lightly golden and spring back when lightly pressed with your finger, 20 to 25 minutes. Remove the pans from the oven and place them on wire racks. Immediately press down on the center of each cupcake with the end of a rolling pin or a 1½-inch-wide glass to form an indentation. Let the cupcakes

the *Cupcake Doctor says...*

I like cherry vanilla ice cream in these cupcakes, but they are delicious with any ice cream of your choice. Even vanilla tastes great in this recipe. And you can use this method with most any cupcake recipe. Create an indentation while the cupcake is warm, fill with ice cream, freeze, garnish, and serve. (Feel free to scoop on more ice cream for a big look.) The soda in this recipe is just for fun. You can use any clear flavor, or just substitute water.

cool in the pan for 5 minutes. Run a dinner knife around the edges of the cupcake liners, lift the cupcakes up from the bottoms of the cups using the end of the knife, and pick them out of the cups carefully with your fingertips. Place them on a wire rack to cool for 15 minutes before filling with ice cream.

4. Meanwhile, prepare the Easy Hot Fudge Sauce.

5. Remove the ice cream from the freezer 5 minutes before using it. Place the cooled cupcakes, still in their liners, back in the pans. With a small (¼ cup) scoop, place a scoop of ice cream in each cupcake well so that the rounded side is up and looks like the rounded top of the cupcake. Cover the pans with plastic wrap and place them in the freezer until time to serve.

6. To serve, remove the cupcakes from the freezer. Remove the paper liner from each cupcake and place the cupcakes on serving plates. Add another scoop of ice cream, if desired. Then spoon sauce over the top of each cupcake and add a squirt of whipped cream, a cherry, and pistachios, if desired.

✿ *Store these ice cream-filled cupcakes, in the baking pans or on a baking sheet covered with plastic wrap, in the freezer for up to 1 month.*

INSIDE-OUT PEANUT BUTTER CUPCAKES

· · · · ·

When traveling, I am often inspired by sweets I see in pastry shops. It's rare that I walk into a shop and walk out empty-handed. I love to taste fancy cookies, but when I get back to my kitchen I invariably try to make them bake-able by you and me. In Raleigh, North Carolina, I sampled a heavy but heavenly chocolate peanut butter cup cookie and I knew this idea could translate into a cupcake. Yes, it takes a bit more time to prepare than the usual cupcake, because you have to make a ganache frosting. But when you bite into that hidden well of fudge inside, you'll realize it was worth it!

Solid vegetable shortening for greasing
     the pans
All-purpose flour for dusting the pans
1 package (18.25 ounces) plain yellow
     cake mix
1⅓ cups water
⅓ cup chunky peanut butter
⅓ cup vegetable oil
3 large eggs
1 teaspoon pure vanilla extract
Double recipe Basic Chocolate Ganache
     (page 332)
3 to 4 peanut butter cups
     (.75-ounce each), chopped, for garnish
     (see "the Cupcake Doctor says")

✿ MAKES 24 CUPCAKES (2½ INCHES EACH)
✿ PREPARATION TIME: 1 HOUR
✿ BAKING TIME: 18 TO 20 MINUTES
✿ ASSEMBLY TIME: 15 MINUTES

5 Ways to Flavor a Ganache Frosting

▼ ▼ ▼

Silky, elegant chocolate ganache frosting is *the* icing on the cupcake, so to speak. Here are ways to flavor it to make my Basic Chocolate Ganache (page 332) even more memorable.

1. With a tablespoon of spirits, such as Kahlúa, bourbon, Chambord, grappa, Madeira, rum, peppermint schnapps, or Amaretto.

2. With a tablespoon of strong brewed coffee or a teaspoon of instant espresso powder.

3. With a teaspoon of vanilla, almond, or peppermint extract.

4. With a teaspoon of vanilla paste. It's more robust than the extract.

5. With 2 tablespoons of your favorite peanut butter.

---

1. Place a rack in the center of the oven and preheat the oven to 350°F. Lightly grease the cupcake cups with vegetable shortening and dust with flour. Shake out the excess flour. Set the pans aside.

2. Place the cake mix, water, peanut butter, oil, eggs, and vanilla in a large mixing bowl and blend with an electric mixer on low speed for 30 seconds. Stop the machine and scrape down the sides of the bowl with a rubber spatula. Increase the mixer speed to medium and beat for 2 minutes more, scraping down the sides again if needed. The batter should be well blended. Spoon or scoop ¼ cup batter into each pre-pared cup, filling it almost two thirds of the way full. Place the pans in the oven.

3. Bake the cupcakes until they spring back when lightly pressed with your finger and a toothpick inserted in the center comes out clean, 18 to 20 minutes. Remove the pans from the oven and place them on wire racks to cool for 2 to 3 minutes. Using the bottom of a small medicine bottle approximately 1¼ inches in diameter or the end of a rolling pin, press into the center of each cupcake to make an indentation approximately ¾ inch deep. Allow the cupcakes to continue to cool in the pans, 40 minutes.

4. Meanwhile, prepare a double recipe of the Basic Chocolate Ganache. Cover the bowl with plastic wrap and place it in the refrigerator to chill for 45 minutes.

5. Run a dinner knife around the edges of the cupcakes, lift the cupcakes up from the bottoms of the cups using the end of the knife, and pick them out of the cups carefully with your fingertips. Place them on a serving platter or cooling rack.

6. When the ganache has cooled and is still spreadable, place a heaping table-spoonful into the well of each cupcake. Then, using a small metal spatula, spread a thin layer of ganache over the top. Immediately sprinkle the chopped peanut butter cups over the ganache so they stick. The cupcakes are ready to serve.

✿ *Store these cupcakes, in a cake saver or under a glass dome, at room temperature for up to one day or in the refrigerator for up to 1 week. Or freeze them, wrapped in*

the Cupcake Doctor says...

Vary this recipe by using smooth peanut butter. Ganache hardens as it cools, and because I don't like waiting for this to happen, I place it in the refrigerator to speed the chilling. If you want to plan ahead and make things easier, prepare the ganache the day before and leave it covered at room temperature or chill it and let it come to room temperature to become spreadable. And chilling the peanut butter cups makes chopping easier, too.

aluminum foil or in a cake saver, for up to 6 months. Thaw the cupcakes overnight in the refrigerator before serving, then set them aside at room temperature for 1 hour to soften the ganache.

CHERRY CHEESECAKE CUPCAKES

• • • • •

What is it about cheese-cake—every smidgen of it—that is so appealing? This cupcake ventures into the creamy texture and subtle flavor of cheese-cake. A soft cheese filling is poured on top of the cupcake before it is baked, and then it is topped with cherry pie filling. The cherry red result is delicious.

28 paper liners for cupcake pans
  (2½-inch size)

❀ **MAKES 28 CUPCAKES (2½ INCHES EACH)**
❀ **PREPARATION TIME: 40 MINUTES**
❀ **BAKING TIME: 18 TO 20 MINUTES**
❀ **ASSEMBLY TIME: 10 MINUTES**

FILLING:

1 package (8 ounces) cream cheese,
  at room temperature
⅓ cup granulated sugar
1 large egg
½ teaspoon pure vanilla extract

CUPCAKES:

1 package (18.25 ounces) plain yellow
  cake mix
1 package (3.4 ounces) vanilla instant
  pudding mix
1 cup whole milk
  (see "the Cupcake Doctor says")
⅔ cup vegetable oil
3 large eggs
1 teaspoon pure almond extract
28 vanilla wafers

TOPPING:

Vegetable oil spray for misting a spoon
1 can (21 ounces) cherry pie filling
¼ cup confectioners' sugar

the Cupcake Doctor says...

Even if you don't keep whole milk in your refrigerator, you might consider buying a quart just for baking. The extra fat in whole milk creates a richer crumb in some recipes, and it is a noticeable addition in this recipe. But if it means running to the store just to buy whole milk, don't do it. Just use the milk you've got on hand.

Note that this recipe makes several more cupcakes than my usual recipes. If you have a 6-cup pan, now's the time to pull it out.

1. Place a rack in the center of the oven and preheat the oven to 350°F. Line 28 cupcake cups with paper liners. Set the pans aside.

2. Prepare the filling: Place the cream cheese in a small mixing bowl and blend with an electric mixer on low speed until the cream cheese has softened, 15 seconds. Add the sugar, egg, and vanilla and continue to beat on low until the ingredients just come together, 1 minute. Set the filling aside.

3. Prepare the cupcake batter: Place the cake mix, pudding mix, milk, oil, eggs, and almond extract in a large mixing bowl. Blend with an electric mixer on low speed for 30 seconds. Stop the machine and scrape down the sides of the bowl with a rubber spatula. Increase the mixer speed to medium and beat 2 minutes more, scraping down the sides again if needed.

4. Place 1 vanilla wafer in the bottom of each cupcake liner. Spoon or scoop ¼ cup batter on top of each vanilla wafer. Gently dollop 1 heaping teaspoon of filling on top of each cupcake. The cup will be nearly full. Do not shake the pans. Place the pans in the oven.

5. Bake the cupcakes until they are golden and spring back when lightly pressed with your finger, 18 to 20 min-

utes. Remove the pans from the oven and place them on wire racks to cool for 5 minutes. Run a dinner knife around the edges of the cupcake liners, lift the cupcakes up from the bottoms of the cups using the end of the knife, and pick them out of the cups carefully with your fingertips. Place them on a wire rack to cool for 15 minutes before topping.

6. Mist a teaspoon with vegetable oil spray and use this to press down on the cupcake to create an indentation. Place a heaping teaspoon of cherry pie filling in the well of each cupcake. Dust with confectioners' sugar. The cupcakes are ready to be served.

✿ *Store these cupcakes, in a cake saver at room temperature, for up to 2 days or in the refrigerator for up to 1 week. Or freeze them, wrapped in aluminum foil or in a cake saver, for up to 6 months. Thaw the cupcakes overnight in the refrigerator before serving.*

5 Ways to Keep Cupcakes Lower in Fat
▼ ▼ ▼

If it's fat that keeps you from baking cupcakes, here are some ideas for keeping them healthy.

1. Fruit purees. Substitute applesauce or pureed prunes or pumpkin or mashed banana for the oil in the recipe. (You can buy prune puree in the healthy/diet section of the supermarket. Do not use baby food.)

2. Substitute reduced-fat sour cream and cream cheese for full-fat versions. Do not substitute the fat-free versions.

3. Forgo the frosting. The cupcakes are all tasty on their own.

4. Eat less. Fill a cupcake with ¼ cup batter, bake these smaller cakes for only 15 to 20 minutes, freeze the extras, and share with your friends.

5. Relax! A recipe for cupcakes makes about 24. A cake recipe serves 12. You're eating half as many calories per serving.

BUTTER PECAN CHEESECAKE CUPCAKES

· · · · ·

Maybe it's the Southern girl in me, but I have always been drawn to the flavor of butter pecan ice cream. And I think peaches and apricots go perfectly with butter pecan. So, naturally, when I came up with this cheesecake cupcake I wanted a dollop of apricot (or peach) preserves on top. These are pretty cupcakes, glistening with preserves and showered with confectioners' sugar. Take them to a tea party, give them to a dear friend, or bring them to a bake sale.

24 paper liners for cupcake pans (2½-inch size)

FILLING:
1 package (8 ounces) cream cheese,
*　　at room temperature*
¼ cup granulated sugar
1 large egg
1 teaspoon pure vanilla extract

CUPCAKES:
1 package (18 ounces) butter pecan
*　　cake mix with pudding (*
*　　see "the Cupcake Doctor says")*
1¼ cups water
⅓ cup vegetable oil
3 large eggs
1 teaspoon pure vanilla extract

✿ **MAKES 22 TO 24 CUPCAKES (2½ INCHES EACH)**
✿ **PREPARATION TIME: 35 MINUTES**
✿ **BAKING TIME: 18 TO 20 MINUTES**
✿ **ASSEMBLY TIME: 10 MINUTES**

TOPPING:

Vegetable oil spray for misting
a spoon

1 cup apricot preserves

½ cup finely chopped pecans, toasted
(see "the Cupcake Doctor says")

2 tablespoons confectioners' sugar

1. Place a rack in the center of the oven and preheat the oven to 350°F. Line 24 cupcake cups with paper liners. Set the pans aside.

2. Prepare the filling: Place the cream cheese in a small mixing bowl and blend with an electric mixer on low speed until the cream cheese has softened, 15 seconds. Add the sugar, egg, and vanilla and continue to beat on low until the ingredients just come together, 1 minute. Set the filling aside.

3. Prepare the cupcake batter: Place the cake mix, water, oil, eggs, and vanilla in a large mixing bowl. Blend with an electric mixer on low speed for 30 seconds. Stop the machine and scrape down the sides

the Cupcake Doctor says...

It's essential to the flavor of this recipe that you begin with a butter pecan cake mix. If you can find one with pudding, that's great; if you can only find a plain mix, go ahead and use it. The toasted pecan garnish accentuates the pecan flavor of the mix, so be sure to toast the nuts. Just place them in the oven when the cupcakes are removed. They need 4 to 5 minutes of toasting, so watch carefully.

of the bowl with a rubber spatula. Increase the mixer speed to medium and beat 2 minutes more, scraping down the sides again if needed.

4. Spoon or scoop ⅓ cup batter into each cupcake liner, filling it three quarters of the way full. Gently dollop about 1 heaping teaspoon of filling on top of each cupcake. Do not shake the pans. The cup will be nearly full. Place the pans in the oven.

5. Bake the cupcakes until they are golden and spring back when lightly pressed with your finger, 18 to 20 minutes. Remove the pans from the oven and place them on wire racks to cool for 5 minutes. Run a dinner knife around the edges of the cupcake liners, lift the cupcakes up from the bottoms of the cups using the end of the knife, and pick them out of the cups carefully with your fingertips. Place them on a wire rack to cool for 15 minutes before filling.

6. Mist a teaspoon with vegetable oil spray and use this to press down on the cupcake to create an indentation. Place a heaping teaspoon of apricot preserves in the well of each cupcake. Sprinkle the pecans over the preserves and dust the entire cupcake with confectioners' sugar. The cupcakes are now ready to serve.

✿ *Store these cupcakes, in a cake saver at room temperature, for up to 2 days or in the refrigerator for up to 1 week. Or freeze them, wrapped in aluminum foil or in a cake saver, for up to 6 months. Thaw the cupcakes overnight in the refrigerator before serving.*

FRESH PEAR AND GINGERBREAD CUPCAKES

WITH A CREAMY LEMON FROSTING

• • • • •

rue confession time: I grew up making gingerbread from a boxed mix. And I like the taste of gingerbread from the box as well as or better than the from-scratch gingerbread I've eaten. So, when I tested this recipe, I had pleasant flashbacks to those early baking days. Too bad I didn't know enough about cooking then to add some diced ripe pear to the recipe . . . or

☘ **MAKES 14 TO 16 CUPCAKES (2½ INCHES EACH)**
☘ **PREPARATION TIME: 15 MINUTES**
☘ **BAKING TIME: 18 TO 20 MINUTES**
☘ **ASSEMBLY TIME: 5 MINUTES**

to use this terrific lemon frosting. Oh well, we live and learn—and bake better as a result!

16 paper liners for cupcake pans
*   (2½-inch size)*
1 package (14.5 ounces) gingerbread mix
1 cup water
1 large egg
1 medium-size ripe pear, peeled, cored,
*   and finely chopped*
1 heaping teaspoon crystallized ginger,
*   finely chopped (optional; see*
*   "the Cupcake Doctor says")*
Creamy Lemon Frosting (page 325)
*   or Sweetened Whipped Cream*
*   (page 349)*

the Cupcake Doctor says...

I used the Betty Crocker gingerbread mix in this recipe. It benefited from the additional crystallized ginger, but this is an expensive ingredient. If you can find it on your spice shelf, use it! You'll love the gingery bite. These cupcakes are still delicious without it, and the ripened pear adds so much flavor. If you like the lemon frosting idea, just whip cream, sweeten it, and spoon it on top of each cupcake. Or, for a lighter alternative, forgo the frosting and dust the tops with confectioners' sugar.

1. Place a rack in the center of the oven and preheat the oven to 350°F. Line 16 cupcake cups with paper liners. Set the pans aside.

2. Place the gingerbread mix, water, egg, pear, and ginger, if desired, in a large mixing bowl. Blend with an electric mixer on low speed for 30 seconds. Stop the machine and scrape down the sides of the bowl with a rubber spatula. Increase the mixer speed to medium and beat until smooth and thickened, 2 minutes more, scraping down the sides again if needed. Spoon or scoop ⅓ cup batter into each lined muffin cup, fill-

ing it three quarters of the way full. (You will get between 14 and 16 cupcakes; remove the empty liners, if any.) Place the pans in the oven.

3. Bake the cupcakes until they spring back when lightly pressed with your finger, 18 to 20 minutes. Remove the pans from the oven and place them on wire racks to cool for 5 minutes. Run a dinner knife around the edges of the cupcake liners, lift the cupcakes up from the bottoms of the cups using the end of the knife, and pick them out of the cups carefully with your fingertips. Place them on a wire rack to cool for 15 minutes before frosting.

4. Meanwhile, prepare the Creamy Lemon Frosting (page 325) or Sweetened Whipped Cream (page 349).

5. Place a heaping tablespoon of frosting on each cupcake and swirl to spread it out with a short metal spatula or a spoon, taking care to cover the tops completely. Place them, uncovered, in the refrigerator until the frosting sets, 20 minutes. The cupcakes are now ready to serve.

❀ *Store the cupcakes, in a cake saver or under a glass dome, at room temperature for up to 3 days or in the refrigerator for up to 1 week. Or freeze them, wrapped in aluminum foil or in a cake saver, for up to 6 months. Thaw the cupcakes overnight in the refrigerator before serving.*

LEMON CHIFFON CUPCAKES

WITH A FROSTY LEMON GLAZE

• • • • •

Chiffon cakes were all the rage 30 to 40 years ago, and this seemingly retro cake deserves another chance in the spotlight. Chiffons, which contain beaten egg whites, are light as angels, and because they also contain egg yolks, oil, and in this recipe, lemon yogurt, they are moist like sponge cakes. Such light but noble cupcakes need just a gossamer but frosty glaze of fresh lemon juice and sugar.

✿ **MAKES 20 TO 22 CUPCAKES (2½ INCHES EACH)**
✿ **PREPARATION TIME: 25 MINUTES**
✿ **BAKING TIME: 20 TO 24 MINUTES**
✿ **ASSEMBLY TIME: 5 MINUTES**

22 paper liners for cupcake pans
   (2½-inch size)
5 large egg whites
½ teaspoon cream of tartar
1 package (18.25 ounces) plain lemon
   cake mix
6 ounces (¾ cup) lemon yogurt
   (see "the Cupcake Doctor says")
½ cup vegetable oil
3 large egg yolks
2 tablespoons pure lemon juice
1 teaspoon grated fresh
   lemon zest
Frosty Lemon Glaze (page 351)

1. Place a rack in the center of the oven and preheat the oven to 350°F. Line 22 cupcake cups with paper liners. Set the pans aside.

2. Place the egg whites and cream of tartar in a medium-size mixing bowl. Beat with an electric mixer on high speed until stiff peaks form, 2 to 3 minutes. Set the bowl aside.

3. Place the cake mix, yogurt, oil, egg yolks, lemon juice, and lemon zest in a large mixing bowl, and with the same beaters used to beat the egg whites (no need to clean them) blend with an electric mixer on low speed for 30 seconds. Stop the machine and scrape down the sides of the bowl with a rubber spatula. Increase the mixer speed to medium and beat for 2 minutes more, scraping down the sides again if needed. The batter should look well blended. Turn the beaten egg whites out on top of the batter, and with the rubber spatula fold the whites into the batter until the mixture is light but well combined. Spoon or scoop ⅓ cup batter into each lined cupcake cup, filling it three quarters of the way full. (You will get between 20 and 22 cupcakes; remove the empty liners, if any.) Place the pans in the oven.

4. Bake the cupcakes until they are golden and spring back when lightly pressed with your finger, 20 to 24 minutes. Remove the pans from the oven and place them on wire racks to cool for 5 minutes. Run a dinner knife around the edges of the cupcake liners, lift the

the Cupcake Doctor says...

Yogurt package sizes seem to be shrinking. Not so long ago, I noticed that my 8-ounce container had shrunk to 6 ounces. But no matter what size yogurt you buy, in this recipe you will need ¾ cup. And feel free to use vanilla instead of lemon yogurt.

cupcakes up from the bottoms of the cups using the end of the knife, and pick them out of the cups carefully with your fingertips. Place them on a wire rack to cool for 15 minutes before frosting.

5. Prepare the Frosty Lemon Glaze.

6. Drizzle the glaze on the top of each cupcake with a spoon. Let the glaze set for at least 5 minutes, then serve.

✿ *Store these cupcakes, in a cake saver or under a glass dome, at room temperature for up to 3 days or in the refrigerator for up to 1 week. Or freeze them, wrapped in aluminum foil or in a cake saver, for up to 6 months. Thaw the cupcakes overnight in the refrigerator before serving.*

MINI LEMON CURD CUPCAKES

WITH LEMONY CREAM

• • • • •

I love these little cupcakes. Oh, they're a bit precious, but this recipe is a snap to assemble and because it makes so many, it's perfect for parties, showers, birthdays, Easter brunch, or a Fourth of July picnic. Lemon curd is an elegant and easy way to doctor up a box of lemon cake mix, and the garnish of fresh strawberries or raspberries makes for a crowning touch.

✿ **MAKES 4 DOZEN MINIATURE CUPCAKES (2 INCHES EACH) OR 24 REGULAR-SIZE CUPCAKES (SEE "BAKING BIGGER CUPCAKES," PAGE 65)**

✿ **PREPARATION TIME: 15 MINUTES**

✿ **BAKING TIME: 15 TO 20 MINUTES**

✿ **ASSEMBLY TIME: 15 TO 20 MINUTES**

48 paper liners for miniature cupcake pans (2-inch size) or 24 paper liners for regular pans (2½-inch size)

1 package (18.25 ounces) plain lemon cake mix

1⅓ cups water

⅓ cup lemon curd (see "Love That Lemon Curd," page 65)

⅓ cup vegetable oil

3 large eggs

Lemony Cream (page 350)

12 strawberries, rinsed, cored, sliced lengthwise and then crosswise into half-moon slices (1 cup) or 48 golden or red raspberries, for garnish

the Cupcake Doctor says...

Miniature paper liners fit the 2-inch pans perfectly, and you can find them in supermarkets, craft stores, and cookware shops. If you don't own a mini cupcake pan, however, you really don't need to invest in one. Buy the foil mini liners, which are sturdy enough to stand on their own on a baking sheet. Just line them up, then spoon in the batter. Silicone miniature cupcake pans, in which no liners are needed, also work well with this recipe.

1. Place a rack in the center of the oven and preheat the oven to 350°F. Line 48 miniature cupcake cups with paper liners (see "the Cupcake Doctor says"). Set the pans aside.

2. Place the cake mix, water, lemon curd, oil, and eggs in a large mixing bowl. Blend on low speed until the ingredients are just incorporated, 30 seconds. Turn off the machine and scrape the sides of the bowl with a rubber spatula. Increase the mixer speed to medium and beat 2 minutes more, scraping down the sides again if needed. The batter should be well blended. Spoon or scoop 2 tablespoons batter into each lined cupcake cup, filling it two thirds of the way full. Place the pans in the oven.

3. Bake the cupcakes until they are golden and spring back when lightly pressed with your finger, 15 to 20 minutes. Remove the pans from the oven and place them on wire racks to cool for 5 minutes. Run a dinner knife around the edges of the cupcake liners, lift the cupcakes up from the bottoms of the cups using the end of the knife, and pick them out of the cups carefully with your fingertips. Place them on a wire rack to cool for 15 minutes before frosting.

4. Meanwhile, prepare the Lemony Cream.

5. Place a heaping tablespoon of frosting on each cupcake and swirl to spread it out with a short metal spatula or a spoon,

taking care to cover the tops completely. Top with strawberry slivers or raspberries and chill or serve.

Baking Bigger Cupcakes: Don't want minis? Spoon the batter into 24 paper-lined 2½-inch cupcake pans and bake at 350°F until just golden and firm to the touch, 20 to 25 minutes.

✿ *Store these cupcakes, uncovered or in a cake saver, in the refrigerator for up to 3 days. Or freeze them, unfrosted, wrapped in aluminum foil or in a cake saver, for up to 6 months. Thaw the cupcakes overnight in the refrigerator before frosting and garnishing.*

Love That Lemon Curd

▼ ▼ ▼

I adore lemon curd, both home-made and from the jar. Of the supermarket varieties I have sampled, my favorite is Dickinson's, which comes in a 10-ounce jar—plenty for this recipe. When you're shopping for curd, read the ingredient list. Curd made with butter tastes better than curd made with margarine.

COCONUT SNOWBALLS

• • • • •

Originally, I was going to call this recipe Coconut Icebox Cupcakes, and that would have been an apt name for them—packed with coconut, they are best stored in the refrigerator (or icebox). But after I saw how beautifully the batter rose into big, rounded tops, and how after piling on whipped cream and shredded coconut they resembled snowballs, I knew their name had to change. No throwing, just joyous eating.

❀ **MAKES 18 TO 20 CUPCAKES (2½ INCHES EACH)**
❀ **PREPARATION TIME: 10 MINUTES**
❀ **BAKING TIME: 18 TO 22 MINUTES**
❀ **ASSEMBLY TIME: 10 TO 15 MINUTES**

20 paper liners for cupcake pans
　(2½-inch size)
1 package (18.25 ounces) plain white
　cake mix
1⅓ cups coconut milk or regular whole milk
　(see "the Cupcake Doctor says")
2 tablespoons vegetable oil
3 large eggs
2 teaspoons coconut flavoring
1 cup (8 ounces) heavy (whipping) cream
2 tablespoons confectioners' sugar
1 bag (7 ounces) sweetened flaked coconut

1. Place a rack in the center of the oven and preheat the oven to 350°F. Line 20 cupcake cups with paper liners. Set the pans aside.

2. Prepare the cupcake batter: Place the cake mix, coconut milk, oil, eggs, and coconut flavoring in a large mixing bowl. Blend with an electric mixer on low speed for 30 seconds. Stop the machine and scrape down the sides of the bowl with a rubber spatula. Increase the mixer speed to medium and beat 2 minutes more, scraping down the sides again if needed. The batter should look well blended. Spoon or scoop ⅓ cup batter into each lined cupcake cup, filling it three quarters of the way full. (You will get between 18 and 20 cupcakes; remove the empty liners, if any.) Place the pans in the oven.

3. Bake the cupcakes until they are lightly golden, nicely domed, and spring back when lightly pressed with your finger, 18 to 22 minutes. Remove the pans from the oven and place them on wire racks to cool for 5 minutes. Run a dinner knife around the edges of the cupcake liners, lift the cupcakes up from the bottoms of the cups using the end of the knife, and pick them out of the cups carefully with your fingertips. Place them on a wire rack to cool for 15 minutes before frosting. Place a large clean mixing bowl and electric mixer beaters in the freezer for 1 minute to chill.

4. Prepare the frosting: Remove the bowl and beaters from the freezer. Pour the cream into the bowl and beat on high speed until the cream has thickened, 1½ minutes. Stop

the Cupcake Doctor says...

Coconut milk is found with the Thai ingredients in your supermarket. It is not the sweetened coconut cream used in tropical drinks. You can buy regular or light coconut milk, and either will work in this recipe. In a pinch, you can even use water instead of milk. And if you don't want to whip cream, go ahead and use 8 ounces of thawed frozen whipped topping, but it will not taste as good as the real thing does in this recipe.

the machine and add the sugar. Beat the cream and sugar on high speed until stiff peaks form, 1 to 2 minutes more.

5. Place a heaping tablespoon of whipped cream frosting on each cupcake, and swirl to spread it out with a short metal spatula or a spoon, taking care to cover the tops completely. Generously sprinkle coconut over the top, and press it down gently so that it stays on. Serve at once or chill until serving time.

✿ *Store these cupcakes, in a cake saver in the refrigerator, for up to 4 days.*

BOBBYE'S ITALIAN CREAM CUPCAKES

• • • • •

Bobbye Adams of Texas sent me a recipe for an Italian cream cake baked in 9-inch layers. I liked it so much I thought I'd try it out as cupcakes, too. Italian cream cake is a white cake filled with finely chopped pecans and coconut. Traditionally a cream cheese frosting goes on top, and I give you two options here. Stick with tradition and spread these pretty cakes with the plain cream cheese frosting, or walk on the wild side and spread on a coconut-flavored cream cheese frosting to bring out the flavor of the shredded coconut inside the cake.

22 paper liners for cupcake pans
    (2½-inch size)
1 package (18.25 ounces) plain white cake
    mix (see "the Cupcake Doctor says")
1⅓ cups water
2 tablespoons vegetable oil
3 large eggs
2 teaspoons coconut flavoring
1 bag (7 ounces) sweetened flaked coconut
1 cup finely chopped pecans
Coconut Cream Cheese Frosting (page 337)
    or plain Cream Cheese Frosting
    (page 336)

✿ **MAKES 20 TO 22 CUPCAKES (2½ INCHES EACH)**
✿ **PREPARATION TIME: 10 MINUTES**
✿ **BAKING TIME: 18 TO 22 MINUTES**
✿ **ASSEMBLY TIME: 10 MINUTES**

1. Place a rack in the center of the oven and preheat the oven to 350°F. Line 22 cupcake cups with paper liners. Set the pans aside.

2. Prepare the cupcake batter: Place the cake mix, water, oil, eggs, and coconut flavoring in a large mixing bowl. Blend with an electric mixer on low speed for 30 seconds. Stop the machine and scrape down the sides of the bowl with a rubber spatula. Increase the mixer speed to medium and beat 2 minutes more, scraping down the sides again if needed.

3. Measure out 1 cup of the coconut and set it aside for the garnish. Add the remaining coconut (about 1 cup) to the batter along with the pecans. Fold them in thoroughly with a rubber spatula. Spoon or scoop ⅓ cup batter into each lined cupcake cup, filling it three quarters of the way full. (You will get between 20 and 22 cupcakes; remove the empty liners, if any.) Place the pans in the oven.

4. Bake the cupcakes until they are lightly golden and spring back when lightly pressed with your finger, 18 to 22 minutes. Remove the pans from the oven and place them on wire racks to cool for 5 minutes. Run a dinner knife around the edges of the cupcake liners, lift the cupcakes up from the bottoms of the cups using the end of the knife, and pick them out of the cups carefully with your fingertips. Place them on a wire rack to cool for 15 minutes before frosting.

the Cupcake Doctor says...

Bobbye Adams prefers a French vanilla cake mix. You can also use a plain yellow cake mix, which I think complements the coconut flavor well.

5. Meanwhile, prepare the Coconut Cream Cheese Frosting or the Cream Cheese Frosting.

6. Place a heaping tablespoon of frosting on each cupcake and swirl to spread it out with a short metal spatula or a spoon, taking care to cover the tops completely. Pat the reserved coconut onto the tops of the cupcakes as garnish. Place them, uncovered, in the refrigerator until the frosting sets, 20 minutes. The cupcakes are ready to serve.

❀ *Store the cupcakes, in a cake saver or under a glass dome, at room temperature for up to 3 days or in the refrigerator for up to 1 week. Or freeze them, wrapped in aluminum foil or in a cake saver, for up to 6 months. Thaw the cupcakes overnight in the refrigerator before serving.*

ORANGE MARMALADE RICOTTA CUPCAKES

WITH MARMALADE BUTTERCREAM

· · · · ·

For nearly a year I lived in the Midlands of England, where I got very accustomed to a morning cup of tea at the kitchen table while reading the London paper and munching buttered wheat toast with orange marmalade. That year opened my eyes to the variety of marmalades out there, made from all types of citrus fruit. I even made my own using the microwave oven (delicious!). Now, back in Nashville, I can bite into this spongy and deeply orange cupcake—with marmalade in the batter, then brushed on top after baking, and added to the frosting—and lovely memories of those less hectic days come rushing back.

24 paper liners for cupcake pans
    (2½-inch size)

CUPCAKES:

1 package (18.25 ounces) plain yellow
    cake mix

1 cup orange juice, purchased or fresh

⅔ cup ricotta cheese or unflavored yogurt
    (see "the Cupcake Doctor says")

⅓ cup plus 3 tablespoons orange marmalade
    (see "the Cupcake Doctor says")

⅓ cup vegetable oil

4 large eggs

✿ **MAKES 22 TO 24 CUPCAKES (2½ INCHES EACH)**

✿ **PREPARATION TIME: 20 MINUTES**

✿ **BAKING TIME: 15 TO 20 MINUTES**

✿ **ASSEMBLY TIME: 5 MINUTES**

MARMALADE BUTTERCREAM:

8 tablespoons (1 stick) butter,
*   at room temperature*

1 heaping tablespoon orange marmalade

2½ cups confectioners' sugar, sifted

2 to 3 tablespoons orange juice,
*   purchased or fresh*

1. Place a rack in the center of the oven and preheat the oven to 350°F. Line 24 cupcake cups with paper liners. Set the pans aside.

2. Prepare the cupcake batter: Place the cake mix, orange juice, ricotta, ⅓ cup of the orange marmalade, oil, and the eggs in a large mixing bowl. Blend with an electric mixer on low speed for 30 seconds. Stop the machine and scrape down the sides of the bowl with a rubber spatula. Increase the mixer speed to medium and beat 2 minutes more, scraping down the sides again if needed. The batter should look thick and well combined. Spoon or scoop ⅓ cup batter into each lined cupcake cup, filling it three quarters of the way full. (You will get between 22 and 24 cupcakes; remove the empty liners, if any.) Place the pans in the oven.

the Cupcake Doctor says...

I used a good supermarket orange marmalade in this recipe, but you can use whatever citrus marmalades you have on your shelf. A bit of almond extract (½ teaspoon) turns this into an orange-almond cupcake. And what, you may ask, does the ricotta contribute to this recipe? It adds richness and structure, making these cupcakes like moist little pound cakes.

3. Bake the cupcakes until they are golden and spring back when lightly pressed with your finger, 15 to 20 minutes. Remove the pans from the oven and place them on wire racks to cool for 5 minutes.

4. Place the remaining 3 tablespoons of marmalade in a small saucepan over low heat. Stir until it thins out, 3 to 4 minutes. Brush this over the tops of the warm cupcakes. Run a dinner knife around the edges of the cupcake liners, lift the cupcakes up from the bottoms of the cups using the end of the knife, and pick them out of the cups carefully with your fingertips. Place them on a wire rack to cool for 15 minutes before frosting.

5. Meanwhile, prepare the Marmalade Buttercream: Place the butter and orange marmalade in a large mixing bowl and beat with an electric mixer on low speed until creamy, 30 seconds. Add 2 cups of the sugar and 2 tablespoons of the orange juice and beat on low until the mixture is combined, 30 seconds. Add the remaining sugar and orange juice and beat until the frosting is spreadable, 30 seconds. Then increase the mixer speed to high and beat until fluffy, 1 minute longer.

6. Place a heaping tablespoon of frosting on each cupcake and swirl to spread it out with a short metal spatula or spoon, taking care to cover the tops completely. The cupcakes are ready to serve.

✿ *Store these cupcakes, in a cake saver or under a glass dome, at room temperature for up to 3 days or in the refrigerator for up to 1 week. Or freeze them, wrapped in aluminum foil or in a cake saver, for up to 6 months. Thaw the cupcakes overnight in the refrigerator before serving.*

RHUBARB CRUMBLE CUPCAKES

• • • • •

Part cupcake, part muffin, these moist nutmeg-scented cupcakes are a breath of springtime. The soft interior contains chopped rhubarb, while on top, contrasting so nicely, is a crunchy oat and cinnamon topping. Serve these at breakfast, place in a lunchbox, or serve with a scoop of vanilla ice cream for dessert.

Vegetable oil spray for misting the pans
All-purpose flour for dusting the pans

CUPCAKES:
1 bag (16 ounces) frozen rhubarb
    (see "the Cupcake Doctor says")
1 package (18.25 ounces) plain white cake mix
1 package (3.4 ounces) vanilla instant
    pudding mix

⅔ cup water
⅓ cup vegetable oil
3 large eggs
1 teaspoon pure vanilla extract
½ teaspoon ground nutmeg
¼ cup all-purpose flour

CRUMBLE TOPPING:
1 cup packed light brown sugar
⅓ cup all-purpose flour
½ teaspoon ground cinnamon
4 tablespoons (½ stick) cold butter
Heaping ⅓ cup old-fashioned oats
    (see "the Cupcake Doctor says")
¼ cup finely chopped pecans

1. Place a rack in the center of the oven and preheat the oven to 350°F. Mist 24 cupcake cups with vegetable oil spray

✿ **MAKES 24 CUPCAKES (2½ INCHES EACH)**
✿ **PREPARATION TIME: 40 MINUTES**
✿ **BAKING TIME: 18 TO 20 MINUTES**

the Cupcake Doctor says...

Rhubarb is easier to chop when it is still frozen. As it thaws, press down on it to extract as much juice as you can. If you would like to use fresh chopped rhubarb, increase the water to 1 cup.

For the best, crunchiest topping, use old-fashioned oats, not quick-cooking oats.

and dust with flour. Shake out the excess flour and set the pans aside.

2. Prepare the cupcake batter: While the oven is heating, coarsely chop the rhubarb while it is still frozen and place it in a colander or strainer to drain. Set it aside to thaw for 20 minutes.

3. Place the cake mix, pudding mix, water, oil, eggs, vanilla, and nutmeg in a large mixing bowl. Blend with an electric mixer on low speed for 30 seconds. Stop the machine and scrape down the sides of the bowl with a rubber spatula. Increase the mixer speed to medium and beat 2 minutes more, scraping down the sides again if needed. Set the batter aside.

4. Prepare the crumble: Place the sugar, flour, and cinnamon in a medium-size mixing bowl. Cut in the butter with two

knives or a pastry blender until coarse crumbs form. Fold in the oats and chopped pecans. Set the topping aside.

5. With a spatula or large spoon, press the juice out of the rhubarb while it is in the colander. Transfer the rhubarb to paper towels and press to remove as much moisture as possible. Place the rhubarb in a small bowl with the flour and toss to coat. Add the rhubarb and flour mixture to the cake batter and fold it in to incorporate well. Spoon or scoop ⅓ cup batter into each prepared cupcake cup, filling it three quarters of the way full. Spoon the topping over each cupcake, pressing it gently into the batter so it adheres. Place the pans in the oven.

6. Bake the cupcakes until they are golden and spring back when lightly pressed with your finger, 18 to 20 minutes. Remove the pans from the oven and place them on wire racks to cool for 5 minutes. Run a dinner knife around the edges of the cupcakes, lift the cupcakes up from the bottoms of the cups using the end of the knife, and pick them out of the cups carefully with your fingertips. Place them on a wire rack to cool for 15 minutes, then serve.

✿ *Store these cupcakes, in a cake saver at room temperature, for up to 3 days. Or freeze them, wrapped in aluminum foil or in a cake saver, for up to 6 months. Thaw the cupcakes overnight in the refrigerator before serving.*

KEY LIME PIE CUPCAKES

WITH COCONUT MERINGUE

• • • • •

Part pie, part cake, these elegant cupcakes with tropical flavors have the best of both worlds. Once baked, they are filled with a traditional Key lime pie filling of sweetened condensed milk and real Key lime juice. Then the cupcakes are topped with a quick coconut-flavored meringue and placed in a hot oven to brown. Variations abound on this elegant dessert. If you are in a hurry, frost them, unfilled, with a little whipped cream, or lighten up the filling mixture with a little whipped cream and use it as a frosting instead. Or just fill the cupcakes and dust them with confectioners' sugar instead of adding the meringue. But if you go all the way, serve them when they are still a little warm, and you will have one stupendous cupcake with a surprise inside.

- ✿ MAKES 24 CUPCAKES (2½ INCHES EACH)
- ✿ PREPARATION TIME: 25 MINUTES
- ✿ BAKING TIME: 18 TO 22 MINUTES
- ✿ ASSEMBLY TIME: 15 MINUTES

24 paper liners for cupcake pans
   (2½-inch size)

CUPCAKES:

1 large lime, scrubbed (for 1 teaspoon zest
   and 2 tablespoons juice)

4 large eggs

1 package (18.25 ounces) plain yellow
   cake mix

1 package (3.4 ounces) vanilla instant
   pudding mix

1¼ cups water

⅓ cup vegetable oil

1 teaspoon coconut flavoring

FILLING:

1 can (14 ounces) sweetened
   condensed milk

⅓ cup Key lime juice
   (see "the Cupcake Doctor says")

COCONUT MERINGUE:

¼ teaspoon cream of tartar

Reserved 3 large egg whites

½ teaspoon coconut flavoring

⅓ cup granulated sugar

1. Place a rack in the center of the oven and preheat the oven to 350°F. Line 24 cupcake cups with paper liners. Set the pans aside.

2. Prepare the cupcake batter: With a citrus zester or fine grater, zest the lime and reserve 1 teaspoon. Cut the lime in half and squeeze the juice over a strainer into a small bowl; you should have 2 tablespoons. Set aside. Separate 3 of the eggs, place the whites in a large clean mixing bowl and the yolks in another mixing bowl.

3. Add the remaining egg, cake mix, pudding mix, water, oil, coconut flavoring and lime zest and juice to the yolks. Blend with an electric mixer on low speed for 30 seconds. Stop the machine and scrape down the sides of the bowl with a rubber spatula. Increase the mixer speed to medium and beat 2 minutes more, scraping down the sides again if needed. The batter should look well blended. Spoon or

the Cupcake Doctor says...

It's important to buy real Key lime juice for this recipe. It has a different flavor from Persian lime juice—it's fresher and more tart tasting. Many supermarkets carry Key lime juice in the juice aisle, so you won't have to visit a specialty store. Once opened, store the bottle in the refrigerator for a month or so. You will have plenty left to make a Key lime pie!

Baked Alaska Cupcakes

It's easy to make a mock Baked Alaska cupcake by topping cake and ice cream with a meringue layer. To check out meringues on cupcakes see the Key Lime Pie Cupcakes, this spread.

First, cut twenty-four ½-inch-deep rounds of angel food cake, layer cake, or pound cake to fit a paper-lined cupcake pan. Top each round of cake with a small scoop of raspberry sorbet, cover with plastic wrap, and freeze for at least 1 hour.

Next, preheat the oven to 450°F. Using 3 egg whites, a pinch of cream of tartar, and ⅓ cup sugar, make a stiff meringue following step 7 on page 78.

Remove the cupcakes from the freezer. Spoon 1 to 2 tablespoons of the meringue over each, thoroughly covering the ice cream, then immediately bake until well browned, 5 to 6 minutes.

Other fun cake and ice cream combinations to try include lemon cake with the raspberry sorbet, angel food cake with pineapple sherbert, and a brownie or chocolate cake with mint chocolate chip ice cream.

scoop ¼ cup batter into each lined cupcake cup, filling it two thirds of the way full. Place the pans in the oven.

4. Bake the cupcakes until they are lightly golden and spring back when lightly pressed with your finger, 18 to 22 minutes. Remove the pans from the oven and place them on wire racks to cool for 5 minutes. Increase the oven heat to 450°F.

5. Run a dinner knife around the edges of the cupcake liners, lift the cupcakes up from the bottoms of the cups using the

end of the knife, and pick them out of the cups carefully with your fingertips. Place them on a wire rack to cool for 15 minutes before filling.

6. Meanwhile, prepare the filling: Place the sweetened condensed milk and Key lime juice in a small bowl and stir to combine. Spoon the mixture into a pastry bag fitted with a medium tip. Press the tip ¼ inch into the top center of each cooked cupcake and squeeze the bag to release about 1 tablespoon filling into the cupcake. Scrape off any excess filling with a rubber spatula. Place the cooled cupcakes nearly side by side on a baking sheet.

7. Prepare the meringue: Add the cream of tartar to the reserved egg whites and beat with an electric mixer on high speed until frothy, 45 seconds. Add the coconut flavoring and 1 tablespoon of the sugar. Continue beating on high, adding 1 table-spoon sugar at a time, until the whites form stiff peaks (if you pull the beaters from the meringue, the meringue should extend from the beaters in straight stiff peaks). Spoon 2 tablespoons meringue onto the top of each cupcake and swirl to spread it just to the edges with a short metal spatula or a spoon. Place the pan in the oven. Bake until the meringue is light nutty brown in color, 5 to 6 minutes. Run a dinner knife around the edges of the cupcake liners, lift the cupcakes up from the bottoms of the cups using the end of the knife, and pick them out of the cups carefully with your fingers. Serve at once, or allow the cupcakes to cool 10 minutes, then serve.

✿ *Store these cupcakes, in a cake saver at room temperature, for up to 3 days.*

PINEAPPLE UPSIDE-DOWN CUPCAKES

• • • • •

If you love pineapple-upside down cake, then you'll love the cupcake version. The buttery cakes release easily onto a platter, with golden sponge cake below and buttery pineapple and brown sugar on top. Whether to add the maraschino cherry is up to you. Many people think the cherry is too retro; others deem it *de rigueur*. I've made it optional; the choice is yours.

Vegetable oil spray for misting the pans
All-purpose flour for dusting the pans

❁ **MAKES 24 CUPCAKES (2½ INCHES EACH)**
❁ **PREPARATION TIME: 45 MINUTES**
❁ **BAKING TIME: 18 TO 20 MINUTES**

TOPPING:

8 tablespoons (1 stick) butter, melted

1 can (20 ounces) crushed pineapple, drained, juice reserved

¾ cup light brown sugar, firmly packed

12 maraschino cherries, halved, drained (optional)

CUPCAKES:

1 package (18.25 ounces) plain yellow cake mix

1 cup sour cream (see "the Cupcake Doctor says")

½ cup pineapple juice reserved from the crushed pineapple

⅓ cup vegetable oil

4 large eggs

1 teaspoon pure vanilla extract

1. Place a rack in the center of the oven and preheat the oven to 350°F. Lightly

the Cupcake Doctor says...

As always, I try to reduce the fat a bit by using reduced-fat sour cream—especially since the cupcake pans are lined with all that delicious butter and brown sugar! I know that someone out there in Readerland is going to want to bake this as a large cake, not cupcakes. To do so, place the topping in the bottom of a 13- by 9-inch pan or large cast-iron skillet (at least 12 inches across). Pour over the batter and bake the cake until the top appears golden and springs back, about 40 minutes.

mist 24 cupcake cups with vegetable oil spray and dust them with flour. Shake out the excess flour. Set the pans aside.

2. Prepare the topping: Measure exactly 1 teaspoon of melted butter into each cupcake cup. Sprinkle 1 packed teaspoon brown sugar on top of the butter. Spread approximately 1 tablespoon drained pineapple on top of the brown sugar. Place 1 cherry half in the center of the pineapple, if desired. Push the cherry down into the pineapple so that it will appear on top of the cupcake when it is turned out. Set the pans aside.

3. Prepare the cupcake batter: Place the cake mix, sour cream, pineapple juice, oil, eggs, and vanilla in a large mixing bowl. Blend with an electric mixer on low speed for 30 seconds. Stop the machine and scrape down the sides of the bowl with a rubber spatula. Increase the mixer speed to medium and beat for 2 minutes more, scraping down the sides again if needed. The batter should be thick and smooth. Spoon or scoop ⅓ cup of the batter into each cupcake cup on top of the pineapple and brown sugar mixture. The cups will be filled nearly to the top. Place the pans in the oven.

4. Bake the cupcakes until they are golden and spring back when lightly pressed with your finger, 18 to 20 minutes. Remove the pans from the oven and immediately run a dinner knife around the edges of the cupcakes and place a platter over the cupcake pan. Quickly turn the pan upside down. The cupcakes with their topping will fall out onto the platter. Cool for 10 to 15 minutes, then serve.

✿ *Store these cupcakes, in a cake saver or under a glass dome, at room temperature for up to 3 days or in the refrigerator for up to 1 week. Or freeze them, wrapped in aluminum foil or in a cake saver, for up to 6 months. Thaw the cupcakes overnight in the refrigerator before serving.*

PRUNE SPICE CUPCAKES

WITH BUTTERSCOTCH MAPLE FROSTING

• • • • •

These cupcakes remind me of a cake my grandmother used to bake. While it was hot in the pan, and with the aroma of cinnamon and nutmeg floating around the kitchen, she would pour a hot buttermilk glaze over the top. That glaze was just too messy for cupcakes, so I added this creamy frosting. The maple flavoring marries beautifully with the prunes, the applesauce, and the spices, and I think even my grandmother would approve.

✿ **MAKES 22 TO 24 CUPCAKES (2½ INCHES EACH)**
✿ **PREPARATION TIME: 15 MINUTES**
✿ **BAKING TIME: 20 TO 23 MINUTES**
✿ **ASSEMBLY TIME: 10 MINUTES**

24 paper liners for cupcake pans
  (2½-inch size)
1 package (18.25 ounces) plain spice
  cake mix
1 tablespoon unsweetened cocoa powder
1 cup chopped pitted prunes
  (about 10 prunes)
1 cup unsweetened applesauce
½ cup water
½ cup vegetable oil
3 large eggs
½ teaspoon ground nutmeg
½ teaspoon ground allspice
Butterscotch Maple Frosting (page 339)

1. Place a rack in the center of the oven and preheat the oven to 350°F. Line 24 cupcake cups with paper liners. Set the pans aside.

2. Prepare the cupcake batter: Place the cake mix and cocoa powder in a large

the *Cupcake Doctor says...*

Not crazy about prunes? Use golden raisins instead. Or really crazy about prunes? Use the orange-flavored prunes. Keep in mind that prunes tend to be softer if purchased in a bag or in a sealed cardboard box. Once you open a box, be sure to seal it well to keep them soft. If the prunes are hard, pour a tablespoon or two of water over them and soften in the microwave oven for 10 to 15 seconds. It is easiest to chop prunes—and all dried fruit—if you first lightly oil the paring knife.

mixing bowl and stir with a wooden spoon to mix. Add the prunes and stir to coat the prunes with the cake mix and cocoa. Add the applesauce, water, oil, eggs, nutmeg, and allspice. Blend with an electric mixer on low speed for 30 seconds. Stop the machine and scrape down the sides of the bowl with a rubber spatula. Increase the mixer speed to medium and blend 1½ minutes more, scraping down the sides again if needed. The batter should look well combined and thickened.

3. Spoon or scoop ⅓ cup batter into each lined cupcake cup, filling it three quarters of the way full. (You will get between 22 and 24 cupcakes; remove the empty liners, if any.) Place the pans in the oven.

4. Bake the cupcakes until they are lightly golden and spring back when lightly pressed with your finger, 20 to 23 minutes. Remove the pans from the oven and place them on wire racks to cool for 5 minutes. Run a dinner knife around the edges of the cupcake liners, lift the cupcakes up from the bottoms of the cups using the end of the knife, and pick them out of the cups carefully with your fingertips. Place them on a wire rack to cool for 15 minutes before frosting.

5. Meanwhile, prepare the Butterscotch Maple Frosting.

6. Place a heaping tablespoon of frosting on each cupcake and swirl to spread it out with a short metal spatula or a spoon, taking care to cover the tops completely. Place them in the refrigerator until the frosting sets, 20 minutes. The cupcakes are now ready to serve.

✿ *Store the cupcakes, in a cake saver or under a glass dome, at room temperature for up to 3 days or in the refrigerator for up to 1 week. Or freeze them, wrapped in aluminum foil or in a cake saver, for up to 6 months. Thaw the cupcakes overnight in the refrigerator before serving.*

TRIPLE BUTTERSCOTCH CUPCAKES

· · · · ·

What do you get when you combine butterscotch cake mix, butterscotch pudding mix, and butterscotch chips? Triple Butterscotch Cupcakes. It's a powerful little cake, appealing to nostalgic adults and children, too. I love the creamy comfort of butterscotch, and to bite into these cupcakes takes me back to my youth when I frequently baked butterscotch blondies and butter-scotch cookies. But I never thought to bake a butterscotch cupcake until I began working on this book. So don't wait as long as I did. Bake them now!

24 paper liners for cupcake pans
    (2½-inch size)
1 package (18.25 ounces) plain
    butterscotch cake mix
    (see "the Cupcake Doctor says")
1 package (3.4 ounces) butterscotch
    instant pudding mix
1 cup water
½ cup vegetable oil
4 large eggs
1 teaspoon pure vanilla extract
Butterscotch Maple Frosting (page 339)
½ cup chopped pecans, for garnish

✿ **MAKES 24 CUPCAKES (2½ INCHES EACH)**
✿ **PREPARATION TIME: 20 MINUTES**
✿ **BAKING TIME: 18 TO 20 MINUTES**
✿ **ASSEMBLY TIME: 15 MINUTES**

1. Place a rack in the center of the oven and preheat the oven to 350°F. Line 24 cupcake cups with paper liners. Set the pans aside.

the Cupcake Doctor says...

If you can't find butterscotch cake mix in your local supermarket, substitute a plain yellow cake mix and a package of either butterscotch or vanilla instant pudding mix. You won't get a triple hit of butterscotch, but the frosting will more than hold its own.

2. Prepare the cupcake batter: Place the cake mix, pudding mix, water, oil, eggs, and vanilla in a large mixing bowl. Blend with an electric mixer on low speed for 30 seconds. Stop the machine and scrape down the sides of the bowl with a rubber spatula. Increase the mixer speed to medium and beat 2 minutes more, scraping down the sides again if needed. Spoon or scoop $\frac{1}{3}$ cup batter into each lined cupcake cup, filling it three quarters of the way full. (You will get between 22 and 24 cupcakes; remove the empty liners, if any.) Place the pans in the oven.

3. Bake the cupcakes until they spring back when lightly pressed with your finger, 18 to 20 minutes. Remove the pans from the oven and place them on wire racks to cool for 5 minutes. Leave the oven on. Run a dinner knife around the edges of the cupcake liners, lift the cupcakes up from the bottoms of the cups using the end of the knife, and pick them out of the cups carefully with your fingertips. Place them on a wire rack to cool for 15 minutes before frosting.

4. Place the pecans in a small baking pan and toast in the oven until aromatic, 3 to 5 minutes.

5. Prepare the Butterscotch Maple Frosting.

6. Place a heaping tablespoon of frosting on each cupcake and swirl to spread it out with a short metal spatula or a spoon, taking care to cover the tops completely. Place them, uncovered, in the refrigerator until the frosting sets, 20 minutes. Sprinkle the toasted pecans over the frosting. The cupcakes are ready to serve.

✿ *Store the cupcakes, in a cake saver or under a glass dome, at room temperature for up to 3 days or in the refrigerator for up to 1 week. Or freeze them, wrapped in aluminum foil or in a cake saver, for up to 6 months. Thaw the cupcakes overnight in the refrigerator before serving.*

WHITE RUSSIAN CUPCAKES

• • • • •

For occasions where just adults will be around, I bake these rich and spongy cupcakes, topped with a silken, sensual whipped cream frosting spiked with Kahlúa. And did I mention chocolate shavings on top? With the Kahlúa and the cream and the vodka, you could say these cupcakes have the components needed for the cocktail known as the White Russian. But I can tell you that they are a whole lot more satisfying than that drink ever was.

✿ **MAKES 22 TO 24 CUPCAKES (2½ INCHES EACH)**
✿ **PREPARATION TIME: 30 MINUTES**
✿ **BAKING TIME: 17 TO 20 MINUTES**
✿ **ASSEMBLY TIME: 10 MINUTES**

24 paper liners for cupcake pans
    (2½-inch size)

CUPCAKES:
1 package (18.25 ounces) plain yellow
    cake mix
1 package (3.4 ounces) vanilla instant
    pudding mix
1 cup vegetable oil
¾ cup whole milk
4 large eggs
¼ cup vodka
¼ cup plus 2 tablespoons Kahlúa
1 teaspoon pure vanilla extract

KAHLUA WHIPPED CREAM:
1 cup (8 ounces) heavy (whipping) cream
2 tablespoons confectioners' sugar
1 tablespoon Kahlúa
2 tablespoons semisweet chocolate shavings
    (see "the Cupcake Doctor says"),
    for garnish

the Cupcake Doctor says...

The key to beautiful chocolate shavings is right in your kitchen drawer. Pulling a sharp vegetable peeler down the edge of a bar of chocolate will produce shavings perfect for decorating these cupcakes. If the chocolate bar is room temperature and you pull firmly and slowly, that curl will be larger and more rounded. If the chocolate bar is cold and you pull quickly, the shavings will be shorter and not curled at all. Should you want a wider curl, pull the vegetable peeler across the top of the bar. This simple garnish can be made in advance and set aside on waxed paper until it is placed on the cupcakes after they are frosted.

1. Place a rack in the center of the oven and preheat the oven to 350°F. Line 24 cupcake cups with paper liners. Set the pans aside.

2. Prepare the cupcake batter: Place the cake mix, pudding mix, oil, milk, eggs, vodka, ¼ cup Kahlúa, and vanilla in a large mixing bowl. Blend with an electric mixer on low speed for 30 seconds. Stop the machine and scrape down the sides of the bowl with a rubber spatula. Increase the mixer speed to medium and beat 2 minutes more, scraping down the sides again if needed. Spoon or scoop ⅓ cup batter into each lined cupcake cup, filling it three quarters of the way full. (You will get between 22 and 24 cupcakes; remove the empty liners, if any.) Place the pans in the oven.

3. Bake the cupcakes until they are golden and spring back when lightly pressed with your finger, 17 to 20 minutes. Remove the pans from the oven and place them on wire racks to cool for 5 minutes. Brush the tops of the cupcakes with the remaining 2 tablespoons Kahlúa. Run a dinner knife around the edges of the cupcake liners, lift the cupcakes up from the bottoms of the cups using the end of the knife, and pick them out of the cups carefully with your fingertips. Place them on a wire rack to cool for 15 minutes before frosting.

4. Meanwhile, prepare the frosting: Place a large, clean mixing bowl and electric mixer beaters in the freezer to chill for 1 minute. Remove the bowl and beaters from the freezer. Pour the cream into the bowl and beat with an electric mixer on high speed until the cream has thickened, 1½ minutes. Stop the machine and add the sugar and Kahlúa. Beat the cream on high speed until stiff peaks form, 1 to 2 minutes more.

5. Place a heaping tablespoon of the whipped cream on each cupcake and swirl to spread it out with a short metal spatula or a spoon, taking care to cover the tops completely. Garnish with chocolate shavings. The cupcakes are ready to serve.

✿ *Store these cupcakes, in a cake saver, in the refrigerator for up to 4 days.*

5 Tips for Frosting Prettier Cupcakes

▼ ▼ ▼

1. Use 1 heaping tablespoon of creamy frosting per cupcake.

2. Spread the frosting on with a short metal spatula or the back of a soupspoon.

3. Apply the frosting just to the edge of the cupcake, allowing a little bit of the cake to peek out.

4. For a finished look, add something on top—a chocolate curl, a nut, a strawberry half.

5. For a clean and sleek look, frost cupcakes with cooked frostings while the frosting is still warm.

BLACK BOTTOM CUPCAKES

• • • • •

My mother used to make a delicious black bottom pie to serve when she entertained. The pie was so named because it contained a ribbon of chocolate over a gingersnap crust, then a fragrant bourbon custard, with whipped cream on top. To emulate those black bottom pie flavors, I have created a cupcake with a gingersnap cookie on the bottom, layers of chocolate cake and bourbon-flavored cake, and a glossy chocolate and bourbon glaze poured over all. Who can resist?

✿ **MAKES 24 CUPCAKES (2½ INCHES EACH)**
✿ **PREPARATION TIME: 40 MINUTES**
✿ **BAKING TIME: 18 TO 20 MINUTES**
✿ **ASSEMBLY TIME: 5 MINUTES**

24 paper liners for cupcake pans
(2½-inch size)

CUPCAKES:
24 gingersnap cookies
1 package (18.25 ounces) plain yellow
cake mix
1 cup water
⅓ cup vegetable oil
⅓ cup bourbon
3 large eggs
1 teaspoon pure vanilla extract
2 tablespoons unsweetened cocoa powder
3 ounces cream cheese, at room temperature

GLAZE:
1 cup semisweet chocolate chips
3 tablespoons butter
2 tablespoons light corn syrup
1 to 2 tablespoons bourbon (optional)

I. Place a rack in the center of the oven and preheat the oven to 350°F. Line 24 cupcake cups with paper liners. Place a gingersnap cookie in each liner. Set the pans aside.

2. Prepare the cupcake batter: Place the cake mix, water, oil, bourbon, eggs, and vanilla in a large mixing bowl. Blend with an electric mixer on low speed for 30 seconds. Stop the machine and scrape down the sides of the bowl with a rubber spatula. Increase the mixer speed to medium and beat 2 minutes more, scraping down the sides again if needed. Measure out 3½ cups of the batter and set it aside.

3. Place the cocoa powder and cream cheese in a medium-size mixing bowl and blend with an electric mixer on low speed until the cocoa is just incorporated into the cream cheese, 15 seconds. Add the batter remaining in the first mixing bowl to the cream cheese mixture and blend on low speed until just combined, 30 seconds. Spoon 1 heaping teaspoon of chocolate batter on top of the gingersnap. Shake the pans back and forth to distribute the batter. Spoon 1 heaping tablespoon of plain batter on top of the chocolate batter. The cups will be two thirds full. Do not shake the pans again, and place them in the oven.

the Cupcake Doctor says...

You can omit the bourbon in both the batter and glaze and you will still have delicious layered cupcakes with a serious chocolate glaze on top, plus the added bite of the gingersnap cookie.

4. Bake the cupcakes until they are golden and spring back when lightly pressed with your finger, 18 to 20 minutes. Remove the pans from the oven and place them on wire racks to cool for 5 minutes. Run a dinner knife around the edges of the cupcake liners, lift the cupcakes up from the bottoms of the cups using the end of the knife, and pick them out of the cups carefully with your fingertips. Place them on a wire rack to cool for 15 minutes before frosting.

5. Meanwhile, prepare the glaze: Place the chocolate chips, butter, and corn syrup in a small saucepan over medium-low heat. Stir until the chocolate and butter have melted and the glaze is well combined, 5 to

7 minutes. Add the bourbon, if desired, and stir to combine. Remove the pan from the heat.

6. While the glaze is still warm, generously drizzle it over the cupcakes. Let the cupcakes rest 20 minutes, then serve.

✿ *Store these cupcakes, in a cake saver or under a glass dome, at room temperature for up to 3 days or in the refrigerator for up to 1 week. Or freeze them, wrapped in aluminum foil or in a cake saver, for up to 6 months. Thaw the cupcakes overnight in the refrigerator before serving.*

HARVEY WALLBANGER CUPCAKES

• • • • •

What could be better to take to an adult birthday party than a pretty platter of Harvey Wallbanger Cupcakes? Harvey was a surfer dude (or so the story goes) along the southern California coast who drank too many cocktails made of vodka, orange juice, and Galliano at a local bar, and banged his head on the wall when leaving. First the drink was named after him, then a cake, and now these cupcakes. This recipe is a bit different than the Bundt cake variation in my first book because here I specifically call for fresh orange juice (you will need two to three large oranges) and fresh orange zest, and the cupcake is covered in a buttercream frosting flavored with orange juice, zest, and Galliano.

✿ **MAKES 22 TO 24 CUPCAKES (2½ INCHES EACH)**
✿ **PREPARATION TIME: 25 MINUTES**
✿ **BAKING TIME: 17 TO 20 MINUTES**
✿ **ASSEMBLY TIME: 10 MINUTES**

24 paper liners for cupcake pans
(2½-inch size)

CUPCAKES:

1 package (18.25 ounces) plain orange
cake mix

1 package (3.4 ounces) vanilla instant
pudding mix

½ cup vegetable oil

½ cup fresh orange juice
(from 2 or 3 large oranges)

⅓ cup Galliano liqueur or other anise
liqueur (see "the Cupcake Doctor says")

4 large eggs

2 tablespoons vodka

1 teaspoon grated fresh orange zest
(from 1 orange)

FRESH ORANGE AND ANISE
BUTTERCREAM:

8 tablespoons (1 stick) butter,
at room temperature

1 teaspoon grated fresh orange zest

3 cups confectioners' sugar, sifted

2 tablespoons fresh orange juice
(from 1 orange)

1 tablespoon Galliano liqueur or
other anise liqueur

the Cupcake Doctor says...

Galliano is an anise liqueur that marries well with orange juice. Both Galliano and vodka are components of the Harvey Wallbanger cocktail, and thus this cake. If you would like to omit the vodka, you can substitute water instead. But you really must use the Galliano, or another anise liqueur, in the cake and frosting.

1. Place a rack in the center of the oven and preheat the oven to 350°F. Line 24 cupcake cups with paper liners. Set the pans aside.

2. Prepare the cupcake batter: Place the cake mix, pudding mix, oil, orange juice, Galliano, eggs, vodka, and orange zest in a large mixing bowl. Blend with an electric mixer on low speed for 30 seconds. Stop the machine and scrape down the sides of the bowl with a rubber spatula. Increase the mixer speed to medium and beat 2 minutes more, scraping down the sides again if needed. Spoon or scoop ⅓ cup batter into each lined cupcake cup, filling it three quarters of the way full. (You will get between 22 and 24 cupcakes; remove the empty liners, if any.) Place the pans in the oven.

3. Bake the cupcakes until they are golden and spring back when lightly pressed with your finger, 17 to 20 minutes. Remove the pans from the oven and place them on wire racks to cool for 5 minutes. Run a dinner knife around the edges of the cupcake liners, lift the cupcakes up from the bottoms of the cups using the end of the knife, and pick them out of the cups carefully with your fingertips. Place them on a wire rack to cool for 15 minutes before frosting.

4. Meanwhile, prepare the Fresh Orange and Anise Buttercream: Place the butter and orange zest in a large mixing bowl. Blend with an electric mixer on low speed until fluffy, 30 seconds. Stop the machine and add the confectioners' sugar, orange juice, and Galliano. Blend with the mixer on low speed until the sugar is well incorporated, 1 minute. Increase the speed to medium and beat until the frosting lightens and is fluffy, 1 minute more.

5. Place a heaping tablespoon of frosting on each cupcake and swirl to spread it out with a short metal spatula or a spoon, taking care to cover the tops completely. The cupcakes are ready to serve.

✿ *Store these cupcakes, in a cake saver or under a glass dome, at room temperature for up to 3 days or in the refrigerator for up to 1 week. Or freeze them, wrapped in aluminum foil or in a cake saver, for up to 6 months. Thaw the cupcakes overnight in the refrigerator before serving.*

Cupcakes for Kids

❀ ❀ ❀

I must warn you that this chapter is totally about fun. Yes, the bright blue Cotton Candy Cupcakes are really decorated with a handful of blue cotton candy. Yes, X marks the spot on the nearly black Buried Treasure Cupcakes because a surprise is buried inside. Yes, the Chocolate Volcano Cupcakes are supposed to peak when baking, and that red, orange, and yellow glaze dripping down the sides should look like searing hot lava. And yes, the green, blue, and red streaks created by miniature M&M candies are supposed to run through the Tie-Dye Cupcakes.

In fact, when I look at the assortment of cupcakes I created, I am amazed at how my sisters and I survived our childhood on just two cupcake flavors (vanilla and chocolate) and one frosting (chocolate) that my mother made. Now, she was a stupendous cook, and it was a delicious and creamy cocoa frosting, the stuff that lured your fingers to the bowl, but it was always the same. And we never thought to ask for anything different. Then, as an adult, I learned of a butterfly cupcake recipe that some lucky children baked. It seems that while I was poking my fingers in chocolate buttercream, other children were fashioning butterfly wings out of cupcake tops, positioning them on cupcake bottoms, and then decorating their works of art before eating them up. Now that I'm a mom, I thought I'd try it out on my children.

One January morning, in the midst of testing cupcake recipes for this book, I baked big almond-flavored cupcakes. I scooped more than enough batter into the cups so that the tops would rise up over the pan and I would be able to slice them off and use them for butterfly wings. Then Amy Baron, a student who was helping me at the time, made buttercream frostings and we tinted them various beautiful shades, like buttercup yellow, cornflower blue, and rose pink. We dyed granulated sugar to match each frosting, fashioned antennae out of licorice, and found other add-ons, like gold dragées, to dress up these little cakes. When my children arrived home from school, the kitchen looked like an art studio. They couldn't wait to create their own butterflies, and my older daughter turned hers into a dragonfly instead. It might have been bleak outside on that January afternoon, but it was bright and glorious inside, with all the warm smells and dazzling colors.

I hope you can tell how much I've loved creating this chapter! There is plenty of whimsy here, including those Butterfly Cupcakes with Pastel Frostings and Lemonade Angel Cakes with Creamy Lemonade Frosting, and Fortune Cookie Cupcakes with a real fortune inside. But don't feel as if you've got to have an art degree (I surely don't) to create special cupcakes for your children. Many kids are drawn to tried-and-true favorite flavors, and for them I've developed Cookie Dough Cupcakes, Cinnamon Toast Cupcakes, and Banana Pudding Cupcakes.

And this chapter is also filled with cupcakes that adults will love as well. The Pineapple Banana Smoothie Cupcakes with Pineapple Buttercream are easy to make in a blender, just like a smoothie. The Malted Milk Cupcakes are sheer nostalgia and will take you back to childhood. The Milk Chocolate Rocky Road Cupcakes, S'mores Cupcakes, and Little Fudge Brownie Bites should come with warning labels because they're so addictive.

I've tossed in two recipes no cupcake book should be without—The Best Birthday Cupcakes with Two Frostings and White on White Cupcakes. The first is a recipe we have used successfully for countless birthday parties, and it works because the birthday boy or girl gets to choose his or her favorite frosting. (If it's not one of the two I offer with the recipe, there are plenty more to choose from.) The second is a recipe that will come in handy during that stage in your child's life when white food is all he or she wants. My recipe is so much better tasting than those supermarket cupcakes, and you can dress them up with little soccer balls, ballerinas, or other fun plastic decorations found at the local craft store.

Enjoy baking these cupcakes with your children, or your parents, depending on your age. Enjoy them for parties or just on that gray day when you want to turn the kitchen into someplace magical.

BUTTERFLY CUPCAKES

WITH PASTEL FROSTINGS

• • • • •

When Stella Himmelreich was growing up in London, she took a home economics course to learn how to bake. One day, the teacher taught her class how to make traditional English butterfly cakes. Now Stella lives in Nashville, Tennessee, and teaches high school algebra, but she hasn't forgotten the good feeling of bringing sponge cake butterflies home to share with her family.

I transformed Stella's childhood butterfly cupcake into one that begins with a cake mix. There is a lot of room here for creativity, so tint the buttercream frosting the pastel colors you prefer. The green frosting is a must since it turns the cupcake bottoms into the grass that acts as the butterflies' perch. Dye granulated sugar to match if you wish (see How to Dye Sugar to Match the Buttercream Frosting, page 100). Red or black licorice becomes antennae, and to add definition, use gold dragées and chocolate sprinkles.

- ✿ **MAKES 22 TO 24 CUPCAKES (2½ INCHES EACH)**
- ✿ **PREPARATION TIME: 15 MINUTES**
- ✿ **BAKING TIME: 20 TO 25 MINUTES**
- ✿ **ASSEMBLY TIME: 40 MINUTES**

24 paper liners for cupcake pans

   (2½-inch size)

1 package (18.25 ounces) plain yellow

   cake mix

1 package (3.4 ounces) vanilla instant

   pudding mix

1 cup whole milk

1 cup vegetable oil

4 large eggs

1 teaspoon pure vanilla extract

1 teaspoon pure almond extract

2 recipes Buttercream Frosting

   (page 318)

Pastel food colorings of your choice

   (see "the Cupcake Doctor says")

24 pieces (3 inches each) red or black

   licorice, split almost to the end

Decorating icing tubes in 2 or 3 colors

Yellow miniature M&M's (for kids) or

   gold dragées (for adults), as

   garnish (optional)

▲▲▲

LITTLE GIRLS' TEA PARTY

·············

Fairy sandwiches: *Peanut butter and jelly, cheese, or ham with crusts removed and bread cut into small shapes*

————

Chocolate chip cookies dusted with confectioners' sugar

————

Fresh strawberries

————

Butterfly Cupcakes with Pastel Frostings

————

Shirley Temples: *Ginger ale with a maraschino cherry and a bit of the cherry juice*

————

Hot cocoa with whipped cream

————

Party favors: *Inexpensive straw hats the girls can decorate with paper or real flowers and ribbons*

————

Activities: *Decorating hats; musical chairs*

▼▼▼

1. Place a rack in the center of the oven and preheat the oven to 350°F. Line 24 muffin cups with paper liners. Set the pans aside.

2. Prepare the cupcake batter: Place the cake mix, pudding mix, milk, oil, eggs, vanilla, and almond extract in a large mixing bowl. Blend with an electric mixer on low speed for 30 seconds. Stop the machine and scrape down the sides of the bowl with a rubber spatula. Increase the mixer speed to medium and beat 2 minutes more, scraping down the sides again if needed. The batter should look well blended. Spoon or scoop a heaping ⅓ cup batter into each lined cupcake cup, filling it almost to the top of the cup. (You will get between 22 and 24 cupcakes; remove the empty liners, if any.) Place the pans in the oven.

3. Bake the cupcakes until they are golden and spring back when lightly pressed with your finger, 20 to 25 minutes. Remove the pans from the oven and place them on wire racks to cool for 10 minutes. With a long serrated knife slice the top off each cupcake and carefully place the cupcake tops on the rack to cool. Run a dinner knife around the edges of the cupcake liners, lift the cupcake bottoms up from the cups using the end of the knife, and pick them out of the cups carefully with your fingertips. Place them on a wire rack to cool for 15 minutes before frosting.

4. Meanwhile, prepare the Buttercream Frosting. Divide the frosting evenly between two bowls. Tint the frosting in one bowl light green for the grass and tint the frosting in the other bowl either blue or yellow or pink. If you wish, you can divide the frosting in the second bowl into two equal batches and tint half of it yellow and the other half blue or pink.

5. Place a heaping tablespoon of frosting on each cupcake bottom and spread it out smoothly with a short metal spatula or a spoon, taking care to cover the area completely. Cut the cupcake tops in half vertically. Spread the top (rounded) side

---

the Cupcake Doctor says...

When making the buttercream frosting, add enough sugar so that the frosting is a little stiffer than usual. You don't want it to slide, especially if you are making the butterflies in warm weather. Choose pastel food colorings for that garden look, and preferably use food coloring pastes, which are more concentrated and won't change the consistency of the frosting. You will need about ¼ teaspoon of the paste to tint 1 recipe of frosting.

---

of each half with a smooth coat of frosting. Turn the halves into butterfly wings by placing them back on the cupcake, with round sides in, straight sides out, and tilted very slightly up in a winglike position. Place a dab of green frosting under each wing so that it stays in place. For the antennae, separate the halves of the licorice piece and secure it in the dab of frosting underneath the wings. Use the decorating icing tubes to pipe a butterfly outline on the frosted wings. Place dots of a contrasting icing color within the outline or use yellow miniature M&M's (for kids), or gold dragées (for adults), if desired. The cupcakes are ready to serve

How to Dye Sugar to Match the Buttercream Frosting

▼ ▼ ▼

What's pretty on butterfly or flower cupcakes—and just about any cupcake recipe for which you tint the frosting—is granulated sugar dyed to match. I guess it's something like having the purse match the shoes—really smart looking. Plus, it adds another dimension to the butterflies, making them glisten and seem more lifelike. The most natural-looking garden and nature colors come from the pastes that are sold in little jars. You can find them at craft stores, cooking stores, and wherever Wilton products are sold.

To dye, put about 1/16 teaspoon of food coloring paste in a small bowl. Add 2 drops of hot tap water and stir this to thin out the paste. Then add 2 tablespoons of granulated sugar and stir. If needed, add another drop of hot tap water and continue to stir until the sugar is dyed the right hue. Spread the sugar out on waxed paper to dry for 20 minutes before using.

(remove the dragées before eating the cupcake).

VARIATION To make flower-topped cupcakes: Proceed with the butterfly recipe through step 3. Frost the cupcake bottoms with your choice of color, pale pink for roses, yellow for daisies, blue for irises—you get the idea. Then cut the top of the cupcake into petal shapes with a small, sharp paring knife and frost them individually before placing them back on the cupcake. You might cut the top into fourths or smaller teardrop pieces and layer these on the cupcake to resemble petals. Place a dab of frosting in the center and sprinkle it with chocolate sprinkles if you are creating a sunflower or daisy that needs a brown center. Color it peach and the petals yellow if you are creating a rose. By dusting the frosting with dyed sugar to match, your flowers will sparkle on the platter just as flowers glisten in the sun after a light rain.

❀ *Store these cupcakes, in a cake saver or under a glass dome, at room temperature for up to 3 days or in the refrigerator for up to 1 week.*

LEMONADE ANGEL CAKES

WITH CREAMY LEMONADE FROSTING

• • • • •

I keep lemonade concentrate in the freezer for recipes such as this one and for making lemonade quickly on sultry summer days. Describing this lemony recipe, the key word is "light." The cupcakes start with an angel food cake mix to which you add the concentrate and water—that's it. And the frosting, too, is flavored with the lemonade.

❀ **MAKES 22 TO 24 CUPCAKES (2½ INCHES EACH)**
❀ **PREPARATION TIME: 10 MINUTES**
❀ **BAKING TIME: 20 TO 22 MINUTES**
❀ **ASSEMBLY TIME: 5 MINUTES**

24 paper liners for cupcake pans (2½-inch size)
1 package (16 ounces) angel food cake mix
¾ cup water
½ cup thawed frozen lemonade concentrate
Creamy Lemonade Frosting (page 327)
16 lemon drops, crushed (see "the Cupcake Doctor says")

1. Place a rack in the center of the oven and preheat the oven to 350°F. Line 24 cupcake cups with paper liners. Set the pans aside.

2. Place the cake mix, water, and lemonade concentrate in a large mixing bowl. Blend with the electric mixer on low speed for 30 seconds. Stop the machine and scrape down the sides of the bowl with a rubber spatula. Increase the mixer speed to medium and beat 2 minutes

Try to find a 6-ounce can of lemonade concentrate. If your local grocery store or supermarket only stocks the bigger cans, make the remaining concentrate into lemonade. Measure the amount that's left over, then add three times as much water to it (for example, ¼ cup concentrate would take ¾ cup water). You can also use raspberry lemonade concentrate.

To crush the lemon drops easily, place them in a sturdy plastic bag, cover with an old dish towel, and on a hard surface (the basement or garage floor, for example) pound them with a hammer five or six times or until you have fine crumbs.

more, scraping down the sides again if needed. The batter should look thick and well combined. Spoon or scoop ⅓ cup batter into each lined cupcake cup, filling it three quarters of the way full. (You will get between 22 and 24 cupcakes; remove the empty liners, if any.) Place the pans in the oven.

3. Bake the cupcakes until they are golden and spring back when lightly pressed with your finger, 20 to 22 minutes. Remove the pans from the oven and place them on wire racks to cool for 5 minutes. Run a dinner knife around the edges of the cupcake liners, lift the cupcakes up from the bottoms of the cups using the end of the knife, and pick them out of the cups carefully with your fingertips. Place them on a wire rack to cool for 15 minutes before frosting.

4. Meanwhile, prepare the Creamy Lemonade Frosting.

5. Place a heaping tablespoon of frosting on each cupcake and swirl to spread it out with a short metal spatula or a spoon, taking care to cover the tops completely. Sprinkle the crushed lemon drops on the frosting. The cupcakes are ready to serve.

✿ *Store the cupcakes, in a cake saver or under a glass dome, at room temperature for up to 3 days or in the refrigerator for up to 1 week. Or freeze them, wrapped in aluminum foil or in a cake saver, for up to 6 months. Thaw the cupcakes overnight in the refrigerator before serving. Garnish just before serving.*

PINEAPPLE BANANA SMOOTHIE CUPCAKES

WITH PINEAPPLE BUTTERCREAM

• • • • •

My girls love to whip up fruit smoothies in the blender, and smoothies are a fun party food. This cupcake is much like a smoothie in that the wet ingredients—the fruit, yogurt, and eggs—are pureed in the blender. Then the smoothie is poured over yellow cake mix and stirred just until everything comes together. I love the tropical flavors of the banana and pineapple, but feel free to use any fruit you have on hand.

✿ **MAKES 22 TO 24 CUPCAKES (2½ INCHES EACH)**
✿ **PREPARATION TIME: 10 MINUTES**
✿ **BAKING TIME: 20 TO 25 MINUTES**
✿ **ASSEMBLY TIME: 10 MINUTES**

24 paper liners for cupcake pans
　　(2½-inch size)

CUPCAKES:

1 ripe medium-size banana, cut into
　　5 to 6 pieces (about 1 cup; see
　　"the Cupcake Doctor says")
1 can (8 ounces) shredded pineapple,
　　drained, and juice reserved
1 cup (8 ounces) vanilla yogurt
½ teaspoon ground cinnamon
3 large eggs
1 package (18.25 ounces) plain yellow
　　cake mix

PINEAPPLE BUTTERCREAM:

4 tablespoons (½ stick) butter,
　　at room temperature
2½ cups confectioners' sugar, sifted
2 to 3 tablespoons reserved pineapple
　　juice
24 dried banana chips, for garnish (optional)

▲▲▲

HAWAIIAN LUAU

· · · · · · · · · · · · ·

Chicken skewers: *Baked nuggets or grilled strips on bamboo skewers (if age appropriate) and sweet-and-sour sauce for dipping*

———

Waikiki watermelon: *Watermelon half filled with chunks of melon, pineapple, and grapes*

———

Coconut or peach ice cream

———

Pineapple Banana Smoothie Cupcakes with Pineapple Buttercream

———

Oahu punch: *Your favorite fruit punch with slices of pineapple floating in it*

———

Party favors: *Grass skirts and leis, toy ukuleles*

———

Activities: *Doing the limbo and dancing the hula to Don Ho music*

▼▼▼

I. Place a rack in the center of the oven and preheat the oven to 350°F. Line 24 cupcake cups with paper liners. Set the pans aside.

2. Prepare the cupcake batter: Place the banana pieces in a blender and pulse to puree, 10 seconds. This makes about ½ cup banana puree. Add the pineapple and pulse until smooth, 10 seconds or more. Add the yogurt, cinnamon, and eggs and pulse until well combined, 30 seconds.

the Cupcake Doctor says...

You can use whatever fruit you have available, especially peeled ripe peaches, pears, bananas, and berries. You need 1½ cups fruit and 1 cup yogurt. There is no need for oil, because the fruit keeps the cupcakes moist.

3. Place the cake mix in a large mixing bowl. Pour the blender mixture over the mix, and stir with a wooden spoon to combine well, 50 strokes. Spoon or scoop ⅓ cup batter into each lined cupcake cup, filling it three quarters of the way full. (You will get between 22 and 24 cupcakes; remove the empty liners, if any.) Place the pans in the oven.

4. Bake the cupcakes until they are golden and spring back when lightly pressed with your finger, 20 to 25 minutes. Remove the pans from the oven and place them on wire racks to cool for 5 minutes. Run a dinner knife around the edges of the cupcake liners, lift the cupcakes up from the bottoms of the cups using the end of the knife, and pick them out of the cups carefully with your fingertips. Place them on a wire rack to cool for 15 minutes before frosting.

5 Kid-Friendly Ways to Frost a Plain Yellow Cupcake

▼ ▼ ▼

1. Cinnamon Cream Cheese Frosting (page 338)

2. Lemony Cream (page 350)

3. Marshmallow Frosting (page 348)

4. Chocolate Buttercream (page 319)

5. Chocolate Syrup Frosting (page 330)

5. Meanwhile, prepare the Pineapple Buttercream: Place the butter in a large mixing bowl, and blend with an electric mixer on low speed just until the butter is creamy, 10 seconds. Add the sugar and 2 table-spoons of the pineapple juice and blend on low until the mixture is creamy and combined. If it seems too thick, add the remaining pineapple juice and continue blending until creamy. Then increase the mixer speed to medium-high and beat the frosting to incorporate air and lighten it, 20 seconds.

6. Place a heaping tablespoon of frosting on each cupcake and swirl to spread it out with a short metal spatula or a spoon, taking care to cover the tops completely. Top each with a banana chip, if desired. Place these cupcakes, uncovered or in a cake saver, in the refrigerator until the frosting sets, 20 minutes. The cupcakes are ready to serve.

✿ *Store the cupcakes, in a cake saver or under a glass dome, at room temperature for up to 3 days or in the refrigerator for up to 1 week. Or freeze them, wrapped in aluminum foil or in a cake saver, for up to 6 months. Thaw the cupcakes overnight in the refrigerator before serving.*

PRETTY IN PINK STRAWBERRY CUPCAKES

• • • • •

My daughters both went through a pink cake stage, from kindergarten through second grade, when the only cake they wanted for their birthdays was strawberry. It helped that they had spring and early summer birthdays, because the local strawberries were in season. I was sad when that phase ended—there is something dazzling about a pink cake. (But in case you're wondering, the pink stage was followed by a white cake stage. Now they're both into chocolate.)

Here are moist and fresh strawberry cupcakes, just right for a birthday sleepover, or any time the occasion calls for pink.

✿ **MAKES 22 TO 24 CUPCAKES (2½ INCHES EACH)**
✿ **PREPARATION TIME: 15 MINUTES**
✿ **BAKING TIME: 20 TO 25 MINUTES**
✿ **ASSEMBLY TIME: 10 MINUTES**

24 paper liners for cupcake pans
(2½-inch size)
1 package (18.25 ounces) plain
white cake mix
1 package (3 ounces) strawberry gelatin
1 cup finely chopped fresh strawberries
with juice, from 1½ cups whole berries
(see "the Cupcake Doctor says")

¾ cup milk

¾ cup vegetable oil

4 large eggs

Strawberry Cream Cheese Frosting
    (page 341)

Pink and white sprinkles, for garnish
    (optional)

24 strawberry slices, for garnish (optional)

1. Place a rack in the center of the oven and preheat the oven to 350°F. Line 24 cupcake cups with paper liners. Set the pans aside.

2. Place the cake mix, gelatin, strawberries and juice, milk, oil, and eggs in a large mixing bowl. Blend with an electric mixer on low speed for 30 seconds. Stop the machine and scrape down the sides of the bowl with a rubber spatula. Increase the mixer speed to medium and beat 2 minutes more, scraping down the sides again if needed. Spoon or scoop ⅓ cup batter into each lined cupcake cup, filling it three quarters of the way full. (You will get between 22 and 24 cupcakes; remove the empty liners, if any.) Place the pans in the oven.

3. Bake the cupcakes until they are lightly golden and spring back when lightly pressed with your finger, 20 to 25 minutes. Remove the pans from the oven and place them on wire racks to cool for

▲▲▲

GIRL-POWER SLEEPOVER

· · · · · · · · · · · · ·

English muffin pizzas: *Jarred tomato sauce and shredded mozzarella or American cheese on English muffin halves run under the broiler*

───────

**Waffle-cut carrot chips
and ranch dressing dip**

───────

Tortilla chips and salsa

───────

Pretty in Pink Strawberry Cupcakes

───────

Fruit-flavored bottled water

───────

Party favors: *Personalized flip-flops*

───────

Activities: *Manicures and pedicures;
playing Twister*

▼▼▼

5 minutes. Run a dinner knife around the edges of the cupcake liners, lift the cupcakes up from the bottoms of the cups using the end of the knife, and pick them out of the cups carefully with your fingertips. Place them on a wire rack to cool for 15 minutes before frosting.

4. Meanwhile, prepare the Strawberry Cream Cheese Frosting.

5. Place a heaping tablespoon of frosting on each cupcake and swirl to spread it out with a short metal spatula or a spoon,

the CupcakeDoctor says...

Although these cupcakes put the season's best berries to good use, they are also perfect for those berries that arrive at your market from far away and have little juice and less flavor than good local berries. If you are using juicy berries, drain them well and use only the juice that clings to them when the berries have been chopped for the cake and the frosting. A pinch of cinnamon picks up the strawberry flavor in the cupcake batter.

taking care to cover the tops completely. Place in the refrigerator, uncovered, and chill until the frosting sets, 20 minutes. Sprinkle the sprinkles over the frosting, and place a strawberry slice in the center of each cupcake, if desired. The cupcakes are ready to serve.

✿ *Store these cupcakes, in a cake saver or under a glass dome, at room temperature for up to 3 days or in the refrigerator for up to 1 week. Or freeze them, wrapped in aluminum foil or in a cake saver, for up to 6 months. Thaw the cupcakes overnight in the refrigerator before serving.*

MONSTER MONKEYS

WITH CINNAMON CREAM CHEESE FROSTING

These fun, big, banana-packed cupcakes appeal to all ages, especially if you love the flavor of fresh banana bread. They're called "monster" because they're baked in cupcake pans with 3-inch cups and are larger than the average cupcake. And they're called "monkey" not only because they contain bananas, but because when I bake them children seem to act like monkeys, jumping around the kitchen and trying to grab one of them as soon as it has been frosted. I like to play up the monkey theme by piping a monkey's face on the frosted cupcake (see "the Cupcake Doctor says" for directions). Decorated or not, these cupcakes are moist and inviting.

❀ **MAKES: 12 LARGE (3-INCH) CUPCAKES OR 20 TO 24 REGULAR (2½-INCH) CUPCAKES**
❀ **PREPARATION TIME: 15 MINUTES**
❀ **BAKING TIME: 24 TO 28 MINUTES FOR LARGE CUPCAKES, 18 TO 20 MINUTES FOR REGULAR SIZE**
❀ **ASSEMBLY TIME: 10 MINUTES**

〰〰〰〰〰〰〰〰〰〰〰〰

the Cupcake Doctor *says...*

Monkey around! To create a monkey's face on top of the frosted cupcake, place two brown M&M candies for eyes and one slightly lower, on its edge and in the center, for the nose. With a squeeze bottle filled with chocolate frosting, or a tube of brown icing from the supermarket, pipe a semicircle for a wide grin. At each end of the grin, anchor a red M&M candy. For ears, secure two mini Oreo cookies in the frosting until they hold (use a little extra frosting if needed). Or use banana chips for the ears. Sprinkle chocolate sprinkles around the edges for fur.

〰〰〰〰〰〰〰〰〰〰〰〰

CUPCAKES:

Vegetable oil spray for misting the pans

All-purpose flour for dusting the pans

1 package (18.25 ounces) plain yellow
　　cake mix

1½ cups mashed bananas, from 3 medium
　　or 4 small bananas

½ cup water

½ cup vegetable oil

3 large eggs

1 teaspoon ground cinnamon

Cinnamon Cream Cheese Frosting (page 338)

1. Place a rack in the center of the oven and preheat the oven to 350°F. Mist the pans with vegetable oil spray and dust with flour. Shake out the excess flour and set the pans aside.

2. Place the cake mix, mashed bananas, water, oil, eggs, and cinnamon in a large mixing bowl. Blend with the electric mixer on low speed for 30 seconds. Stop the machine and scrape down the sides of the bowl with a rubber spatula. Increase the mixer speed to medium and beat 2 minutes more, scraping down the sides again if needed. The batter should look thick and well combined. Spoon or scoop ½ cup of batter (for the large cups) or ⅓ cup batter (for the regular cups) into each prepared cup, filling it three quarters of the way full. Place the pans in the oven.

3. Bake the cupcakes until they are golden and spring back when lightly pressed with your finger, 24 to 28 minutes for large cupcakes, 18 to 20 minutes for regular size. Remove the pans from the oven and place them on wire racks to cool for 5 minutes. Run a dinner knife around the edges of the cupcakes, lift the cupcakes up from the bottoms of the cups using the end of the knife, and pick them out of the cups carefully with your fingertips. Place them on a wire rack to cool for 15 minutes before frosting.

4. Meanwhile, prepare the Cinnamon Cream Cheese Frosting.

5. Place 2 to 3 tablespoons of frosting on each cupcake and swirl to spread it out with a short metal spatula or a spoon, taking care to cover the tops completely. Place, uncovered, in the refrigerator and chill until the frosting sets, 20 minutes. The cupcakes are ready to serve.

✿ *Store the cupcakes, in a cake saver or under a glass dome, at room temperature for up to 3 days or in the refrigerator for up to 1 week. Or freeze them, wrapped in aluminum foil or in a cake saver, for up to 6 months. Thaw the cupcakes overnight in the refrigerator before serving.*

CINNAMON TOAST CUPCAKES

• • • • •

Remember those lazy childhood mornings when you didn't think you could ever pull yourself out from under the warm covers of your bed, but then you'd catch a whiff of something wonderful cooking in the kitchen? For me it was cinnamon toast that made getting up worthwhile. Here is a cupcake that captures the alluring aroma and taste of cinnamon toast in its batter, in its frosting, and in the cinnamon-sugar mixture that's sprinkled on top. And if children don't devour the entire batch, I know plenty of nostalgic grown-ups who will come running to the kitchen for them.

24 paper liners for cupcake pans
   (2½-inch size)
1 package (18.25 ounces) plain yellow
   cake mix
1 package (3.4 ounces) vanilla instant
   pudding mix
1¼ cups whole milk
¾ cup vegetable oil
3 large eggs
1 tablespoon ground cinnamon
Cinnamon Cream Cheese Frosting
   (page 338)
1 tablespoon cinnamon sugar for sprinkling
   (see "the Cupcake Doctor says")

✿ MAKES 20 TO 24 CUPCAKES (2½ INCHES EACH)
✿ PREPARATION TIME: 15 MINUTES
✿ BAKING TIME: 18 TO 22 MINUTES
✿ ASSEMBLY TIME: 10 MINUTES

Mix and Match

Perhaps the very thing that inspired me to write the first *Cake Mix Doctor* book—my need to modify recipes—is what keeps readers doctoring up *my* recipes. I have learned that if I call for a Bundt pan, someone will want to make the cake in layers. If I say chocolate, they'll yearn for vanilla. So to be a step ahead of the game, I've scrambled some of the cupcake recipes and frostings in this chapter just in case you feel the need to change things. And I promise that the results are delicious. Of course, you'll still come up with your own! Keep me posted.

✿ Cinnamon Toast Cupcakes (page 112) with Butterscotch Maple Frosting (page 339)

✿ Cookie Dough Cupcakes (page 124) with Mocha Buttercream Frosting (page 323)

✿ Chocolate Volcano Cupcakes (page 126) with Easy Hot Fudge Sauce (page 356)

✿ Malted Milk Cupcakes (page 129) with Coconut Pecan Frosting (page 346)

✿ The Best Birthday Cupcakes (page 138) with White Chocolate Peppermint Cream Cheese Frosting (page 343)

✿ A Cupcake Zoo (page 150) with Lemony Cream (page 350)

✿ Plum Good Cupcakes (page 152) with Cinnamon Cream Cheese Frosting (page 338)

✿ White on White Cupcakes (page 166) with Basic Chocolate Ganache (page 332)

I. Place a rack in the center of the oven and preheat the oven to 350°F. Line 24 cupcake cups with paper liners. Set the pans aside.

2. Place the cake mix, pudding mix, milk, oil, eggs, and cinnamon in a large mixing bowl. Blend with an electric mixer on low speed for 30 seconds. Stop the machine

the Cupcake Doctor says...

You can buy cinnamon and sugar already combined in a handy canister for sprinkling on buttered toast or these cupcakes. Or make your own by combining 1 tablespoon sugar and ¼ teaspoon ground cinnamon.

and scrape down the sides of the bowl with a rubber spatula. Increase the mixer speed to medium and blend 1½ to 2 minutes more, scraping down the sides again if needed. The batter should look thick and well combined. Spoon ⅓ cup batter into each lined cupcake cup, filling it three quarters full. (You will get between 20 and 24 cupcakes; remove the empty liners, if any.) Place the pans side by side in the oven.

3. Bake the cupcakes until they are golden and spring back when lightly pressed with your finger, 18 to 22 minutes. Remove the pans from the oven and place them on wire racks to cool for 5 minutes. Run a dinner knife around the edges of the cupcake liners, lift the cupcakes up from the bottoms of the cups using the end of the knife, and pick them out of the cups carefully with your fingertips. Place them on a wire rack to cool for 15 minutes before frosting.

4. Meanwhile, prepare the Cinnamon Cream Cheese Frosting.

5. Place a heaping tablespoon of frosting on each cupcake and swirl to spread it out with a short metal spatula or a spoon, taking care to cover the tops completely. Sprinkle the frosting with the cinnamon-sugar mixture. Place these cupcakes, uncovered or in a cake saver, in the refrigerator until the frosting sets, 20 minutes. The cupcakes are ready to serve.

✿ *Store the cupcakes, in a cake saver or under a glass dome, at room temperature for up to 3 days or in the refrigerator for up to 1 week. Or freeze them, wrapped in aluminum foil or in a cake saver, for up to 6 months. Thaw the cupcakes overnight in the refrigerator before serving.*

JELLY DOUGHNUT CUPCAKES

• • • • •

I can't recall what I loved best about jelly doughnuts when I was younger—the warm, fresh dough, the sweet surprise of jelly inside, or the confectioners' sugar on top that always wound up on the tip of my nose. All those pleasant memories are here in this amazingly easy cupcake that smacks of child-hood. Yet instead of a doughnut you have a sweet and sturdy cupcake baked to house whatever flavor of jelly or preserves you decide to squirt inside after they cool. I fill a pastry bag full of jelly, but you could just as easily cut a small plug in the top of each cupcake, spoon in the jelly, replace the plug, and cover up the incision with fresh berries and sugar. Yum.

24 paper liners for cupcake pans
    (2½-inch size)
1 package (18.25 ounces) plain yellow
    cake mix
1 package (3.4 ounces) vanilla instant
    pudding mix
1 cup whole milk
1 cup vegetable oil
4 large eggs
1 jar (12 ounces) blueberry or strawberry
    preserves, or your favorite jelly
½ cup confectioners' sugar
24 whole blueberries or 12 strawberries
    cut in half lengthwise, for garnish

✿ **MAKES 22 TO 24 CUPCAKES (2½ INCHES EACH)**
✿ **PREPARATION TIME: 15 MINUTES**
✿ **BAKING TIME: 18 TO 20 MINUTES**
✿ **ASSEMBLY TIME: 20 MINUTES**

the Cupcake Doctor says...

This recipe is a great way to clean out all those half-empty jars of jelly in your refrigerator. Use them to fill these cupcakes. And if your kids are fans of peanut butter and grape jelly, squirt a little of each into the center of the cupcakes.

1. Place a rack in the center of the oven and preheat the oven to 350°F. Line 24 cupcake cups with paper liners. Set the pans aside.

2. Place the cake mix, pudding mix, milk, oil, and eggs in a large mixing bowl. Blend with an electric mixer on low speed for 30 seconds. Stop the machine and scrape down the sides of the bowl with a rubber spatula. Increase the mixer speed to medium and beat 1½ to 2 minutes more, scraping down the sides again if needed. Spoon or scoop a heaping ¼ cup batter into each lined cupcake cup, filling it two thirds of the way full. (You will get between 22 and 24 cupcakes; remove the empty liners, if any.) Place the pans side by side in the oven.

3. Bake the cupcakes until they are golden and spring back when lightly pressed with your finger, 18 to 20 minutes. Remove the pans from the oven and place them on wire racks to cool for 5 minutes. Run a dinner knife around the edges of the cupcake liners, lift the cupcakes up from the bottoms of the cups using the end of the knife, and pick them out of the cups carefully with your fingertips. Place them on a wire rack to cool for 15 minutes before filling.

4. Fit a pastry bag with a metal tip that has a large round hole and spoon about ½ cup preserves into the bag. Insert the whole tip into the top center of the cupcake. Generously squirt 2 teaspoons to 1 tablespoon preserves into each cupcake (you may need to wipe the tip clean as you go). Continue filling the cupcakes, refilling the pastry bag as needed. When done, sift the cupcake tops with confectioners' sugar. Garnish each cupcake with a whole blueberry or strawberry half to cover the pastry tip hole. The cupcakes are ready to serve.

✿ *Store these cupcakes, in a cake saver or under a glass dome, at room temperature for up to 3 days or in the refrigerator for up to 1 week. Or freeze them, wrapped in aluminum foil or in a cake saver, for up to 6 months. Thaw the cupcakes overnight in the refrigerator before serving.*

How to Handle a Pastry Bag Like a Pro

A pastry bag is the key to transforming the basic cupcake into something with a surprise inside. With this simple bag you can squirt pudding, jelly, or flavored whipped cream into the heart of a baked cupcake, providing flavor, texture, and sheer fun. Open a clean pastry bag and slide a metal or plastic tip down to the point of the bag so that only about half of the tip is exposed. Then, using a rubber spatula, fill the bag about half full with soft pudding, jelly, or whipped cream. Close the top of the bag and roll it down as you would a tube of toothpaste. With one hand, cradle the tip of the bag, gently piercing the cupcake with it. With the other hand, support the weight of the bag and gently squeeze it to push some of the contents through the tip and into the cake. Then release the pressure and gently pull the tip out of the cake. It's that easy. With practice you will become more accustomed to using a pastry bag. You can find them in fancy cookware shops or in the baking aisle of the supermarket.

COTTON CANDY CUPCAKES

• • • • •

Believe it or not, I am a health-conscious parent who serves three vegetables every night with dinner, keeps fresh fruit in the house, and buys low-fat milk for my children. And may I add that my children do not eat sweets every day! But, with that said, here are some fun, nutrition-free cupcakes your children will adore come party time. Why? They're blue and they contain cotton candy. Few kids can resist cotton candy.

✿ **MAKES 22 TO 24 CUPCAKES (2½ INCHES EACH)**
✿ **PREPARATION TIME: 20 MINUTES**
✿ **BAKING TIME: 17 TO 20 MINUTES**
✿ **ASSEMBLY TIME: 10 MINUTES**

24 paper liners for cupcake pans
　　(2½-inch size)

CUPCAKES:
1 package (18.25 ounces) plain white
　　cake mix
1½ cups blueberry yogurt
　　(2 cartons, 6 ounces each)
¼ cup water
¼ cup vegetable oil
3 large egg whites
　　(see "the Cupcake Doctor says")
5 to 6 drops blue food coloring
　　(see "the Cupcake Doctor says")

COTTON CANDY BUTTERCREAM:
3 ounces (½ bag; about 4 cups) blue cotton
　　candy (see "the Cupcake Doctor says")
4 tablespoons (½ stick) butter,
　　at room temperature
3 cups confectioners' sugar, sifted
3 tablespoons milk

1. Place a rack in the center of the oven and preheat the oven to 350°F. Line 24 cupcake cups with paper liners. Set the pans aside.

2. Prepare the cupcake batter: Place the cake mix, yogurt, water, oil, egg whites, and food coloring in a large mixing bowl. Blend with an electric mixer on low speed for 30 seconds. Stop the machine and scrape down the sides of the bowl with a rubber spatula. Increase the mixer speed to medium and beat 2 minutes more, scraping down the sides again if needed. Spoon or scoop ¼ cup batter into each lined cupcake cup, filling it two thirds of the way full. (You will get between 22 and 24 cupcakes; remove the empty liners, if any.) Place the pans in the oven.

3. Bake the cupcakes until they are lightly golden and spring back when lightly pressed with your finger, 17 to 20 minutes. Remove the pans from the oven and place them on wire racks to cool for 5 minutes. Run a dinner knife around the edges of the cupcake liners, lift the cupcakes up from the bottoms of the cups using the end of the knife, and pick them out of the cups carefully with your fingertips. Place them on a wire rack to cool for 15 minutes before frosting.

4. Meanwhile, prepare the Cotton Candy Buttercream: Measure out 2½ cups cot-

▲▲▲

UNDER THE BIG TOP CIRCUS PARTY

Hot dogs and the fixings: *Mustard, ketchup, sweet pickle relish, and toasted buns*

Popcorn and Cracker Jack

Cotton Candy Cupcakes

Various Sodas

Party favors: *Clown glasses, glow-in-the-dark light wands*

Activities: *Dressing up as clowns, bareback riders, animal trainers, and ringmaster*

▼▼▼

ton candy and set it aside for the frosting. Measure out 1 to 1½ cups of the cotton candy and set it aside for the garnish. If any cotton candy is left, let the kids eat it while the cupcakes are baking. Place the butter in a large mixing bowl and blend with an electric mixer on low speed until creamy, 30 seconds. Add the 2½ cups cotton candy and blend on low until it is incorporated. The mixture will be blue and grainy. Add the sugar and milk and blend on low until the frosting comes together and is nearly smooth, 1 to 1½ minutes. It will still be a little grainy.

the Cupcake Doctor says...

The reason you want to use only egg whites in the cake batter is that this helps keep the batter blue. Yolks turn the batter slightly green. Cotton candy can be found at candy stores and in many supermarkets in sealed 6-ounce plastic bags. A 3-ounce clump of cotton candy yields enough for this recipe. If you want to use pink cotton candy, use strawberry yogurt and pink food coloring in the cupcake batter. When using food coloring, it is best to add a little at a time; you can always add more, but you can't remove it if you add too much.

Increase the mixer speed to medium-high and beat the frosting to incorporate air so that it is fluffy, 30 seconds.

5. Place a heaping tablespoon of frosting on each cupcake and swirl to spread it out with a short metal spatula or a spoon, taking care to cover the tops completely. Tear the cotton candy reserved for garnish into 24 pieces and press a piece into the top of each cupcake. The cupcakes are ready to serve.

✿ *Store these cupcakes, in a cake saver or under a glass dome, at room temperature for no more than two days. They are best eaten fresh because the cotton candy hardens as it rests at room temperature.*

S'MORES CUPCAKES

• • • • •

When the sky darkens, the stars appear, and a bonfire is lit, that's the time for ghost stories and s'mores, those irresistible campfire dessert sandwiches made from graham crackers, fire-toasted marshmallows, and chocolate candy bars. This cupcake with s'mores topping is perfect for sleepovers, complete with haunted-house decorations.

24 paper liners for cupcake pans (2½-inch size)

7 whole graham crackers, coarsely chopped (see "the Cupcake Doctor says")

1 cup sour cream

1 package (18.25 ounces) plain German chocolate cake mix

1 package (3.4 ounces) vanilla instant pudding mix

½ cup water

½ cup vegetable oil

4 large eggs

1 cup milk chocolate chips

Marshmallow Frosting (page 348)

2 Hershey's milk chocolate bars (1.55 ounces each), broken into 24 small pieces (total), for garnish

✿ **MAKES 22 TO 24 CUPCAKES (2½ INCHES EACH)**
✿ **PREPARATION TIME: 20 MINUTES**
✿ **BAKING TIME: 19 TO 22 MINUTES**
✿ **ASSEMBLY TIME: 15 MINUTES**

▲ ▲ ▲

COWBOY CAMP-OUT

·············

Hamburgers or pulled pork barbecue:
With ketchup, mustard,
tomato slices, cheese,
and toasted buns

———

Bronco baked beans:
Seasoned with chili seasonings

———

Hash browns or potato salad

———

S'mores Cupcakes

———

Sarsaparilla *(root beer in tin cups)*

———

Party favors: *Cowboy hats and/or*
sheriff badges

———

Activities: *Telling ghost stories;*
pin the tail on the donkey;
dodgeball

▼ ▼ ▼

I. Place a rack in the center of the oven and preheat the oven to 350°F. Line 24 cupcake cups with paper liners. Set the pans aside.

2. Place 1 scant tablespoon of chopped graham cracker crumbs in the bottom of each liner. Set these aside. Reserve the remaining graham cracker crumbs for garnish. Set aside 3 tablespoons of the sour cream for the frosting.

3. Place the cake mix, pudding mix, remaining sour cream, water, oil, and eggs in a large mixing bowl. Blend with an electric mixer on low speed for 30 seconds. Stop the machine and scrape down the sides of the bowl with a rubber spatula. Increase the mixer speed to medium and beat 2 minutes more, scraping down the sides again if needed. The batter should look thick and well combined. Fold in the chocolate chips, making sure they are well distributed throughout the batter. Spoon or scoop ¼ cup batter into each lined cupcake cup, filling it two thirds of the way full. (You will get between 22 and 24 cupcakes; remove the empty liners, if any.) Place the pans in the oven.

4. Bake the cupcakes until they spring back when lightly pressed with your finger, 19 to 22 minutes. Remove the pans from the oven and place them on wire racks to cool for 5 minutes. Run a dinner

the Cupcake Doctor says...

Do not use finely crushed graham crackers that come in a box. They do not adhere to the bottom of the cupcake. For increased flavor, use chocolate graham crackers or cinnamon graham crackers.

Cupcake Toppers

Ever wonder where to buy cupcake toppers, those little plastic toys and objects used to decorate the top of frosted cupcakes? They're nice to have when you don't have the time to pipe on elaborate frosting embellishments. And let's face it, kids love pulling these out of the cake and licking off the frosting. Begin with the baking aisle of your supermarket for fun stick-ins and curvy candles. If you can't find what you need, go to a craft store that sells Wilton cake decorating supplies. You'll find an assortment of seasonal plastic trinkets and those tried and true clowns, soccer balls, and ballerinas. For a larger selection, head to:

✿ The Wilton catalog or www.wilton.com. I found a dazzling array of candles, and cake toppers like flags, circus animals, jungle animals, dinosaurs, and dolls. To get a catalog call toll-free, (800) 794-5866.

✿ The Sweet Celebrations catalog. I found great happy birthday picks, and ones topped with tennis balls, soccer balls, hearts, clowns, and balloons. Call their toll-free number for a copy: (800) 328-6722.

knife around the edges of the cupcake liners, lift the cupcakes up from the bottoms of the cups using the end of the knife, and pick them out of the cups carefully with your fingertips. Place them on a wire rack to cool for 15 minutes before frosting.

5. Meanwhile, prepare the Marshmallow Frosting.

6. Carefully remove the liner from each cupcake, taking care that the graham cracker crumbs don't fall off, before you frost them. Place a heaping tablespoon of frosting on each cupcake and swirl to spread it out with a short metal spatula or spoon, taking care to cover the tops completely. Garnish with the reserved coarsely chopped graham crackers and a piece of milk chocolate. The cupcakes are ready to serve.

✿ *Store these cupcakes; in a cake saver or under a glass dome, in the refrigerator for up to 1 week.*

COOKIE DOUGH CUPCAKES

WITH CHOCOLATE BUTTERCREAM

• • • • •

The idea for this recipe had been in my head for a while, but the first two times I bought frozen cookie dough, it vanished before I had a chance to test my idea. My children are like bloodhounds when it comes to sniffing out new foods, and I normally don't buy frozen cookie dough. When they found it, they ate it. It was particularly frustrating because I was trying to develop a recipe that kids would love—and my kids weren't letting me!

The next go-around I put a sign on the dough that said, "Don't touch, or you'll have Mom after you." These cupcakes are best eaten a bit warm, with the centers still gooey. Need I say that they don't last long?

24 paper liners for cupcake pans
   (2½-inch size)
1 package (18.25 ounces) plain yellow
   cake mix
1 package (3.4 ounces) vanilla instant
   pudding mix
1 cup whole milk
1 cup vegetable oil
4 large eggs
1 teaspoon pure vanilla extract
1 package (1 pound) frozen cookie dough
   (see "the Cupcake Doctor says")
Chocolate Buttercream (page 319)

✿ MAKES 22 TO 24 CUPCAKES (2½ INCHES EACH)
✿ PREPARATION TIME: 15 MINUTES
✿ BAKING TIME: 23 TO 27 MINUTES
✿ ASSEMBLY TIME: 10 MINUTES

I. Place a rack in the center of the oven and preheat the oven to 350°F. Line 24 cupcake cups with paper liners. Set the pans aside.

2. Place the cake mix, pudding mix, milk, oil, eggs, and vanilla in a large mixing bowl. Blend with an electric mixer on low speed for 30 seconds. Stop the machine and scrape down the sides of the bowl with a rubber spatula. Increase the mixer speed to medium and beat 2 minutes more, scraping down the sides again if needed. The batter should look well blended. Spoon or scoop a heaping ¼ cup batter into each lined cupcake cup, filling it two thirds of the way full. (You will get between 22 and 24 cupcakes; remove the empty liners, if any.) Cut the frozen dough pieces in half to make 24 pieces. Place a frozen cookie dough piece on top of each cupcake. Place the pans in the oven.

3. Bake the cupcakes until they are golden and spring back when lightly pressed with your finger, 23 to 27 minutes. Remove the pans from the oven and place them on wire racks to cool for 5 minutes. Run a dinner knife around the edges of the cupcake liners, lift the cupcakes up from the bottoms of the cups using the end of the knife, and pick them out of the cups carefully with your fingertips. Place them on a wire rack to cool for

the Cupcake Doctor says...

If you use the 18-ounce logs of refrigerated chocolate chip cookie dough (instead of the 1-pound packages of frozen dough), cut them into 24 equal pieces and freeze them before using them in this recipe. It's important to use frozen dough, because you don't want it to bake completely and become a cookie. You want the center to be gooey when you bite into it.

15 minutes before frosting. They may sink a bit in the center.

4. Meanwhile, prepare the Chocolate Buttercream.

5. Place a heaping tablespoon of frosting on each cupcake and swirl to spread it out with a short metal spatula or a spoon, taking care to cover the tops completely. The cupcakes are ready to serve.

✿ *Store these cupcakes, in a cake saver or under a glass dome, at room temperature for up to 3 days or in the refrigerator for up to 1 week. Or freeze them, wrapped in aluminum foil or in a cake saver, for up to 6 months. Thaw the cupcakes overnight in the refrigerator before serving.*

CHOCOLATE VOLCANOES

WITH WHITE CHOCOLATE LAVA GLAZE

• • • • •

During my years as a newspaper food writer, I received many "help" calls from frustrated cooks whose layer cakes were rising to peaks and domes in the center. For this fun recipe, I wanted to create that peak so these chocolate cupcakes would rise up and look as if they were about to erupt, like a volcano. To create the peak, the sudden rise, you need to add more leavening than usual, but just the right amount or the cake (in this case, the cupcakes) will fall flat. I added 1 teaspoon baking soda to the batter and a little vinegar to make the soda more active, and I baked these at a higher temperature than most of the cupcakes in this book to force them quickly upwards. After you pour a delicious white chocolate glaze over them and decorate them with colored sugar sprinkles, you will have a science experiment and a moist, chocolatey, kid-friendly cupcake all in one!

✿ **MAKES 22 TO 24 CUPCAKES (2½ INCHES EACH)**
✿ **PREPARATION TIME: 20 MINUTES**
✿ **BAKING TIME: 11 TO 13 MINUTES**
✿ **ASSEMBLY TIME: 10 MINUTES**

the Cupcake Doctor says...

Unflavored vinegar is best, but you can use cider vinegar. Cake mixes already contain a perfect amount of leavening, and that's why it's tricky to get them to peak in the center! I tried this recipe many times and came up with the ratio of 2 tablespoons vinegar and 1 teaspoon baking soda. If you are more interested in eating a moist chocolate cupcake with white chocolate glaze than you are in creating a science experiment, forgo the vinegar and soda in the batter and the sugar sprinkle garnish.

Vegetable oil spray for misting the pans
All-purpose flour for dusting the pans

CUPCAKES:

1 package (18.25 ounces) plain chocolate
    cake mix
1⅓ cups water
½ cup vegetable oil
3 large eggs
2 tablespoons distilled white vinegar
    (see "the Cupcake Doctor says")
2 tablespoons unsweetened cocoa powder
1 teaspoon baking soda
1 teaspoon pure vanilla extract

WHITE CHOCOLATE LAVA GLAZE:

¼ cup milk
¼ cup granulated sugar
2 tablespoons butter
1 cup white chocolate chips
Red, yellow, and orange sugar sprinkles, or
    1 package (.33 ounce) Pop Rocks candy,
    for garnish

I. Place a rack in the center of the oven and preheat the oven to 400°F. Mist 24 cupcake cups with vegetable oil spray and dust with flour. Shake out the excess flour and set the pans aside.

2. Prepare the cupcake batter: Place the cake mix, water, oil, eggs, vinegar, cocoa powder, baking soda, and vanilla in a large mixing bowl. Blend with an electric mixer on low speed for 30 seconds. Stop the machine and scrape down the sides of the bowl with a rubber spatula. Increase the mixer speed to medium and beat 2 minutes more, scraping down the sides again if needed. Spoon or scoop ¼ cup batter into each prepared cupcake cup, filling it two thirds of the way full. (You will get between 22 and 24 cupcakes). Place the pans in the oven.

3. Bake the cupcakes until they peak and spring back when lightly pressed with your finger, 11 to 13 minutes. Watch the cupcakes closely because they can burn at this high heat. Remove the pans from the oven and place them on wire racks to cool for 5 minutes. Run a dinner knife around the edges of the cupcakes, lift the cupcakes up from the bottoms of the cups using the end of the knife, and pick them out of the cups carefully with your finger-tips. Place them on a wire rack to cool for 15 minutes before glazing.

4. Meanwhile, prepare the glaze: Place the milk, sugar, and butter in a small saucepan over medium heat. Cook, stir-ring, until the sugar dissolves, the butter melts, and the mixture begins to come to a boil, 3 to 4 minutes. Turn off the heat and stir in the white chocolate chips until they are dissolved and the glaze is smooth.

5. Place the cupcakes on a serving plate or place waxed paper under the baking rack to catch runoff glaze. With a serving spoon, ladle the hot glaze over the cup-cakes and immediately sprinkle them with the sugar or the candy so that the colors melt into the glaze. The cupcakes are ready to serve.

✿ *Store these cupcakes, in a cake saver or under a glass dome, at room temperature for up to 3 days or in the refrigerator for up to 1 week.*

▲▲▲

CASTAWAY PARTY

· · · · · · · · · · · · ·

Crunchy fish nuggets on spears
(toothpicks, if age appropriate):
Buy frozen at the supermarket

———

Roasted potatoes with island tartar sauce: *Mix mayonnaise with sweet pickle relish for the sauce*

———

Survival salad of fresh pineapple pieces and shredded coconut

———

Raw vegetable kebabs: *Tomato, bell pepper, and cucumber chunks on skewers (if age appropriate)*

———

Chocolate Volcano Cupcakes with White Chocolate Lava Glaze

———

Desert island punch: *Your favorite juice punch*

———

Party favors: *Seashells, sailor knot bracelets*

———

Activities: *Face painting; bongo drumming; making your own message in a bottle*

▼▼▼

MALTED MILK CUPCAKES

• • • • •

One Saturday I offered up a half dozen different cupcakes created for kids to my own personal panel of experts (my three children); my husband walked by, spotted this one, and declared it his hands-down favorite. It is gorgeous, with milk chocolate chips inside, and it bakes up big and pretty in the pan. On top is a creamy frosting flavored with malted milk. For added crunch, sprinkle crushed malted milk candy balls over the frosting just before serving.

❁ **MAKES 22 TO 24 CUPCAKES (2½ INCHES EACH)**
❁ **PREPARATION TIME: 20 MINUTES**
❁ **BAKING TIME: 18 TO 20 MINUTES**
❁ **ASSEMBLY TIME: 10 MINUTES**

24 paper liners for cupcake pans (2½-inch size)
1 package (18.25 ounces) plain yellow cake mix
1 box (3.8 ounces) instant chocolate pudding mix
1 cup sour cream
⅓ cup vegetable oil
¼ cup water
¼ cup sugar
4 large eggs
1 teaspoon vanilla extract
1 cup milk chocolate chips
Malted Milk Buttercream (page 324)
40 malted milk balls, coarsely crushed, for garnish (see "the Cupcake Doctor says")

1. Place a rack in the center of the oven and preheat the oven to 350°F. Line 24 cupcake cups with paper liners. Set the pans aside.

2. Place cake mix, pudding mix, sour cream, oil, water, sugar, eggs, and vanilla in a large mixing bowl. Blend with an electric mixer on low speed for 30 seconds, until the ingredients are well blended, then stop the machine and scrape down the sides of the bowl with a rubber spatula. Increase the mixer speed to medium and beat for 2 minutes more, scraping down the sides again if needed. The batter should look smooth and thickened. Fold in the chocolate chips, making sure they are well distributed throughout the batter. Spoon or scoop ⅓ cup batter into each lined cupcake cup, filling it three quarters of the way full. (You will get between 22 and 24 cupcakes; remove the empty liners, if any.) Place the pans in the oven.

3. Bake the cupcakes until they spring back when lightly pressed with your finger, 18 to 20 minutes. Remove the pans from the oven and place them on wire racks to cool for 5 minutes. Run a dinner knife around the edges of the cupcake liners, lift the cupcakes up from the bottoms of the cups using the end of the knife, and pick them out of the cups carefully with your fingertips. Place them on a wire rack to cool for 15 minutes before frosting.

4. Meanwhile, prepare the Malted Milk Buttercream.

5. Place a heaping tablespoon of frosting on each cupcake and swirl to spread it out

the Cupcake Doctor says...

Crush malted milk balls by placing them in a sturdy plastic bag and pounding the bag with a wooden rolling pin or mallet. If you store the cupcakes, the malted milk ball garnish will soften. These cupcakes are best served the day they are made, when the balls are crunchy. If you must hold them for longer storage, place the malted milk garnish on the cupcakes just before serving, or use grated semisweet chocolate instead, or go without a garnish. They are delicious on their own.

with a short metal spatula or a spoon, taking care to cover the tops completely. Garnish with crushed malted milk balls. The cupcakes are ready to serve.

✿ *Store these cupcakes, in a cake saver or under a glass dome, at room temperature for up to 3 days or in the refrigerator for up to 1 week. Or freeze them ungarnished, wrapped in aluminum foil or in a cake saver, for up to 6 months. Thaw the cupcakes overnight in the refrigerator before serving.*

ROCKY ROAD CUPCAKES

• • • • •

G et ready to pour the milk! This is a crowd-pleasing recipe sure to suit all kids and any adult with a particularly sweet tooth. A bit more subtle in flavor than some of the other chocolate cupcakes, this batter contains chocolate cake mix plus vanilla pudding, and milk chocolate chips that are folded in at the last minute. The Milk Chocolate Rocky Road Frosting is the crowning touch.

✿ **MAKES 22 TO 24 CUPCAKES (2½ INCHES EACH)**
✿ **PREPARATION TIME: 20 MINUTES**
✿ **BAKING TIME: 18 TO 20 MINUTES**
✿ **ASSEMBLY TIME: 10 MINUTES**

24 paper liners for cupcake pans
(2½-inch size)

CUPCAKES:
1 package (18.25 ounces) plain
devil's food cake mix
1 package (3.4 ounces) vanilla instant
pudding mix
1 cup whole milk
½ cup vegetable oil
3 large eggs
1 teaspoon pure vanilla extract
1 cup milk chocolate chips

MILK CHOCOLATE ROCKY ROAD FROSTING:
¾ cup granulated sugar
5 tablespoons butter
⅓ cup whole milk
1 cup milk chocolate chips
¾ cup coarsely chopped unsalted dry-
roasted peanuts (see "the Cupcake
Doctor says")
1 heaping cup miniature marshmallows

the Cupcake Doctor says...

If you wish, omit the peanuts, but it won't be a true rocky road frosting. The reason I use pudding mix in this recipe is to help keep the chocolate chips suspended throughout the batter.

I. Place a rack in the center of the oven and preheat the oven to 350°F. Line 24 cupcake cups with paper liners. Set the pans aside.

2. Prepare the cupcake batter: Place the cake mix, pudding mix, milk, oil, eggs, and vanilla in a large mixing bowl. Blend with an electric mixer on low speed for 30 seconds. Stop the machine and scrape down the sides of the bowl with a rubber spatula. Increase the mixer speed to medium and beat 2 minutes more, scraping down the sides again if needed. Fold in the chocolate chips until they are well distributed. Spoon or scoop ⅓ cup batter into each lined cupcake cup,

filling it three quarters of the way full. (You will get between 22 and 24 cupcakes; remove the empty liners, if any.) Place the pans in the oven.

3. Bake the cupcakes until they spring back when lightly pressed with your finger, 18 to 20 minutes. Remove the pans from the oven and place them on wire racks to cool for 5 minutes. Run a dinner knife around the edges of the cupcake liners, lift the cupcakes up from the bottoms of the cups using the end of the knife, and pick them out of the cups carefully with your fingertips. Place them on a wire rack to cool for 15 minutes before frosting.

4. Meanwhile, prepare the Milk Chocolate Rocky Road Frosting: Place the sugar, butter, and milk in a small saucepan over medium-low heat and cook, stirring constantly, until the mixture comes to a boil, 3 to 4 minutes. Boil, stirring constantly, for 1 minute. Remove the pan from the heat, add the milk chocolate chips, and stir until they are melted. Let the pan rest off the heat to cool slightly but not completely, 3 to 4 minutes. Fold in the peanuts and marshmallows until they are well combined and the heat from the frosting begins to melt the marshmallows.

5. Place a heaping tablespoon of frosting on each cupcake and swirl to spread it out with a short metal spatula or a spoon, taking care to cover the tops completely. The cupcakes are ready to serve.

✿ *Store these cupcakes, in a cake saver or under a glass dome, at room temperature for up to 3 days or in the refrigerator for up to 1 week. Or freeze them, wrapped in aluminum foil or in a cake saver, for up to 6 months. Thaw the cupcakes overnight in the refrigerator before serving.*

Tote That Cupcake
▼ ▼ ▼

Cupcakes are lunch-bag and lunchbox favorites, but getting them to school intact can be a bit of a trial. I've found that 1-cup round plastic containers with snap-on plastic lids make the perfect cupcake carriers. They're light, secure, and unbreakable. And if the frosting gets smooshed on the lid, well, it's easy to lick off. These plastic containers are readily available in supermarkets and mart-type stores.

LITTLE FUDGE BROWNIE BITES

It's ironic that these bite-size chewy chocolate cupcakes show up in the children's chapter when they are a mainstay of our school's parent meeting refreshment table. In fact, I think these tiny cupcakes alone are responsible for luring so many busy parents to meetings on weeknights. Yet kids love them, too. They're the perfect size for lunchboxes and for nibbling at the playground. And this recipe is a snap to prepare for either grown-ups or children.

- **MAKES 24 MINIATURE CUPCAKES**
- **PREPARATION TIME: 10 MINUTES**
- **BAKING TIME: 12 TO 14 MINUTES**

Vegetable spray for misting the pans
All-purpose flour for dusting the pans
1 package (20 ounces) brownie mix (see "the Cupcake Doctor says")
⅓ cup water
5 tablespoons butter, melted
1 large egg
1 teaspoon pure vanilla extract
½ cup semisweet chocolate chips

1. Place a rack in the center of the oven and preheat the oven to 350°F. Lightly mist mini cupcake (2-inch size) cups with vegetable oil spray. Dust with flour, shake out the excess flour, and set the pans aside.

2. Place the brownie mix, water, butter, egg, vanilla, and chocolate chips in a large mixing bowl. Stir to combine for 50 strokes, or until the batter is smooth. Spoon or scoop a scant ¼ cup batter into each prepared cup, filling

the Cupcake Doctor says...

I love using the Ghirardelli brownie mix (it contains chocolate chips) in this recipe, but you can use any brownie mix you like, as long as it is about 20 ounces in weight. If the brownie mix doesn't include chocolate chips, add an extra ½ cup.

it three quarters full. Place the pans in the oven.

3. Bake the cupcakes until they puff up and the edges are crisp but the centers still soft, 12 to 14 minutes. Remove the pans from the oven and place them on wire racks to cool for 5 minutes. They will sink as they cool. Run a dinner knife around the edges of the cupcakes, lift the cupcakes up from the bottoms of the cups using the end of the knife, and pick them out of the cups carefully with your fingertips. Place them on a wire rack to cool for 15 minutes. The cupcakes are ready to serve.

✿ *Store these cupcakes, in a cake saver or under a glass dome, at room temperature for up to 5 days. Or freeze them, wrapped in aluminum foil or in a cake saver, for up to 6 months. Thaw the cupcakes overnight in the refrigerator before serving.*

COOKIES AND CREAM CUPCAKES

• • • • •

One of the most child-friendly recipes in one of my previous books, *Chocolate from the Cake Mix Doctor,* is the Cookies and Cream Cake, a white cake loaded with crushed Oreos. Once the cake is slathered with whipped cream frosting, more crushed Oreos are added. Here it is, in much the same spirit, but with a twist. In addition to the crushed Oreos in the batter, there is also half an Oreo in the bottom of each cupcake cup. Indulgence? You bet. Overkill? Never!

✿ **MAKES 22 TO 24 CUPCAKES (2½ INCHES EACH)**
✿ **PREPARATION TIME: 20 MINUTES**
✿ **BAKING TIME: 18 TO 20 MINUTES**
✿ **ASSEMBLY TIME: 10 MINUTES**

24 paper liners for cupcake pans
(2 ½-inch size)
30 Oreo cookies (see "the Cupcake Doctor says")
1 package (18.25 ounces) plain white cake mix
1 cup sour cream
½ cup vegetable oil
3 large eggs
1 teaspoon pure vanilla extract
Buttercream Frosting (page 318)

I. Place a rack in the center of the oven and preheat the oven to 350°F. Line 24 cupcake cups with paper liners. Set the pans aside.

2. Count out 12 Oreos and separate the top and bottom wafers. Make sure each has some of the icing on it. Place one wafer, icing side up, in the bottom of each paper liner. Set them aside. Place the remaining 18 Oreos between sheets of waxed paper or in a large, closed zipper-lock bag and crush them by rolling over them with a rolling pin. Set these crumbs aside.

3. Place the cake mix, sour cream, oil, eggs, and vanilla in a large mixing bowl. Blend with an electric mixer on low speed for 30 seconds. Stop the machine and scrape down the sides of the bowl with a rubber spatula. Increase the mixer speed to medium and beat 1½ minutes more, scraping down the sides again if needed. Measure out 1½ cups of the crushed Oreos and fold these into the batter until well incorporated. Set aside the remaining crushed Oreos for garnish. Spoon or scoop ⅓ cup batter into each lined cupcake cup, filling it three quarters of the way full. (You will get between 22 and 24 cupcakes; remove the empty liners, if any.) Place the pans in the oven.

4. Bake the cupcakes until they are lightly golden and spring back when lightly pressed with your finger, 18 to 20 minutes. Remove the pans from the oven and place them on wire racks to cool for 5 minutes. Run a dinner knife around the edges of the cupcake liners, lift the cupcakes up from the bottoms of the cups using the end of the knife, and pick them out of the cups carefully with your fingertips. Place them on a wire rack to cool for 15 minutes before frosting.

the CupcakeDoctor says...

Instead of plain Oreos, substitute mint or chocolate-stuffed Oreos. But don't use double-stuff Oreos, because they won't work in this recipe.

5. Meanwhile, prepare the Buttercream Frosting.

6. Place a heaping tablespoon of frosting on each cupcake and swirl to spread it out with a short metal spatula or a spoon, taking care to cover the tops completely. Sprinkle the reserved cookie crumbs over the tops, gently pressing them into the frosting so that they stick. The cupcakes are now ready to serve.

✿ *Store these cupcakes, in a cake saver or under a glass dome, at room temperature for up to 3 days or in the refrigerator for up to 1 week. If you plan to freeze them, don't add the cookie-crumb topping. Wrap them in aluminum foil or in a cake saver and freeze for up to 6 months. Thaw the cupcakes overnight in the refrigerator and top with cookie crumbs before serving.*

THE BEST BIRTHDAY CUPCAKES

WITH TWO FROSTINGS

• • • • •

This sturdy and inviting pound cake–like cupcake is the one featured big on the cover. Delicious on its own, it is wonderful spread with a lip-smacking-good creamy chocolate frosting made with the birthday boy or girl's favorite chocolate syrup. Should your child tend to favor pastels, or if it is springtime, opt for a cream cheese frosting crammed with fresh berries. Either way, you can't lose. And happy birthday!

✿ **MAKES 22 TO 24 CUPCAKES (2½ INCHES EACH)**

✿ **PREPARATION TIME: 15 MINUTES**

✿ **BAKING TIME: 24 TO 27 MINUTES**

✿ **ASSEMBLY TIME: 10 MINUTES**

24 paper liners for cupcake pans (2½-inch size)

1 package (18.5 ounces) plain butter recipe golden cake mix

1 package (8 ounces) reduced-fat cream cheese, at room temperature (see "the Cupcake Doctor says")

½ cup sugar

½ cup water

½ cup vegetable oil

4 large eggs

1 tablespoon pure vanilla extract

Chocolate Syrup Frosting (page 330) or Strawberry Cream Cheese Frosting (page 341)

Colored sprinkles or candy cake decorations, for garnish

Birthday candle and candle holder

I. Place a rack in the center of the oven and preheat the oven to 350°F. Line 24 cupcake cups with paper liners. Set the pans aside.

You Say It's Your Birthday

▼ ▼ ▼

And you're gonna have a good time! Did you know that throughout history, birthdays weren't celebrated with as much hullabaloo as they are now? At first, birthday celebrations were a way of warding off evil spirits. Family and friends would gather for a meal and to extend good wishes in hopes of bringing good luck. The idea of blowing out candles on a cake came from the ancient Greeks and Romans, who believed that the flame would carry this wish to the gods.

But what would a birthday party today be without cake, candles, ice cream, and singing "Happy Birthday to You"? This melody was written in the early 1890s by Mildred Hill, with lyrics by her sister Patty, who was a teacher, as a way for students to greet their teacher ("Good Morning to You"). It is thought that forty years later, Patty added the birthday lyrics we use today.

2. Place the cake mix, cream cheese, sugar, water, oil, eggs, and vanilla in a large mixing bowl. Blend on low speed with an electric mixer for 30 seconds, until the ingredients are well blended, then stop the machine and scrape down the sides. Increase the mixer speed to medium and beat for 1½ to 2 minutes more, scraping down the sides again if needed. The batter should be smooth and thickened. Spoon or scoop ¼ cup batter into each lined cupcake cup, filling it two thirds of the way full. (You will get between 22 and 24 cupcakes; remove the empty liners, if any.) Place the pans in the oven.

3. Bake the cupcakes until they are golden and spring back when lightly pressed with your finger, 24 to 27 minutes. Remove the pans from the oven and place them on wire racks to cool for 5 minutes. Run a dinner knife around the edges of the cupcake liners, lift the cupcakes up from the bottoms of the cups using the end of the knife, and pick them out of the cups carefully with your fingertips. Place them on a wire rack to cool for 15 minutes before frosting.

4. Meanwhile, prepare the Chocolate Syrup Frosting or the Strawberry Cream Cheese Frosting.

the Cupcake Doctor says...

Be sure that the cream cheese has softened to room temperature before you begin blending it into the cake mix. If it's not soft, unwrap it and place it on a microwave-safe plate. Place it in the microwave oven on high power for 20 seconds or until soft, repeating for another 10 seconds if needed. Have fun selecting the candle, as there are so many choices these days. Look for a bright neon color or wavy candle.

5. Place a heaping tablespoon of frosting on each cupcake and swirl to spread it out with a short metal spatula or spoon, taking care to cover the tops completely. Sprinkle the sprinkles over the frosting and place a birthday candle in a candle holder in the cupcake for the birthday boy or girl. (If using the Strawberry Cream Cheese Frosting, place the cupcakes, uncovered or in a cake saver, in the refrigerator until the frosting sets, 20 minutes.) The cupcakes are ready to serve.

✿ *Store either the strawberry-frosted cupcakes or the chocolate-frosted cupcakes, in a cake saver or under a glass dome, at room temperature for up to 3 days or in*

▲▲▲

OLD-FASHIONED PATIO BIRTHDAY PARTY

Dad's grilled sausages:
Dad knows what to do

———

Mom's macaroni salad:
Your favorite recipe for this

———

Jell-O salad: *And this, too*

———

Watermelon wedges: *Buy seedless or remove the seeds*

———

Chips and onion dip

———

Celery sticks stuffed with peanut butter

———

The Best Birthday Cupcakes with Two Frostings

———

Mini sodas piled in a bucket of ice

———

Party favors: *Goody bags with rubber balls and trading cards for the boys; chiffon scarves and big sunglasses for the girls*

———

Activities: *Pin the tail on the donkey; croquet; hide-and-seek*

▼▼▼

the refrigerator for up to 1 week. Or freeze them, wrapped in aluminum foil or in a cake saver, for up to 6 months. Thaw the cupcakes overnight in the refrigerator before serving.

BURIED TREASURE CAKES

• • • • •

All children love to find treasures—and adults never outgrow this. So, I thought it would be fun to create a cupcake with a surprise treasure inside.

When I was developing this recipe, I tested it using different candies to see which ones stayed intact when baked into the cupcakes. M&M's and Skittles were our favorites. The dark chocolate frosting, which looks almost black, is made by adding Dutch-process cocoa powder. And if you pipe a white X in the middle of each cupcake, that X will mark the spot under which the candy treasure is buried.

Serve these to some budding pirates, and by all means come up with your own treasures and your own way of decorating these fun cupcakes.

✿ **MAKES 22 TO 24 CUPCAKES (2½ INCHES EACH)**
✿ **PREPARATION TIME: 20 MINUTES**
✿ **BAKING TIME: 14 TO 16 MINUTES**
✿ **ASSEMBLY TIME: 10 MINUTES**

24 paper liners for cupcake pans
  (2½-inch size)

1 package (18.25 ounces) white cake mix
  with pudding (see "the Cupcake
  Doctor says")

¾ cup all-purpose flour (see "the Cupcake
  Doctor says")

1½ cups milk or water

½ cup vegetable oil

3 large eggs

1 teaspoon pure vanilla extract

72 M&M's or Skittles

Dark Chocolate Buttercream (page 321)

1 white decorating pen
  (see "the Cupcake Doctor says")

1. Place a rack in the center of the oven and preheat the oven to 400°F. Line 24 cupcake cups with paper liners. Set the pans aside.

2. Place the cake mix, flour, milk, oil, eggs, and vanilla in a large mixing bowl. Blend with an electric mixer on low speed for 30 seconds. Stop the machine and scrape down the sides of the bowl with a rubber spatula. Increase the mixer speed to medium and beat 2 minutes more, scraping down the sides again if needed. Spoon or scoop ¼ cup batter into each lined cupcake cup, filling it two thirds of the way full. (You will get between 22 and 24 cupcakes; remove the empty liners, if

▲ ▲ ▲

SHIVER ME TIMBERS PIRATE PARTY

Walk the plank franks and beans:
Baked beans mixed with sliced frankfurters in a casserole dish. Top with shredded cheese and bake at 350°F until bubbly, 20 to 25 minutes.

Fruit salad with oranges, apples, and grapes

Buried Treasure Cakes

Grape juice

Party favors: Eye patches; beads; hoop earrings; chocolate gold coins; fake tattoos

Activities: Treasure hunt

▼ ▼ ▼

any.) Place 3 M&M's or Skittles on top of each cupcake (they will sink into the batter). Place the pans in the oven.

3. Bake the cupcakes until they are lightly golden and spring back when lightly pressed with your finger, 14 to 16 minutes. Remove the pans from the oven and place them on wire racks to cool for 5 minutes. Run a dinner knife around the edges of the cupcake liners, lift the cupcakes up from the bottoms of the cups using the end of the knife, and pick them out of the cups carefully with your fingertips. Place them on a wire rack to cool for 15 minutes before frosting.

4. Meanwhile, prepare the frosting. Place a heaping tablespoon of frosting on each cupcake and spread it out with a short metal spatula or a spoon, taking care to cover the tops completely. With a white decorating pen or melted white chocolate in a squeeze bottle, pipe an X on top of each cupcake. The cupcakes are ready to serve.

VARIATION Berried Treasure Cakes: Excuse the play on words, but I could not resist omitting the candy and placing a quarter of a large strawberry on top of the batter before it went into the oven. If it works, I've got a real "berried treasure," I thought. Well, it did, and beautifully. I frosted the results with dark chocolate frosting, but you might enjoy a lighter, more pastel Strawberry Cream Cheese Frosting (page 341) instead.

the Cupcake Doctor says...

To get these cupcakes to rise quickly and surround the treasure inside, I bake them at 400°F. I used Betty Crocker sour cream white cake mix. The additional flour adds structure to the batter and helps the batter bake up and around the candy. White frosting decorating pens are available at Williams-Sonoma. Decorating pens are 1.6 ounces each, come in an array of colors, and contain enough frosting (which hardens) to decorate one cake or a batch of cupcakes.

✿ *Store these cupcakes, in a cake saver or under a glass dome, at room temperature for up to 3 days or in the refrigerator for up to 1 week. Or freeze them, wrapped in aluminum foil or in a cake saver, for up to 6 months. Thaw the cupcakes overnight in the refrigerator before serving.*

CARAMEL SPICED APPLE CUPCAKES

• • • • •

If you look quickly at these cupcakes you might think that you are looking at caramel apples. But look again and you'll see that they are actually soft, blush-pink cupcakes coated in velvety melted caramel and decorated with a popsicle stick and crushed peanuts. The pinkish color comes from finely chopped spiced apple rings that are folded into the batter. No doubt about it, these cupcakes are as much fun to make as they are to eat.

24 paper liners for cupcake pans
   (2½-inch size)

CUPCAKES:
1 jar (14.5 ounces) red spiced apple rings,
   drained
1 package (18.25 ounces) plain yellow
   cake mix
1 package (3.4 ounces) vanilla instant
   pudding mix
¾ cup water
½ cup vegetable oil
3 large eggs

❀ **MAKES 22 TO 24 CUPCAKES (2½ INCHES EACH)**
❀ **PREPARATION TIME: 25 MINUTES**
❀ **BAKING TIME: 18 TO 20 MINUTES**
❀ **ASSEMBLY TIME: 15 MINUTES**

GLAZE:

45 to 50 caramels (from a 14-ounce bag)

⅓ cup evaporated milk

1 teaspoon pure vanilla extract

½ cup unsalted peanuts, chopped

24 wooden craft sticks (optional)

1. Place a rack in the center of the oven and preheat the oven to 350°F. Line 24 cupcake cups with paper liners. Set the pans aside.

2. Prepare the cupcake batter: Place the drained apple rings in the food processor and in on-off pulse motions finely chop them, 15 seconds. Place the cake mix, pudding mix, chopped apple rings, water, oil, and eggs in a large mixing bowl. Blend with an electric mixer on low speed for 30 seconds. Stop the machine and scrape down the sides of the bowl with a rubber spatula. Increase the mixer speed to medium and beat 2 minutes more, scraping down the sides again if needed. The batter should look well combined. Spoon or scoop ¼ cup batter into each lined muffin cup, filling it two thirds of the way full. (You will get between 22 and 24 cupcakes; remove the empty liners, if any.) Place the pans side by side in the oven.

3. Bake the cupcakes until they are golden and the top springs back when lightly pressed with your finger, 18 to 20

▲▲▲

HARVEST BIRTHDAY PARTY

•••••••••••

Turkey burgers (on buns) or turkey sub sandwiches: *With lettuce, tomato, roasted red peppers, onion slices (if your kids like them), and a mild vinaigrette, all on a sub roll*

———

Vegetable chips

———

Waldorf salad: *Apple and celery chunks and walnut pieces mixed with mayonnaise*

———

Caramel Spiced Apple Cupcakes

———

Apple cider

———

Party favors: *Miniature pumpkins and Indian corn, candy corn*

———

Activities: *Apple bobbing; decorating and carving pumpkins*

▼▼▼

minutes. Remove the pans from the oven and place them on wire racks to cool for 5 minutes. Run a dinner knife around the edges of the cupcake liners, lift the cupcakes up from the bottoms of the cups using the end of the knife, and pick them out of the cups carefully with your fingertips. Place them on a wire rack to cool for 15 minutes before glazing.

4. Meanwhile, prepare the caramel glaze: Unwrap the caramels and place them in a medium-size saucepan. Add the evaporated milk. Stir with a wooden spoon over medium heat until all the caramels are melted, 5 to 6 minutes. Stir in the vanilla.

5. Immediately spoon the warm caramel glaze over the top of each cooled cupcake and sprinkle the chopped peanuts around the edges. Push a craft stick in the center of each cupcake, if desired. The cupcakes are ready to serve.

✿ *Store these cupcakes, in a cake saver or under a glass dome, at room temperature for up to 3 days or in the refrigerator for up to 1 week. Or freeze them (without the craft sticks), wrapped in aluminum foil or in a cake saver, for up to 6 months. Thaw the cupcakes overnight in the refrigerator before serving.*

BANANA PUDDING CUPCAKES

• • • • •

I f my family was asked to select the most comforting cupcake from this book, it would be these. The batter is filled with fresh banana, and the finished cupcakes have a vanilla pudding center and whipped cream and crushed vanilla wafers on top. You can eat them right from your hands, but we prefer to place them on small plates and eat them with a spoon, as you would banana pudding.

24 paper liners for cupcake pans
(2½-inch size)

❀ **MAKES 22 TO 24 CUPCAKES (2½ INCHES EACH)**
❀ **PREPARATION TIME: 20 MINUTES**
❀ **BAKING TIME: 18 TO 20 MINUTES**
❀ **ASSEMBLY TIME: 20 MINUTES**

36 vanilla wafers

3 medium-size ripe bananas

1 package (18.25 ounces) plain yellow
  cake mix

½ cup vegetable oil

¼ cup milk

3 large eggs

1 teaspoon pure vanilla extract

FILLING:

2 cups milk

1 package (3 ounces) cook and serve
  vanilla pudding mix

3 tablespoons butter

1 teaspoon pure vanilla extract

TOPPING:

1 cup heavy (whipping) cream

1 tablespoon sugar

2 medium-size ripe bananas,
  cut into 24 slices

the Cupcake Doctor says...

The riper the banana, the more flavorful this cupcake. If you're pressed for time, forgo the real whipped cream and sugar and plop a dollop of whipped topping on top of each cupcake. But I don't have to tell you that real cream makes this cupcake sublime.

1. Place a rack in the center of the oven and preheat the oven to 350°F. Line 24 cupcake cups with paper liners. Count out 12 vanilla wafers for the garnish and set them aside. Place the remaining 24 vanilla wafers flat-side down in the bottom of the cupcake liners. Set the pans aside.

2. Prepare the cupcake batter: Slice the bananas and place them in a large mixing bowl. Mash with a potato masher or fork until the bananas are smooth, 1 minute; you will have about 1¼ cups. Place the cake mix, oil, milk, eggs, and vanilla in the bowl with the banana puree. Blend with an electric mixer on low speed for 30 seconds. Stop the machine and scrape down the sides of the bowl with a rubber spatula. Increase the mixer speed to medium and beat 2 minutes more, scraping down the sides again if needed. Spoon or scoop ⅓ cup batter into each lined cupcake cup, filling it three quarters of the way full. (You will get between 22 and 24 cupcakes; remove the empty liners, if any.) Place the pans in the oven.

3. Bake the cupcakes until they are golden and spring back when lightly pressed with your finger, 18 to 20 minutes. Remove the pans from the oven and place them on wire racks to cool for 5 minutes. Run a dinner knife around the edges of the cupcake liners, lift the cupcakes up from the bottoms of the cups using the end of the knife, and pick them out of the cups carefully with your fingertips. Place them on a wire rack to cool for 15 minutes before filling.

4. Meanwhile, prepare the filling: Place the milk in a medium-size saucepan. Whisk in the pudding mix until incorporated. Place the pan over medium heat and continue to whisk as the mixture comes to a full boil, 3 to 4 minutes. Remove the pan from the heat and stir in the butter and vanilla. Pour the pudding into a medium-size bowl to cool for 20 minutes.

5. Meanwhile, prepare the topping: Place a large mixing bowl and electric mixer beaters in the freezer to chill. Place the reserved 12 vanilla wafers in a small plastic bag and crush by rolling over the bag with a rolling pin. Remove the bowl and beaters from the freezer. Pour the cream into the bowl and beat on high speed until the cream has thickened, 1½ minutes. Stop the machine and add the sugar. Beat the cream and sugar on high speed until stiff peaks form, 1 to 2 minutes more.

6. To assemble the cupcakes, remove the paper liners and place the cupcakes on a serving platter. Spoon ½ cup of the cooled pudding into a pastry bag fitted with a wide tip. Pipe a generous amount of pudding into the cupcake through the center of the top (1 to 2 tablespoons), allowing about 1 teaspoon of the pudding to overflow onto the surface of the cupcake. Repeat with the remaining cupcakes. Sprinkle the vanilla wafer crumbs on top of the pudding. Dollop about 1 tablespoon of the whipped cream on top of the crumbs. Just before serving, stand a banana slice in the whipped cream. The cupcakes are ready to serve.

✿ *Store these cupcakes, without the banana garnish, lightly covered in the refrigerator for 1 day. Add the banana slice just before serving. Or freeze the unfilled cupcakes, wrapped in aluminum foil or in a cake saver, for up to 6 months. Thaw the cupcakes overnight in the refrigerator before filling, garnishing, and serving.*

A CUPCAKE ZOO

WITH CARAMEL PAN FROSTING

• • • • •

Who can resist light chocolate cupcakes with creamy caramel frosting and topped with a children's favorite—animal crackers? Lined up on a serving platter and dusted with confectioners' sugar, it's like having a mini zoo at a children's party. They are also great for toting to a picnic or a birthday party away from home, because the caramel frosting hardens and isn't messy.

✿ **MAKES 22 TO 24 CUPCAKES (2½ INCHES EACH)**
✿ **PREPARATION TIME: 20 MINUTES**
✿ **BAKING TIME: 18 TO 20 MINUTES**
✿ **ASSEMBLY TIME: 10 MINUTES**

24 paper liners for cupcake pans
　　(2½-inch size)
1 package (18.25 ounces) plain yellow
　　cake mix
1 package (3.8 ounces) chocolate instant
　　pudding mix
1¼ cups whole milk
½ cup vegetable oil
3 large eggs
1 teaspoon pure vanilla extract
Caramel Pan Frosting (page 345)
3 boxes (2⅛ ounces each) animal crackers
　　(you need 24 unbroken crackers;
　　see "the Cupcake Doctor says")
1 tablespoon confectioners' sugar

I. Place a rack in the center of the oven and preheat the oven to 350°F. Line 24 cupcake cups with paper liners. Set the pans aside.

2. Place the cake mix, pudding mix, milk, oil, eggs, and vanilla in a large mixing bowl. Blend with an electric mixer on low speed for 30 seconds. Stop the machine

the Cupcake Doctor says...

Instead of decorating the top of each cupcake with an animal cracker, you can buy zoo motif hard candy decorations at the supermarket.

and scrape down the sides of the bowl with a rubber spatula. Increase the mixer speed to medium and beat 2 minutes more, scraping down the sides again if needed. Spoon or scoop ⅓ cup batter into each lined cupcake cup, filling it three quarters of the way full. (You will get between 22 and 24 cupcakes; remove the empty liners, if any.) Place the pans in the oven.

3. Bake the cupcakes until they are golden and spring back when lightly pressed with your finger, 18 to 20 minutes. Remove the pans from the oven and place them on wire racks to cool for 5 minutes. Run a dinner knife around the edges of the cupcake liners, lift the cupcakes up from the bottoms of the cups using the end of the knife, and pick them out of the cups carefully with your fingertips. Place them on a wire rack to cool for 15 minutes before frosting.

4. Meanwhile, prepare the frosting.

5. Place a heaping tablespoon of frosting on each cupcake and swirl to spread it out

SAFARI PARTY

Grilled steak cubes:
On a skewer (if age appropriate)

Monkey fruit salad: *A mix of grapes, melon balls, and lots of banana slices*

Animal feed snacks: *Bowls of potato sticks, trail mix, gummy worms, peanuts in the shell*

A Cupcake Zoo with Caramel Pan Frosting

Jungle punch: *Your favorite fruit punch*

Party favors: *Little stuffed animals*

Activities: *Create a "petting zoo" with pets and stuffed animals, giving them names and habitats*

with a short metal spatula or a spoon, taking care to cover the tops completely. Immediately stand one animal cracker in the frosting of each cupcake and lightly dust with confectioners' sugar. The cupcakes are ready to serve.

✿ *Store these cupcakes, in a cake saver or under a glass dome, at room temperature for up to 5 days. Or freeze them, wrapped in aluminum foil or in a cake saver, for up to 6 months. Thaw the cupcakes overnight in the refrigerator before serving.*

PLUM GOOD CUPCAKES

WITH POLKA DOT FROSTING

● ● ● ● ●

Polka dots are so much fun to wear, and this recipe proves they're fun to eat as well. These moist, subtle plum and spice cupcakes with a rich cream cheese frosting tinted golden yellow are fit for a party at the palace. When some of the cupcakes are piped with purple polka dots and decorated with yellow miniature M&M's, the result is a platter of very regal cupcakes, perfect for the prince or princess on your party list. (This is also lovely for adults when decorated with gold dragées.)

✿ MAKES 20 TO 22 CUPCAKES (2½ INCHES EACH)
✿ PREPARATION TIME: 15 MINUTES
✿ BAKING TIME: 17 TO 19 MINUTES
✿ ASSEMBLY TIME: 10 MINUTES

22 paper liners for cupcake pans
(2½-inch size)

CUPCAKES:
1 package (18.25 ounces) plain yellow
cake mix
2 packages (3.5 ounces each)
strained plums with apples baby food
(see "the Cupcake Doctor says")
1 cup sour cream
⅓ cup vegetable oil
3 large eggs
1 teaspoon ground cinnamon
¼ teaspoon ground nutmeg

POLKA DOT FROSTING:
4 ounces (½ package) cream cheese,
at room temperature
2 tablespoons butter, at room temperature
1 teaspoon pure vanilla extract
2 cups confectioners' sugar, sifted
2 to 3 drops yellow food coloring
Purple icing decorating pen
Yellow miniature M&M's or hard candies

1. Place a rack in the center of the oven and preheat the oven to 350°F. Line 22 cupcake cups with paper liners. Set the pans aside.

2. Prepare the cupcake batter: Place the cake mix, plums, sour cream, oil, eggs, cinnamon, and nutmeg in a large mixing bowl. Blend with an electric mixer on low speed for 30 seconds. Stop the machine and scrape down the sides of the bowl with a rubber spatula. Increase the mixer speed to medium and beat 2 minutes more, scraping down the sides again if needed. Spoon or scoop ⅓ cup batter into each lined cupcake cup, filling it three quarters of the way full. (You will get between 20 and 22 cupcakes; remove the empty liners, if any.) Place the pans in the oven.

3. Bake the cupcakes until they are golden and spring back when lightly pressed with your finger, 17 to 19 minutes. Remove the pans from the oven and place them on wire racks to cool for 5 minutes. Run a dinner knife around the edges of the cupcake liners, lift the cupcakes up from the bottoms of the cups using the end of the knife, and pick them out of the cups carefully with your fingertips. Place them on

▲▲▲

KING (OR QUEEN) OF THE ROUND TABLE

King's fried chicken legs:
Use a favorite recipe

Cottage fries

Bunches of fresh grapes

Plum Good Cupcakes with Polka Dot Frosting

Grape juice: *Call it mead*

Party favors: *Crowns, purple capes, swords, magic sets*

Activities: *Drawing your own coat of arms; knighting and naming ceremony when guests arrive; pretend magic show*

▼▼▼

a wire rack to cool for 15 minutes before frosting.

4. Meanwhile, prepare the Polka Dot Frosting: Place the cream cheese and butter in a large mixing bowl, and blend with an electric mixer on low speed until creamy. Add the vanilla and sugar and blend on low until the sugar is incorporated, 30 seconds. Increase the speed to medium-high and beat to incorporate air and lighten the frosting, 30 seconds more.

the Cupcake Doctor says...

I used Gerber's Prunes with Apples, which comes in a plastic container and is packed two per package. For a fun flavor twist for adults, frost these cupcakes with Caramel Pan Frosting (page 345) and forgo the polka dots.

Add 2 drops of the food coloring and beat to blend, adding another drop if needed to tint the frosting a golden color.

5. Place a heaping tablespoon of frosting on each cupcake and spread it out smoothly with a short metal spatula or a spoon, taking care to cover the tops completely. Make random dots about ¼ inch wide on the frosting, using the purple icing pen. Between these dots, make random tiny dots. Center miniature M&M's on each of the larger dots. Place the cupcakes, uncovered, in the refrigerator until the frosting sets, 20 minutes. The cupcakes are ready to serve.

✿ *Store the cupcakes, in a cake saver or under a glass dome, at room temperature for up to 3 days or in the refrigerator for up to 1 week. Or freeze them, wrapped in aluminum foil or in a cake saver, for up to 6 months. Thaw the cupcakes overnight in the refrigerator before serving.*

TIE-DYE CUPCAKES

WITH PSYCHEDELIC BUTTERCREAM

I was thinking of calling these M&M cupcakes, but after the cupcakes came out of the oven I saw how the miniature candies had streaked the top of the cake. It reminded me of the tie-dye T-shirts of the 1960s. They are fun to serve at a sixties theme party or most anytime. Have fun frosting these little cakes. You can dye the frosting hot, fun colors or fold the little candies into a plain buttercream so the colors run. Groovy.

✿ **MAKES 22 TO 24 CUPCAKES (2½ INCHES EACH)**
✿ **PREPARATION TIME: 20 MINUTES**
✿ **BAKING TIME: 17 TO 20 MINUTES**
✿ **ASSEMBLY TIME: 10 MINUTES**

24 paper liners for cupcake
pans (2½-inch size)

CUPCAKES:
1 package (18.25 ounces)
plain yellow cake mix
1 package (3.4 ounces) vanilla instant
pudding mix
1 cup whole milk
½ cup vegetable oil
4 large eggs
1 teaspoon pure vanilla extract
¾ cup miniature M&M's
(see "the Cupcake Doctor says")

PSYCHEDELIC BUTTERCREAM:
4 tablespoons butter (½ stick),
at room temperature
3 cups confectioners' sugar, sifted
3 to 4 tablespoons milk
Bright blue, green, and pink food coloring
(see "the Cupcake Doctor says")
½ cup miniature M&M's (optional)

the Cupcake Doctor says...

It's important to use miniature M&M's because the regular M&M's will sink instead of creating a streaked, tie-dye effect on top. Try to distribute the colors well, using some of each (the blue M&M's create the most noticeable streak). It is less expensive to buy the minis in the 12-ounce bag rather than several of the small bags. As for food coloring, I love the Wilton teal, sky blue, leaf green, and pink in this recipe.

Instead of dying the frosting bright colors and topping with the M&M's, you can use a plain buttercream frosting and fold the M&M's into it, then let it rest in a warm place for an hour. Stir. The M&M colors will streak through the frosting.

I. Place a rack in the center of the oven and preheat the oven to 350°F. Line 24 cupcake cups with paper liners. Set the pans aside.

2. Prepare the cupcake batter: Place the cake mix, pudding mix, milk, oil, eggs, and vanilla in a large mixing bowl. Blend with an electric mixer on low speed for 30 seconds. Stop the machine and scrape down the sides of the bowl with a rubber spatula. Increase the mixer speed to medium and beat 2 minutes more, scraping down the sides again if needed. Spoon or scoop a heaping ¼ cup batter into each lined cupcake cup, filling it two thirds full. (You will get between 22 and 24 cupcakes; remove the empty liners, if any.) Place 16 miniature M&M's on top of each cupcake. Make sure to get a good mix of colors. Place the pans in the oven.

3. Bake the cupcakes until they are golden and spring back when lightly pressed with your finger, 17 to 20 minutes. Remove the pans from the oven and place them on wire racks to cool for 5 minutes. Run a dinner knife around the edges of the cupcake liners, lift the cupcakes up from the bottoms of the cups using the end of the knife, and pick them out of the cups carefully with your fingertips. Place them on a wire rack to cool for 15 minutes before frosting.

4. Meanwhile, prepare the Psychedelic Buttercream: Place the butter in a medium-size mixing bowl and blend with an electric mixer on low speed until creamy. Add the sugar and 3 tablespoons of the milk. Blend on low until the ingredients just come together, adding up to another tablespoon of milk if needed to make the frosting spreadable. Increase the mixer speed to medium-high and beat in air to make the frosting fluffy, 30 seconds longer. Divide the frosting into two or three bowls for tinting. If you are using liquid colors, you'll need about 2 drops of color per bowl; if using paste, about ⅛ teaspoon. Stir the colors into the frosting to blend.

5. Place small dollops of each colored frosting on each cupcake and swirl them together with the edge of a short metal spatula to resemble a tie-dye pattern, taking care to cover the tops completely. Or, decorate the top with miniature M&M's, if desired. The cupcakes are ready to serve.

✿ *Store these cupcakes, in a cake saver or under a glass dome, at room temperature for up to 3 days or in the refrigerator for up to 1 week. Or freeze them, wrapped in aluminum foil or in a cake saver, for up to 6 months. Thaw the cupcakes overnight in the refrigerator before serving.*

▲▲▲

WOODSTOCK PEACE-IN

∙∙∙∙∙∙∙∙∙∙∙∙∙∙

Cheese and vegetable quesadillas: *Slices of Muenster cheese, mushrooms, and grilled peppers sandwiched between flour tortillas and toasted on a griddle or in a large skillet*

Hot chicken wings

Love Bug snack mix: *Trail mix with granola and M&Ms*

Frozen yogurt with berries

Tie-Dye Cupcakes

Apple juice

Party favors: *Tinted granny glasses; love beads; peace symbol necklaces*

Activities: *Beading; weaving; making tie-dye T-shirts*

▼▼▼

NEAPOLITAN SUNDAE CUPCAKES

• • • • •

Neapolitan ice cream is perfect for parties and picnics because with ribbons of chocolate, vanilla, and strawberry, it has a flavor for everyone, and the same goes for these festive cupcakes. After baking, the cupcake is topped with whipped cream, drizzled with chocolate, and crowned with a cherry. Serve it with spoons, as you would a sundae.

24 paper liners for cupcake pans
   (2½-inch size)

✿ **MAKES 22 TO 24 CUPCAKES (2½ INCHES EACH)**
✿ **PREPARATION TIME: 25 MINUTES**
✿ **BAKING TIME: 18 TO 20 MINUTES**
✿ **ASSEMBLY TIME: 10 MINUTES**

CUPCAKES:

*1 package (18.25 ounces) plain white
   cake mix*

*1 package (3.4 ounces) vanilla instant
   pudding mix*

*1 container (6 ounces) low-fat
   vanilla yogurt*

½ cup vegetable oil

½ cup water

4 large eggs

½ cup chocolate syrup

*3 tablespoons strawberry gelatin powder
   from a 3-ounce box*

TOPPING:

*1 container (8 ounces) frozen whipped
   topping, thawed*

1 cup chocolate syrup or sauce

24 maraschino cherries

Chocolate sprinkles (optional)

*Chopped peanuts, pecans, or
   walnuts (optional)*

▲▲▲

MAMA MIA!
ITALIAN ARTIST PARTY

Leaning tower of pizza: *Order in pizzas and serve them on cake stands*

Spaghetti and a selection of sauces

Mona Lisa melon balls and strawberries

Neapolitan Sundae Cupcakes

Gelato: *Italian ice cream in a variety of flavors*

Italian fruit nectars

Party favors: *Big T-shirts to decorate, painters' caps or berets, watercolor sets*

Activities: *Drawing portraits of each other (with watercolors or crayons); playing bocce ball*

▼▼▼

I. Place a rack in the center of the oven and preheat the oven to 350°F. Line 24 cupcake cups with paper liners. Set the pans aside.

2. Place the cake mix, pudding mix, yogurt, oil, water, and eggs in a large mixing bowl. Blend with an electric mixer on

the Cupcake Doctor says...

To arrive at the three neat layers of chocolate, then vanilla, and then strawberry cake, you must take care to spoon one batter on top of the other and not to spread the batter out to reach the sides. Don't even tilt the pan.

low speed for 1 minute. Stop the machine and scrape down the sides of the bowl with a rubber spatula. Increase the mixer speed to medium and blend 1½ to 2 minutes more, scraping down the sides again if needed. The batter should look well combined and thickened.

3. Divide the batter equally into 3 small mixing bowls (approximately 2 cups batter in each). To one bowl, stir in the chocolate syrup until it is incorporated. To the second bowl, stir in the strawberry gelatin until it is incorporated. Leave the batter in the third bowl plain. Beginning with the chocolate batter, spoon a heaping tablespoon of batter into each lined muffin cup. Next, carefully spoon 1 tablespoon plain batter on top of the chocolate. Do not spread out the batter and do not let it touch the sides of the liner. Finally, gently spoon 1 tablespoon strawberry batter on top of the plain, not letting it touch the sides. (You will fill 22 to 24 cupcakes; remove the empty liners, if any.) Place the pans side by side in the oven.

4. Bake the cupcakes until they spring back when lightly pressed with your finger, 18 to 20 minutes. Remove the pans from the oven and place them on wire racks to cool for 5 minutes. Run a dinner knife around the edges of the cupcake liners, lift the cupcakes up from the bottoms of the cups using the end of the knife, and pick them out of the cups carefully with your fingertips. Place them on a wire rack to cool for 15 minutes before frosting.

5. Dollop a heaping tablespoon of whipped topping on top of each cupcake, then drizzle with chocolate syrup or sauce. Top with a cherry and, if desired, sprinkle with chocolate sprinkles and nuts, as you would a sundae. The cupcakes are ready to serve.

✿ *Store these cupcakes, without the toppings, in a cake saver or under a glass dome at room temperature for up to 3 days. Or freeze them, topless, wrapped in aluminum foil or in a cake saver, for up to 6 months. Thaw the cupcakes overnight in the refrigerator before topping and serving.*

5 Ways to Top This Cupcake:

▼ ▼ ▼

1. Slice two bananas and scatter the slices around the whipped topping, then drizzle on the chocolate syrup and add the cherry, as you might a banana split.

2. Spoon lightly sweetened sliced strawberries over the top and omit the chocolate syrup or sauce.

3. Omit the chocolate sauce and the cherry and add warm caramel or butterscotch sauce, then a sprinkling of toasted pecans.

4. For a neat look and an easy traveler, don't dollop, just spread the top of the cupcakes with whipped topping as you might frosting. Sprinkle on the chocolate sprinkles or grated semisweet chocolate.

5. Make an M&M sundae cupcake by omitting the cherry and the nuts and chocolate sprinkles and just shower miniature M&M's over the whipped topping and chocolate sauce.

PEANUT BUTTER SURPRISES

• • • • •

If your kids love the combination of chocolate and peanut butter, then they'll love these peanut butter cupcakes with a chocolate Hershey's Kiss baked inside. Topped with a smooth chocolate buttercream frosting, garnished with chopped Reese's Peanut Butter Cups, they make another wonderful surprise-filled dessert.

✿ MAKES: 22 TO 24 CUPCAKES (2½ INCHES EACH)
✿ PREPARATION TIME: 40 MINUTES
✿ BAKING TIME: 18 TO 20 MINUTES
✿ ASSEMBLY TIME: 10 MINUTES

24 paper liners for cupcake pans
    (2½-inch size)
24 Hershey's Kisses
1 package (18.25 ounces) plain yellow
    cake mix
1⅓ cups water
⅓ cup smooth peanut butter
⅓ cup vegetable oil
3 large eggs
1 teaspoon pure vanilla extract
8 Reese's Peanut Butter Cups (.75 ounce
    each; see "the Cupcake Doctor says"),
    for garnish
Chocolate Buttercream (page 319)

1. Place a rack in the center of the oven and preheat the oven to 350°F. Line 24 cupcake cups with paper liners. Set the pans aside. Unwrap 24 Hershey's Kisses and set them aside.

2. Place the cake mix, water, peanut butter, oil, eggs, and vanilla in a large mixing bowl. Beat with an electric mixer on low

the Cupcake Doctor says...

Although they make a fun garnish, feel free to omit the Peanut Butter Cups. If you do use them they are easier to chop if they have first been frozen. For variation, garnish with white chocolate Peanut Butter Cups.

speed until blended, 30 seconds. Stop the machine and scrape down the sides of the bowl with a rubber spatula. Increase the mixer speed to medium and beat for 2 minutes longer, scraping down the sides again if necessary. The batter should be well blended. Spoon or scoop ¼ cup batter into each lined cupcake cup, filling it two thirds of the way full. (You will get between 22 and 24 cupcakes; remove the empty liners, if any.) Gently place 1 Kiss on top of each cupcake. Do not press the Kiss into the batter. Meanwhile, place the Peanut Butter Cups in the freezer for at least 30 minutes. Place the pans in the oven.

3. Bake the cupcakes until they are golden and spring back when lightly pressed with your finger, 18 to 20 minutes. Remove the pans from the oven and place them on wire racks to cool for 5 minutes. Run a dinner knife around the edges of the cupcake liners, lift the cupcakes up from the bottoms of the cups using the end of the knife, and pick them out of the cups carefully with your fingertips. Place them on a wire rack to cool for 15 minutes before frosting.

4. Meanwhile, prepare the Chocolate Buttercream. Remove the Peanut Butter Cups from the freezer and coarsely chop them.

5. Place a heaping tablespoon of frosting on each cupcake and swirl to spread it out with a short metal spatula or metal spoon, taking care to cover the tops. Garnish with chopped Peanut Butter Cups. The cupcakes are ready to serve.

✿ *Store these cupcakes, in a cake saver or under a glass dome, at room temperature for up to 3 days or in the refrigerator for up to 1 week. Or freeze them, wrapped in aluminum foil or in a cake saver, for up to 6 months. Thaw the cupcakes overnight in the refrigerator before serving.*

FORTUNE COOKIE CUPCAKES

• • • • •

When Peg Lee of Houston's Central Market found out I was writing a book on cupcakes, she told me about one she used to make when her children were little. She would write a fortune message on a strip of parchment paper, seal it in foil, then tuck it into the cupcake batter. I could hardly wait to get back to my kitchen to start testing Peg's idea. It worked perfectly; the parchment paper fortunes became hidden as the cupcakes baked up golden and glorious. Flavor these cupcakes with almond, lemon, or orange.

24 paper liners for cupcake pans
    (2½-inch size)
1 package (18.25 ounces) plain yellow
    cake mix
1 package (3.4 ounces) vanilla instant
    pudding mix
1¼ cups milk
½ cup vegetable oil
3 large eggs
1 teaspoon almond extract or
    ½ teaspoon lemon or orange extract
¼ cup confectioners' sugar

1. Place a rack in the center of the oven and preheat the oven to 350°F. Line 24 cupcake cups with paper liners. Set the pans aside. Measure a strip of parchment that's 12 inches long and 2 inches wide

✿ **MAKES 22 TO 24 CUPCAKES (2½ INCHES EACH)**
✿ **PREPARATION TIME: 20 MINUTES**
✿ **BAKING TIME: 20 TO 22 MINUTES**
✿ **ASSEMBLY TIME: 5 MINUTES**

the Cupcake Doctor says...

If you don't have parchment paper, you can use ordinary white typing paper, but you must seal it in aluminum foil before placing it in the cupcake. A ballpoint is the best pen to use on parchment paper. Tell children to look for the surprise inside (you don't want them eating it).

To dress up a cupcake that needs little decoration, use stencils and confectioners' sugar. Many cake stencils have a small pattern in the center—or one to the side—that is the same size as the top of a cupcake. Place this over the cupcake, sift the confectioners' sugar over the stencil, and carefully lift the stencil.

into ½-inch-long segments. Cut the strip into 24 pieces (2 x ½ inch each). Write the fortunes on one side of each parchment piece with a ballpoint pen. (For ideas, see Fabulous Fortunes on the facing page.) Fold the fortunes in half, wrap each in a small piece of aluminum foil, and set aside.

2. Place the cake mix, pudding mix, milk, oil, eggs, and almond extract in a large mixing bowl. Blend with an electric mixer on low speed for 30 seconds. Stop the machine and scrape down the sides of

▲▲▲

RING IN THE CHINESE NEW YEAR

Fried rice served with chopsticks:
Buy this and the egg rolls from your favorite Chinese carry-out restaurant.

Crunchy egg rolls

Fortune Cookie Cupcakes

Favorite juice in Chinese teapots

Party favors: *Chinese paper kites*

Activities: *Creating a Chinese dragon; flying kites; fortune cookie treasure hunt*

▼▼▼

the bowl with a rubber spatula. Increase the mixer speed to medium and beat 2 minutes more, scraping down the sides again if needed. Spoon or scoop ⅓ cup batter into each lined cupcake cup, filling it three quarters of the way full. (You will get between 22 and 24 cupcakes; remove the empty liners, if any.) Gently press a fortune into the center of each cupcake with a toothpick or a fork, sinking it into the batter so it cannot be seen. Place the pans in the oven.

3. Bake the cupcakes until they are golden and spring back when lightly pressed with your finger, 20 to 22 minutes.

Fabulous Fortunes

My six-year-old son, John, flipped when he found a fortune inside his cupcake that predicted what he might be when he grows up. Here are some ideas:

✿ President of the United States

✿ Famous ballerina

✿ Firefighter

✿ Painter

✿ Author

✿ Teacher

✿ Poet

✿ Olympic runner

✿ Doctor

✿ Movie star

✿ Banker

✿ Baseball player

✿ Veterinarian

✿ Cowboy

If you're making these cupcakes for a party, consider having the fortunes match party favors or gifts:

✿ You have won a new ball.

✿ Your party gift is a paint set.

✿ Congratulations! You're the owner of a brand new action figure.

Or, just select a fun phrase for each fortune, such as:

✿ You're fun to be with.

✿ You have a nice smile.

✿ You are a hard worker.

✿ You are a good sport.

✿ You will get a special surprise.

✿ You have lots of good friends.

Remove the pans from the oven and place them on wire racks to cool for 5 minutes. Run a dinner knife around the edges of the cupcake liners, lift the cupcakes up from the bottoms of the cups using the end of the knife, and pick them out of the cups carefully with your fingertips. Place them on a wire rack to cool for 15 minutes before garnishing.

4. Place a cake stencil on top of each cupcake and sift the confectioners' sugar over the cupcake to cover the pattern. Carefully lift off the stencil to reveal the sugar design. Or, forgo the stencil and simply dust confectioners' sugar over each cupcake. The cupcakes are ready to serve.

✿ *Store these cupcakes, in a cake saver or under a glass dome, at room temperature for up to 5 days. Or freeze them, wrapped in aluminum foil or in a cake saver, for up to 6 months. Thaw the cupcakes overnight in the refrigerator before serving.*

WHITE ON WHITE CUPCAKES

• • • • •

These simple yet elegant cupcakes with fluffy buttercream frosting are beautiful for those occasions when only white will do. If you would rather make them sleek and sassy, add a white chocolate glaze (page 126) instead. Dress up the tops with little plastic dolls or valentine hearts, or dress it down with a single white chocolate curl or one red raspberry.

24 paper liners for cupcake pans
    (2½-inch size)
1 cup (6 ounces) white chocolate chips
1 package (18.25 ounces) plain white
    cake mix
1 cup whole milk
⅓ cup vegetable oil
1 large egg
3 large egg whites
1 teaspoon pure vanilla extract
Buttercream Frosting (page 318)
    (see "the Cupcake Doctor says")
White chocolate curls (see box on page 168),
    for garnish

✿ **MAKES 22 TO 24 CUPCAKES (2½ INCHES EACH)**
✿ **PREPARATION TIME: 15 MINUTES**
✿ **BAKING TIME: 17 TO 20 MINUTES**
✿ **ASSEMBLY TIME: 10 MINUTES**

1. Place a rack in the center of the oven and preheat the oven to 350°F. Line 24 cupcake cups with paper liners. Set the pans aside.

▲ ▲ ▲

HERE COMES THE BRIDE PARTY

I do dip *(ranch dressing) with veggies like carrots and celery sticks*

Party mints

Honeymoon ham and biscuits:
Slices of ham sandwiched between buttered biscuit halves

Groom's grilled cheese sandwiches:
Trim the crusts off before grilling. Cut the grilled sandwiches into quarters.

White on White Cupcakes *wrapped in bridal netting with satin ribbon: Cut circles out of cardboard. Place the cardboard on a large square of netting and a cupcake on the cardboard. Pull the corners of the netting over the frosting and tie with the ribbon.*

Sherbet punch: *Your favorite punch with scoops of sherbet in it*

Party favors: *Wedding veils that you make at the party, big fake diamond rings, disposable cameras, flower bouquets*

Activities: *Wearing white; decorating the wedding veils with ribbons and sequins; having makeup and hair done; playing bride and taking pictures; tossing bouquet*

▼ ▼ ▼

2. Place the white chocolate chips in a medium-size glass mixing bowl in the microwave oven on high power for 50 seconds to 1 minute. Remove the bowl from the oven and stir with a small rubber spatula until it is smooth. Set it aside to cool slightly.

3. Place the cake mix, milk, oil, egg, egg whites, vanilla, and melted white chocolate in a large mixing bowl. Blend with an electric mixer on low speed for 30 seconds. Stop the machine and scrape down the sides of the bowl with a rubber spatula. Increase the mixer speed to medium and beat 2 minutes more, scraping down the sides again if needed. Spoon or scoop ¼ cup batter into each lined cupcake cup, filling it two thirds of the way full. (You will get between 22 and 24 cupcakes; remove the empty liners, if any.) Place the pans in the oven.

4. Bake the cupcakes until they are lightly golden and spring back when

the Cupcake Doctor says...

One recipe of the frosting will provide a good dollop for each cupcake, but if you want to blanket them in frosting, prepare 1½ recipes.

White Chocolate Curls

▼ ▼ ▼

It's easy to make white chocolate curls if you have a 6- to 8-ounce bar of white chocolate and a sharp vegetable peeler. Place the white chocolate on a counter at room temperature for 1 hour to soften slightly, and let it sit flat side up (the side that has no impressed designs or the name of the chocolate on it). Drag the vegetable peeler across the top of the chocolate bar (I find it easier to pull toward me). The softer the chocolate and the longer you drag the peeler, the bigger the curl. If you work with cool chocolate, you will make white chocolate shavings, which look beautiful mounded up in the center of this cupcake. Curls or shavings—it's a win-win situation.

lightly pressed with your finger, 17 to 20 minutes. Remove the pans from the oven and place them on wire racks to cool for 5 minutes. Run a dinner knife around the edges of the cupcake liners, lift the cupcakes up from the bottoms of the cups using the end of the knife, and pick them out of the cups carefully with your fingertips. Place them on a wire rack to cool for 15 minutes before frosting.

5. Meanwhile, prepare the Buttercream Frosting.

6. Place a heaping tablespoon of frosting on each cupcake and swirl to spread it out with a short metal spatula or a spoon, taking care to cover the tops completely. Garnish with a white chocolate curl. The cupcakes are ready to serve.

❀ *Store these cupcakes, in a cake saver or under a glass dome, at room temperature for up to 3 days or in the refrigerator for up to 1 week. Or freeze them, wrapped in aluminum foil or in a cake saver, for up to 6 months. Thaw the cupcakes overnight in the refrigerator before serving.*

Cupcake Painting

My children love to paint. Give them a packet of inexpensive watercolors, a handful of brushes, and a stack of paper and they are set to go. So it seemed likely that they would enjoy painting cupcakes as well.

To test my theory, I baked some really basic cupcakes. I made Buttercream Frosting (page 318) using the lower-fat method with just 4 tablespoons of butter. Then I liberally spread the frosting over the cooled cupcakes. On some I smoothed the frosting for a flat canvas, and on some I swirled it so they could paint along the lines and create colorful flowers.

Then I gathered food coloring paste in pretty blue, soft green, buttery yellow, and peach, and four small glass bowls. With a small clean paintbrush I dabbed about ⅛ teaspoon of the food coloring into each bowl and added 1 tablespoon water to each. With a clean brush as a whisk, I mixed the color into the water.

When everything was ready, I let the children have at it. My ten-year-old daughter, Litton, loved this activity, and the fact that it was storming outside made the task all the more fun. She created a yellow and peach rose using the lines of the frosting as a guide. She painted a stained-glass window. She painted a rainbow. She became a cupcake artist. If you have cupcakes, white frosting (preferably homemade), food colorings, and children to entertain, a cupcake painting party is a blast. You could use the batter from the White on White Cupcakes, the Butterfly Cupcakes (page 97), A Cupcake Zoo (page 150), or the Best Birthday Cupcakes (page 138).

Celebration Cupcakes

When writing a cookbook, you often have to make recipes when they aren't necessarily in season. Let's just say that in a four-week period my family celebrated a year's worth of holidays, from Valentine's Day through Christmas. It was exhilarating and festive, but somewhat discombobulating.

Finding St. Patrick's Day cupcake liners in June is not easy. And there was something not quite right about serving snowmen in summer, either. The Easter Basket Cupcakes? Well, I know that I'm baking them again this spring. And the Halloween Spider

Cupcakes are at the top of my list for fall.

This chapter includes some of the most fun recipes in this book. They are guaranteed to make you smile while honoring the holiday and setting the party scene. The cupcakes underneath the decorations are moist and true to the Cupcake Doctor's high standards!

With this chapter, I conquered my long-standing fear of decorating. I can bake a pretty cake, but decorating it? For me, this chapter was a feat. I don't normally roam supermarket aisles in search of the right green candy for a pumpkin cake stem, but I did here. I don't rack my brain figuring out how to make an edible Pilgrim's hat, either, but I did here.

Because I want you to be able to bake and decorate these cupcakes with ease, I have taken special care to make the recipes clear, and I have offered up several suggestions and options for decorations, because I know it's tough to find every ingredient everywhere. Plus, when you use a little creativity with the ingredients you've got on hand, you're going to enjoy baking more. In order to make this a stress-free zone, I consulted with a half dozen creative friends and we bounced easy ideas off each other.

As the months and seasons pass, I know you'll have fun flipping these pages to find the right cupcakes for the right party. There are Mardi Gras Cupcakes that are gold and glitzy, Groundhog Day Cupcakes that are so cute, Kiss Me Cakes, in a sweetheart shape and with a combination of chocolate and fresh raspberry flavors, as well as the individual Strawberry Rose Cakes.

I've also included recipes for Election Cupcakes, incorporating flavors of early America, green-colored and Bailey's-flavored St. Patrick's Pistachio Cupcakes, the previously mentioned Easter Basket Cupcakes, and brightly decorated cinnamon and chocolate Cinco de Mayo Cupcakes. For the patriotic holidays, there are Stars and Stripes Cupcakes arranged on a platter to resemble the American flag, as well as the Fireworks Confetti Cupcakes, decorated inside and out.

And for fall, there are Little Pumpkin Cinnamon Cakes and Halloween Spider Cupcakes, as well as Pilgrims' Hats, which children adore. For winter parties, there are Snowman Cupcakes made by stacking marshmallows on cupcakes, and Holiday Gift Cupcakes, which resemble wrapped presents, for large family gatherings.

Every cupcake in this chapter is a personal favorite—fun, festive, and relatively easy. They look stunning on a platter and they taste great, too!

MARDI GRAS CUPCAKES

• • • • •

What better day than Fat Tuesday, or Mardi Gras, the day before the Christian season of Lent begins, to forget about calories? Whereas King Cake might be the traditional sweet on Mardi Gras, these fun cupcakes are an easy version. They resemble the famed cake with its white glaze and purple, gold, and green sugars on top. But instead of a time-consuming yeast bread dough, you make a quick cream cheese–pound cake batter. In keeping with Mardi Gras tradition, you might want to tuck something inside a few cupcakes—a pecan half, for example. If you find the pecan in your cupcake, good luck will come your way.

24 paper cupcake liners (2½-inch size)

CUPCAKES:
1 package (18.25 ounces) plain yellow
    cake mix
1 package (8 ounces) cream cheese,
        at room temperature
½ cup water
½ cup vegetable oil
¼ cup granulated sugar
4 large eggs
½ teaspoon pure vanilla extract
½ teaspoon pure almond extract
2 to 3 pecan halves (optional)

✿ **MAKES 22 TO 24 CUPCAKES (2½ INCHES EACH)**
✿ **PREPARATION TIME: 15 TO 20 MINUTES**
✿ **BAKING TIME: 16 TO 20 MINUTES**
✿ **COOLING TIME: 30 MINUTES**
✿ **ASSEMBLY TIME: 10 MINUTES**

GLAZE:

2 cups confectioners' sugar, sifted

2 to 2½ tablespoons milk

GARNISH:

Purple, green, and yellow or
gold sprinkles

Chocolate gold coins (optional)

Gold dragées (optional)

I. Place a rack in the center of the oven and preheat the oven to 350°F. Line 24 cupcake cups with paper liners. Set the pans aside.

2. Prepare the cupcake batter: Place the cake mix, cream cheese, water, oil, sugar, eggs, and vanilla and almond extracts in a large mixing bowl. Blend with an electric mixer on low speed for 30 seconds. Stop the machine and scrape down the sides of the bowl with a rubber spatula. Increase the mixer speed to medium and beat 2 minutes more, scraping down the sides again if needed. Spoon or scoop ⅓ cup batter into each lined cupcake cup, filling it three quarters of the way full. (You will get

The Lowdown on Dragées

▼ ▼ ▼

I adore decorative little gold and silver dragées, and place them on butterfly and Mardi Gras cupcakes. Yet controversy surrounds them. Dragées are not for sale or distribution in California, and the Food and Drug Administration says they are "nonedible" and the jars must read "for decoration only" because they contain a trace amount of metal (silver). Dragées are sold in Europe for consumption and used widely for cake and cookie decoration. They add a real visual impact and come in gold, silver, copper, pearl, pink, blue, and more colors, but you or the person eating the cupcake should remove them before eating. (Make sure you remove any dragées before serving cupcakes to children.) If you do not live in California and are able to purchase dragées for decoration, two good on-line sources are www.beryls.com (Beryl's of Springfield, Virginia) and www.sugarcraft.com (Sugarcraft of Hamilton, Ohio).

the Cupcake Doctor says...

It need not be Mardi Gras to enjoy these cupcakes. They are perfect for any occasion for which you might want to decorate with two or three colors. They might be your school colors, or the colors of the season, or just the favorite colors of the birthday boy or girl. But the gold coins and dragées turn these cupcakes into an instant party.

between 22 and 24 cupcakes; remove the empty liners, if any.) If desired, push pecans deeply into the center of 2 or 3 cupcakes so they cannot be seen. Place the pans in the oven.

3. Bake the cupcakes until they are golden and spring back when lightly pressed with your finger, 16 to 20 minutes. Remove the pans from the oven and place them on wire racks to cool for 5 minutes. Run a dinner knife around the edges of the cupcake liners, lift the cupcakes up from the bottoms of the cups using the end of the knife, and pick them out of the cups carefully with your fingertips. Place them on a wire rack to cool completely for 30 minutes before glazing.

4. Meanwhile, prepare the glaze: Place the confectioners' sugar and milk in a small mixing bowl and whisk to combine until smooth.

5. With a soup spoon, drizzle the glaze over the cooled cupcakes. Immediately garnish with sugar sprinkles, shaking on the colors in three separate strips. Add chocolate coins and gold dragées, if desired. The cupcakes are ready to serve. (Remove the dragées before serving the cupcakes.)

✿ *Store these cupcakes, in a cake saver or under a glass dome, at room temperature for up to 3 days or in the refrigerator for up to 1 week. Or freeze them, wrapped in aluminum foil or in a cake saver, for up to 6 months. Thaw the cupcakes overnight in the refrigerator before serving.*

Sweet Words:
A Decorating Sugar Glossary

You may be familiar with granulated and confectioners' sugars, but did you know there is a world of decorating sugars for festive cupcakes?

✿ Coarse sugar: Also called decorating sugar. A coarser texture than granulated sugar, it is used to top cookies and cakes after they have been frosted. It comes in an array of colors.

✿ Dragées: These sugar-coated pellets come in pastels, silver, white, pearl, gold, and more. They create a festive look on holiday cakes, butterfly cupcakes, and all sorts of other recipes. (Dragées are inedible and should be removed before enjoying a cake.)

✿ Edible glitter: Made of gum arabic and water, these flakes come in all sorts of colors and add texture and color to decorating. Wilton's version is called Cake Sparkles.

✿ Jimmies: Another word for long sugar sprinkles (see below) in a variety of colors.

✿ Nonpareils: These tiny, colored sugar pellets are pretty to look at, but be sure to shake on nonpareils when the frosting is still wet or they will roll off the cake and onto the floor. ("Nonpareil" means "without equal" in French.)

✿ Sanding sugar: This sugar, also used to top cookies and cakes, is finer in texture than coarse or decorating sugar. It, too, is available in colors.

✿ Sprinkles: The classic—tiny candies that come in all colors and are used to shake or "sprinkle" over cakes and ice cream.

✿ Sprinkles in shapes: These slightly larger sprinkles come in the shape of stars, bears, shamrocks, flowers, dinosaurs, and hearts, or assortments for various seasons and holidays.

GROUNDHOG DAY CUPCAKES

• • • • •

This cupcake is almost too cute to eat. Buried in loads of creamy chocolate frosting that's covered in chocolate sprinkles, and complete with a little frosting head with eyes and a nose, these ground-hog cupcakes would make any win-ter party a lot of fun. Serve them on Groundhog Day in February or see "the Cupcake Doctor says" for instructions on how to turn this cupcake into another animal for a different occasion.

✿ MAKES 22 TO 24 CUPCAKES (2½ INCHES EACH)
✿ PREPARATION TIME: 15 MINUTES
✿ BAKING TIME: 18 TO 20 MINUTES
✿ ASSEMBLY TIME: 45 MINUTES

24 paper liners for cupcake pans
  (2 ½-inch size)

CUPCAKES:
1 package (18.25 ounces) plain German
  chocolate cake mix
1¼ cups buttermilk
⅓ cup vegetable oil
4 large eggs
1 teaspoon pure vanilla extract

PALE CHOCOLATE FROSTING:
8 tablespoons (1 stick) butter, at room
  temperature
4 cups confectioners' sugar, sifted
1 tablespoon unsweetened cocoa powder
3 to 4 tablespoons milk
1 teaspoon pure vanilla extract
4 containers (1.75 ounces each, 1 cup total)
  chocolate sprinkles

HEAD FROSTING AND FACE:

3 tablespoons butter, at room temperature

2 ½ cups confectioners' sugar, sifted

1 teaspoon unsweetened cocoa powder

3 to 4 teaspoons milk

48 miniature chocolate chips

24 brown M&M's

Sliced almonds

1. Place a rack in the center of the oven and preheat the oven to 350°F. Line 24 cupcake cups with paper liners. Set the pans aside.

2. Prepare the cupcake batter: Place the cake mix, buttermilk, oil, eggs, and vanilla in a large mixing bowl. Blend with an electric mixer on low speed for 30 seconds. Stop the machine and scrape down the sides of the bowl with a rubber spatula. Increase the mixer speed to medium and beat 2 minutes more, scraping down the sides again if needed. Spoon or scoop ⅓ cup batter into each lined cupcake cup, filling it three quarters of the way full. (You will get between 22 and 24 cupcakes; remove the empty liners, if any.) Place the pans in the oven.

3. Bake the cupcakes until they spring back when lightly pressed with your finger, 18 to 20 minutes. Remove the pans from the oven and place them on wire racks to cool for 5 minutes. Run a dinner knife around the edges of the cupcake liners, lift the cupcakes up from the bottoms of the cups using the end of the knife, and pick them out of the cups carefully with your fingertips. Place them on a wire rack to cool for 15 minutes before frosting.

4. Meanwhile, prepare both frostings, starting with the pale chocolate: Place the butter in a large mixing bowl. Blend with an electric mixer on low speed until fluffy, 30 seconds. Stop the machine and add the confectioners' sugar, cocoa powder, 3 tablespoons milk, and vanilla. Blend with the mixer on low speed until the sugar is incorporated, 1 minute. Increase the speed to medium and beat until light and fluffy, 1 minute more. Blend in up to 1 tablespoon milk if the frosting seems too stiff.

5. Place the chocolate sprinkles in a small bowl and set aside.

6. Prepare the frosting used to make the head: Place the butter in a large mixing bowl. Blend with an electric mixer on low speed until fluffy, 30 seconds. Stop the machine and add the confectioners' sugar,

the CupcakeDoctor says...

You can easily turn this groundhog into a dog. Use a #21 (star) tip with some of the frosting used for the head to pipe small ears on the sides of the face. With a wave motion, pipe on a tail at the edge opposite the head so that it appears curled. To make a turkey, omit the chocolate sprinkles and make rows of sliced almonds standing on end in the pale chocolate frosting. Pull the face frosting down in the front with a toothpick to create a sagging neck. And to make pigs, frost with a pink buttercream frosting, cover in pink sprinkles, then pipe on a head frosting tinted pink with food coloring to make the face, ears, and tail.

cocoa powder, and 3 teaspoons milk. Blend with the mixer on low speed until the sugar is incorporated, 1 minute. Increase the speed to medium and beat until light and as stiff as peanut butter, 1 minute more. If the frosting is too stiff, add another teaspoon of milk. Set aside.

7. Place a heaping tablespoon of the pale chocolate frosting on each cupcake and spread it out smoothly with a short metal spatula or a spoon, taking care to cover the tops completely. Immediately dip the cupcake tops in the sprinkles to coat.

8. Fill a pastry bag fitted with a #12 tip (5⁄16 inch wide) with two thirds of the frosting for the head. To create the head, point the pastry bag tip toward one edge of the cupcake top and squeeze the frosting from the bag in a small spiral about 1 inch wide and ½ inch deep. For the ears, pipe 1 small dot of frosting on both sides of the top of the spiral. For the face, place an M&M in the center of the spiral for the nose and 2 mini chocolate chips slightly above it for the eyes. Tuck 2 trimmed almond slices below the nose for the groundhog's teeth. Repeat with the remaining cupcakes, adding more frosting to the pastry bag as needed. Place these cupcakes, uncovered or in a cake saver, in the refrigerator until the frosting sets, 20 minutes. The cupcakes are ready to serve.

✿ *Store the cupcakes, in a cake saver or under a glass dome, at room temperature for up to 3 days or in the refrigerator for up to 1 week.*

KISS ME CAKES

• • • • •

It doesn't need to be Valentine's Day to make these sumptuous chocolate brownie hearts, filled with gooey chocolate ganache and topped with fresh raspberries. They're a perfect ending to an anniversary or birthday meal, or for a quiet dinner party with friends. For these cakes, you will need two pans with heart-shaped cups that are about 3 inches wide and 1¼ inches deep. If you don't have them, any round 2½-inch to 3-inch tart pan will do. The crusts can be baked a day or two ahead and kept refrigerated.

✿ **MAKES 20 HEARTS**
✿ **PREPARATION TIME: 10 MINUTES**
✿ **BAKING TIME: 12 TO 15 MINUTES**
✿ **ASSEMBLY TIME: 20 MINUTES**

GANACHE FILLING:

¾ cup heavy (whipping) cream

8 ounces semisweet chocolate chips or
*   chunks (1⅓ cups)*

1 tablespoon Chambord
*   (black raspberry liqueur, optional)*

CRUSTS:

Solid vegetable shortening or
*   butter for greasing the pans*

All-purpose flour for dusting the pans

1 package (20 ounces) brownie mix

5 tablespoons unsalted butter, melted

⅓ cup water

1 large egg

1 teaspoon pure vanilla extract

GARNISH:

2 pints fresh raspberries

1 tablespoon confectioners' sugar

1 tablespoon chocolate decorating icing
*   (optional)*

the Cupcake Doctor says...

The chilling takes time in this recipe, which is why it is best prepared a day ahead. The chilling period makes lifting the tart crusts out of the pans so much easier. If you leave the crusts in the refrigerator overnight to chill, cover them with plastic wrap. If the brownie starts to stick when you press it into the pan to create the crust, wet the spoon or knife under cool running water.

1. Prepare the ganache filling: Place the cream in a small saucepan and bring to a boil over medium heat. Place the chocolate in a large stainless steel or glass bowl. When the cream just begins to come to a boil, remove it from the heat and pour it over the chocolate. Stir the cream and chocolate with a wooden spoon until the chocolate melts and the mixture is smooth and thickened. Stir in the Chambord, if desired, and set the ganache aside.

2. Prepare the crusts: Place a rack in the center of the oven and preheat the oven to 350°F. Brush the tart pans with the shortening or soft butter and dust with flour. Shake out the excess flour. Set the pans aside.

3. Place the brownie mix, melted butter, water, egg, and vanilla in a large mixing bowl. Blend with a wooden spoon until the ingredients are well blended and the mixture is smooth, 100 strokes. Spoon a heaping tablespoon batter into each heart cup, filling it nearly full. You should fill 20 cups. Place the pans in the oven.

4. Bake the crusts until they are firm around the edges but still soft in the center, 12 to 15 minutes. Remove the pans from the oven and place them on wire racks. Immediately

10 More Cupcakes for Anniversaries and Birthdays

▼ ▼ ▼

1. Key Lime Cream Cakes (page 282)

2. Holiday Gift Cupcakes (page 216)

3. White on White Cupcakes (page 166)

4. Butterfly Cupcakes with Pastel Frostings (page 97)

5. German Chocolate Cupcakes with Chocolate Shavings (page 27)

6. Coconut Snowballs (page 66)

7. Strawberry Rose Cakes (page 182)

8. The Best Birthday Cupcakes with Two Frostings (page 138)

9. Mardi Gras Cupcakes (page 172)

10. Bobbye's Italian Cream Cupcakes (page 68)

---

press down on each brownie heart with the back of a small spoon or a small knife so that the brownie forms a compact crust in the pan. Let them cool in the pan on the rack for 15 minutes, then place the pans in the refrigerator for 30 minutes to chill completely and make unmolding easier. Run a knife around the edges of each heart, lift it up, and place it on a serving platter.

5. Place a heaping tablespoon ganache onto each crust, spread it out smoothly with a short metal spatula or a spoon, taking care to cover the top completely.

6. Just before serving, place from 4 to 6 raspberries in the center of heart on top of the ganache filling. Dust the tops with confectioners' sugar and serve. If you wish, use the decorating icing to pipe a Cupid's arrow on each serving plate.

✿ *Store the hearts, lightly covered with plastic wrap, on a platter in the refrigerator for up to 4 days.*

STRAWBERRY ROSE CAKES

If you have a pan with twelve sweetheart rose–patterned cups and you're looking for a fast and easy recipe for Valentine's Day, here is a beauty (so to speak). The recipe is the simple strawberry cake I recommend for girls' birthdays in *Cake Mix Doctor*, but the batter is baked in these pretty molds shaped like roses. Because the recipe makes 24 roses, you will have to bake a batch, let it cool, then clean the pan before baking a second batch. You can also use a "bouquet cakelet" pan, yielding 12 slightly larger flowers; they require 28 to 32 minutes cooking time.

✿ **MAKES 24 ROSE CUPCAKES (2 INCHES EACH)**
✿ **PREPARATION TIME: 10 MINUTES**
✿ **BAKING TIME: 24 TO 27 MINUTES PER BATCH**
✿ **ASSEMBLY TIME: 5 MINUTES**

*Solid vegetable shortening for greasing
    the pans*
Flour for dusting the pans
*1 package (18.25 ounces) plain white
    cake mix*
1 package (3 ounces) strawberry gelatin
*1 cup mashed fresh strawberries with juice
    (1½ cups whole berries)*
¾ cup milk
¾ cup vegetable oil
4 large eggs
Confectioners' sugar, for dusting

5 More Cupcakes for Your Love on Valentine's

▼ ▼ ▼

1. Pretty in Pink Strawberry Cupcakes (page 106)

2. Little Fudge Brownie Bites (page 134)

3. Brooklyn Blackout Cupcakes (page 24)

4. Warm Chocolate Cupcakes with Molten Centers and Cinnamon Crème Anglaise (page 29)

5. Red Velvet Cupcakes with White Chocolate Peppermint Cream Cheese Frosting (page 36)

1. Place a rack in the center of the oven and preheat the oven to 350°F. Brush the vegetable shortening inside the rose cups, making sure to cover all the surfaces. Dust with flour and shake out the excess. Set the pan aside.

2. Place the cake mix, gelatin, mashed strawberries and juice, milk, oil, and eggs in a large mixing bowl. Blend with an electric mixer on low speed for 30 seconds. Stop the machine and scrape down the sides of the bowl with a rubber spatula. Increase the mixer speed to medium and beat 2 minutes more, scraping down the sides again if needed. Spoon or scoop ⅓ cup batter into each prepared cup, filling it three quarters of the way full. Place the pan in the oven.

3. Bake the cupcakes until they are lightly golden and spring back when lightly pressed with your finger, 24 to 27 minutes. Remove the pan from the oven and place it on a wire rack to cool for 15 minutes. Leave the oven on. The cupcakes will shrink and settle into the cups as they cool. Run a dinner knife around the edges of the cupcake roses to loosen them, then invert the pan onto a rack and lift off the pan. Let the cupcake roses continue to cool rose-side-up for 30 minutes. Repeat with the remaining batter.

4. Dust the roses with the confectioners' sugar. The cupcakes are ready to serve.

❧ *Store these cupcakes, in a cake saver or under a glass dome, at room temperature for up to 3 days or in the refrigerator for up to 1 week. Or freeze them, wrapped in aluminum foil or in a cake saver, for up to 6 months. Thaw the cupcakes overnight in the refrigerator before serving.*

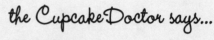

the Cupcake Doctor says...

This recipe creates a pink sweetheart rose cupcake, but you could just as easily make a red rose with the red velvet Holiday Gift Cupcakes recipe (page 216) or a yellow rose with the Best Birthday Cupcakes yellow cake recipe (page 138). For a pretty presentation, place these roses on a silver platter with rose petals and fresh strawberries. No rose pan? Use a regular cupcake pan, lined with paper liners. Bake the cupcakes about 18 to 20 minutes and frost with Cream Cheese Frosting (page 336).

ELECTION CUPCAKES

• • • • •

The history of the sweet yeast cake known as Election Cake or Hartford Election Cake is fascinating. A rich cake seasoned with sherry and nutmeg and crammed with dried fruit and nuts, it was served at election feasts in the early years of this country. These fun cupcakes might be served in February for Presidents' Day or in November as Election Day Cupcakes. Of course, they rely on a modern cake mix, but they contain the traditional nutmeg, sherry, and currants.

✿ **MAKES 22 TO 24 CUPCAKES (2½ INCHES EACH)**
✿ **PREPARATION TIME: 15 MINUTES**
✿ **BAKING TIME: 15 TO 18 MINUTES**
✿ **ASSEMBLY TIME: 15 MINUTES**

CUPCAKES:

1 cup dried currants (half of a 10-ounce box)

⅔ cup cream sherry

*24 paper liners for cupcake pans
  (2½-inch size)*

*1 package (18.25 ounces) white cake mix
  with pudding*

⅓ cup all-purpose flour

1 cup sour cream

⅓ cup vegetable oil

3 large eggs

1 teaspoon pure vanilla extract

¾ teaspoon ground nutmeg

ORANGE BUTTERCREAM FROSTING:

*8 tablespoons (1 stick) unsalted butter,
  at room temperature*

3 ½ cups confectioners' sugar, sifted

1 teaspoon grated orange zest

2 to 3 tablespoons fresh orange juice

GARNISH:

Ground nutmeg

*Candied Orange Zest (recipe follows;
  optional)*

1. Prepare the cupcake batter: Place the currants and sherry in a small microwave-safe bowl and microwave on high power to warm the sherry, 20 seconds. Stir, and let the currants soak for 5 minutes.

2. Place a rack in the center of the oven and preheat the oven to 350°F. Line 24 cupcake cups with paper liners. Set the pans aside.

3. Strain the sherry from the currants into a large mixing bowl and add the cake mix, flour, sour cream, oil, eggs, vanilla, and nutmeg. Blend with an electric mixer on low speed for 30 seconds. Stop the machine and scrape down the sides of the bowl with a rubber spatula. Increase the mixer speed to medium and beat 2 minutes more, scraping down the sides again if needed. Blend in the currants on low speed, 10 to 15 seconds. Spoon or scoop a heaping ¼ cup batter into each lined cupcake cup, filling it two thirds of the way full. (You will get between 22 and 24 cupcakes; remove the empty liners, if any.) Place the pans in the oven.

4. Bake the cupcakes until they are lightly golden and spring back when lightly pressed with your finger, 15 to 18 minutes. Remove the pans from the oven and place them on wire racks to cool for 5 minutes. Run a dinner knife around the

the Cupcake Doctor says...

Plumping dried fruit such as currants in liquid in the microwave is a fast alternative to letting the fruit sit in the liquid for half an hour before baking. If you are a traditionalist, however, go ahead and let it sit! I know the orange zest garnish is "over the top," but it is truly delicious and crowns these lovely cupcakes. To save time, you can prepare the candied zest the day ahead of baking. It stores well in a covered plastic container.

edges of the cupcake liners, lift the cupcakes up from the bottoms of the cups using the end of the knife, and pick them out of the cups carefully with your fingertips. Place them on a wire rack to cool for 15 minutes before frosting.

5. Meanwhile, prepare the Orange Buttercream Frosting: Place the butter in a large mixing bowl. Blend with an electric mixer on low speed until fluffy, 30 seconds. Stop the machine and add the confectioners' sugar, orange zest, and 2 tablespoons of the orange juice. Blend with the mixer on low speed until the sugar is incorporated, 1 minute. Increase the speed to medium and beat until light and fluffy, 1 minute more. If the frosting seems too thick, add up to 1 tablespoon more orange juice, 1 teaspoon at a time, until it is a spreadable consistency.

6. Place a heaping tablespoon of frosting on each cupcake, and swirl to spread it out with a short metal spatula or a spoon, taking care to cover the tops completely. Garnish with the Candied Orange Zest, if desired, or ground nutmeg. The cupcakes are ready to serve.

✿ *Store these cupcakes, in a cake saver or under a glass dome, at room temperature for up to 3 days or in the refrigerator for up to 1 week. Or freeze them, wrapped in aluminum foil or in a cake saver, for up to 6 months. Thaw the cupcakes overnight in the refrigerator before serving.*

CANDIED ORANGE ZEST

• • • •

Thin strips of candied zest are just the right garnish for Election Cupcakes or any elegant cake where orange is an ingredient. Make it the day before you bake.

2 medium-size oranges

2 cups granulated sugar

1¼ cups water

Granulated sugar, to coat

1. Scrub and dry two oranges and then cut off the zest in thin long strands, using a vegetable peeler. Make sure the strands have no bitter white pith attached.

2. Place the sugar and water in a medium-size saucepan over medium heat. Stir until the sugar dissolves and the syrup comes to a simmer. Drop the zest into the pan and stir so that each strand is completely submerged in the syrup. Allow this to barely simmer until the zest is translucent, 1 to 1½ hours. With metal tongs, transfer the zest to a wire rack. While the zest is still pliable, curl it or twist it to your liking. Sprinkle with granulated sugar to coat and let it dry for several hours or overnight.

✿ *Store the zest in a tightly covered plastic container at room temperature for up to 1 week.*

ST. PATRICK'S PISTACHIO CUPCAKES

• • • • •

This cupcake had been on my mind, so when it was time to work on the celebration chapter, I knew what I would bake for St. Patrick's Day. It is a pretty shade of green, tinted both by pistachio pudding mix and a drop of food coloring. The frosting is pure Irish indulgence—whipped cream and Bailey's Irish Cream liqueur. And you can choose from an assortment of toppings—crushed chocolate mint sandwich cookies, green sugar sprinkles in the shape of a shamrock, or simply a sprig of fresh mint. Enjoy!

24 paper liners for cupcake pans
　　(2½-inch size), preferably green
　　or white with shamrocks

CUPCAKES:
1 package (18.25 ounces) plain white
　　cake mix
1 package (3.4 ounces) pistachio instant
　　pudding mix
1 cup ginger ale
1 cup vegetable oil
¼ cup Bailey's Irish Cream
　　liqueur (optional)
3 large eggs
2 to 3 drops green
　　food coloring

✿ **MAKES 22 TO 24 CUPCAKES (2½ INCHES EACH)**
✿ **PREPARATION TIME: 10 MINUTES**
✿ **BAKING TIME: 18 TO 22 MINUTES**
✿ **ASSEMBLY TIME: 15 MINUTES, LONGER IF MORE ELABORATE GARNISH**

BAILEY'S WHIPPED CREAM FROSTING:

2 cups heavy (whipping) cream

2 tablespoons confectioners' sugar

3 tablespoons Bailey's Irish Cream liqueur

Crushed chocolate mint sandwich

> *cookies, green shamrock candy*

> *(see "the Cupcake Doctor says"),*

> *or mint sprigs, for garnish*

1. Place a rack in the center of the oven and preheat the oven to 350°F. Line 24 cupcake cups with paper liners. Set the pans aside.

2. Prepare the cupcake batter: Place the cake mix, pudding mix, ginger ale, vegetable oil, Bailey's liqueur, if desired, eggs, and 2 drops of the green food coloring in a large mixing bowl. Blend with an electric mixer on low speed for 30 seconds. Stop the machine and scrape down the sides of the bowl with a rubber spatula. Add another drop of food coloring if the batter seems too light. Increase the mixer speed to medium and beat 2 minutes more, scraping down the sides again if needed. Spoon or scoop ⅓ cup batter into each lined cupcake cup, filling it three quarters of the way full. (You will get between 22 and 24 cupcakes; remove the empty liners, if any.) Place the pans in the oven.

3. Bake the cupcakes until they are lightly golden and spring back when

the Cupcake Doctor says...

Look for shamrock cupcake liners in cake decorating stores and craft stores, such as Michael's. Top your cupcakes with some fun garnishes: crushed mint chocolate sandwich cookies (you'll need 12), York Swoops (they come 18 to a box), halved Andes Mints candy, a mini Milano Mint cookie (a 5-ounce bag contains 24), or Wilton green Color Mist Food Color Spray (1.5-ounce can) sprayed onto the frosting over a shamrock stencil. Order it from Wilton (www.Wilton.com) or buy it at a Michael's store.

lightly pressed with your finger, 18 to 22 minutes. Remove the pans from the oven and place them on wire racks to cool for 5 minutes. Run a dinner knife around the edges of the cupcake liners, lift the cupcakes up from the bottoms of the cups using the end of the knife, and pick them out of the cups carefully with your fingertips. Place them on a wire rack to cool for 15 minutes before frosting.

4. Meanwhile, prepare the Bailey's Whipped Cream Frosting: Chill a large, clean mixing bowl and electric mixer beaters in the freezer for a few minutes while assembling the ingredients. Pour the cream into the chilled bowl and beat with the electric mixer on high speed until it thickens, 1½ minutes. Stop the machine and add the confectioners' sugar. Beat the cream on high speed until stiff peaks form, 1 to 2 minutes, then fold in the Bailey's Irish Cream.

5. Place a heaping tablespoon of frosting on each cupcake and swirl to spread it out with a short metal spatula or a spoon, taking care to cover the tops completely. Garnish as desired. The cupcakes are ready to serve.

✿ *Store these cupcakes in a cake saver in the refrigerator for up to 3 days.*

A Shamrock Topper

Here's how to create a fun shamrock candy garnish for your cupcakes. Look for bags of confectionary coating wafers, sometimes called Candy Melts (made by Wilton), at craft stores and shops that sell cake-decorating and candy-making supplies. They come in all shades of chocolate, and also green. Place the contents of the entire 14-ounce bag of green wafers in a medium-size glass bowl in the microwave oven on high power for 20-second intervals, removing and stirring, then returning to the microwave, until they have melted and are smooth.

Using the outline of a small shamrock cookie cutter, draw as many shamrock shapes as will fit on a piece of cardboard. Place a sheet of parchment paper or waxed paper over the cardboard. With a small clean paintbrush or pastry bag fitted with a small tip, brush or pipe the melted green wafers onto the paper, filling in the outline of the shamrock below. Once one shamrock is made, move to the next one. Once the parchment is filled, slide the cardboard out from under it, place a fresh sheet of parchment over the cardboard, and repeat the process until you have created 24 shamrocks. Let these harden on the kitchen counter for an hour, or, if you are in a hurry, place the parchment on baking sheets in the refrigerator for 15 to 20 minutes. Run a small spatula underneath the shamrocks to loosen them, and place them on the cupcakes as a garnish.

EASTER BASKET CUPCAKES

• • • • •

Who needs the Easter basket full of chocolate eggs when you've got this winning Easter basket cupcake, topped with tinted coconut to resemble grass and garnished with jelly bean eggs? The waffle bowls can be found in the supermarket with all the ice cream toppings. For a special presentation, decorate with cute yellow marshmallow Peeps and arrange on a platter with wheat grass surrounding the little baskets. It's best to eat these cupcakes with a fork.

CUPCAKES:

1 box (7 ounces) waffle bowls (10 to a box)

1 package (18.25 ounces) plain white cake mix

1 package (3.4 ounces) vanilla instant pudding mix

½ cup milk

½ cup vegetable oil

2 large whole eggs

2 large egg whites

1 tablespoon coconut flavoring

Buttercream Frosting (page 318)

BASKETS:

¾ cup sweetened flaked coconut

2 to 3 drops green food coloring

Assorted jelly beans

10 strawberry-flavored Twizzlers (9½ inches long)

❁ MAKES 10 BASKETS (4 INCHES EACH)

❁ PREPARATION TIME: 10 MINUTES

❁ BAKING TIME: 24 TO 27 MINUTES

❁ COOLING TIME: 30 MINUTES

❁ ASSEMBLY TIME: 25 MINUTES

the Cupcake Doctor says...

This same cupcake batter may be baked in regular-size lined cupcake pans for 16 to 20 minutes, then topped with frosting, coconut grass, and jelly beans. Cut a smaller length of Twizzler and stick it on both sides of the cupcake for the handle.

1. Place a rack in the center of the oven and preheat the oven to 350°F. Wrap the outside of each waffle bowl in an 8-inch aluminum foil square, carefully tucking the edges of the foil just inside the top of the bowl. Place the bowls on a baking sheet and set aside.

2. Place the cake mix, pudding mix, milk, oil, eggs, egg whites, and coconut flavoring in a large mixing bowl. Blend with an electric

mixer on low speed for 30 seconds. Stop the machine and scrape down the sides of the bowl with a rubber spatula. Increase the mixer speed to medium and beat 2 minutes more, scraping down the sides again if needed. Fill each bowl with a heaping ½ cup of batter. Place the baking sheet in the oven.

3. Bake the cupcakes until they are lightly golden and spring back when lightly pressed with your finger, 24 to 27 minutes. Remove the pan from the oven and place it on a wire rack to cool for 5 minutes. Gently peel off the aluminum foil and allow the bowls to cool to room temperature, 30 minutes.

4. Meanwhile, prepare the Buttercream Frosting.

5. Place the coconut in a plastic bag with 2 drops of the green food coloring. Shake well until the coconut turns green. If the color isn't strong enough, add another drop of color, and shake again.

6. To assemble, place 2 heaping tablespoons of frosting on each cupcake and spread it out smoothly with a short metal spatula or a spoon, taking care to cover the tops completely. Immediately sprinkle on coconut to resemble grass and place a pile of jelly beans on the coconut to resemble eggs. To create the basket handle, insert one end of a Twizzler in one side of the cupcake near the edge, then bend it over the cupcake and insert the other end on the opposite side. The cupcakes are ready to serve.

✿ *Store these cupcakes for up to 1 day at room temperature. After a day, the cake will begin to pull away from the sides of the bowl.*

Holiday Cupcake Supplies

Let's face it. Holiday and special-day cupcakes are just plain fun. They're as enjoyable to look at as they are to eat. You might want to keep these supplies on hand to make sure you have all the right stuff to make the decorating festive.

Pans: Plain cupcake pans will do. But so will pans with heart- and star-shaped cups, as well as cups in the shape of flowers. Shop for these pans once the particular holiday has passed to find the best prices.

Cupcake liners: Sure, you can use pastel paper liners from the supermarket in a pinch, but why not splurge here with fancy foil liners during the winter holidays and festive patterned ones of the season? See page 19 for mail-order sources, or check out your local cake-decorating shop or craft stores.

Sprinkles and baubles: Check out those same mail-order sources for extra-fancy dragées and big, bold sprinkles to top cupcakes. Look for the Wilton seasonal sprinkles packaged in a large canister for easy shaking. Check out the coarse colored decorating sugars and icings in a tube from Williams-Sonoma.

Extras: When you're shopping, go ahead and buy fun decorating touches like edible spray mists or colored Candy Melts, which you can pipe into a shape for garnishing the top of a cupcake (both from Wilton). Stash these in a baking drawer in your kitchen for when you need that something extra—that mist of peppermint green on a St. Patrick's cupcake, for example.

CINCO DE MAYO CUPCAKES

• • • • •

The fifth of May, or Cinco de Mayo, is the day Mexicans commemorate their victory over the French in 1862. It is not the official Mexican independence day, but it is an important holiday and is celebrated with parades, food, and music in Mexico and in areas of the United States where there are large populations of people of Mexican heritage. The top of these colorful cinnamon and chocolate cupcakes is frosted to resemble the Mexican flag with three vertical stripes— green, white, and red. A chocolate round in the center of the white stripe on the cupcake represents the seal on the Mexican flag.

24 paper liners for cupcake pans
(2½-inch size)

CUPCAKES:
1 package (18.25 ounces) plain German
chocolate cake mix
1 cup buttermilk
½ cup vegetable oil
3 large eggs
1 teaspoon pure vanilla
extract
1 teaspoon cinnamon

✿ **MAKES 22 TO 24 CUPCAKES (2½ INCHES EACH)**
✿ **PREPARATION TIME: 10 MINUTES**
✿ **BAKING TIME: 16 TO 20 MINUTES**
✿ **ASSEMBLY TIME: 30 MINUTES**

FROSTING:

Buttercream Frosting (page 318)

2 to 3 drops red food coloring

2 to 3 drops green food coloring

24 chocolate Candy Melts (confectionery
    decorating wafers, about 1 inch in
    diameter), for garnish

1. Place a rack in the center of the oven and preheat the oven to 350°F. Line 24 cupcake cups with paper liners. Set the pans aside.

2. Prepare the cupcake batter: Place the cake mix, buttermilk, oil, eggs, vanilla extract, and cinnamon in a large mixing bowl. Blend with an electric mixer on low speed for 30 seconds. Stop the machine and scrape down the sides of the bowl with a rubber spatula. Increase the mixer speed to medium and beat 2 minutes more, scraping the sides down again if needed. Spoon or scoop ⅓ cup batter into each lined cupcake cup, filling it three quarters of the way full. (You will get between 22 and 24 cupcakes; remove the empty liners, if any.) Place the pans in the oven.

3. Bake the cupcakes until they spring back when lightly pressed with your finger, 16 to 20 minutes. Remove the pans from the oven and place them on wire racks to cool for 5 minutes. Run a dinner

the Cupcake Doctor says...

The best chocolate confectionery coating wafers for these cupcakes are Wilton Light Cocoa Candy Melts (they come in a 14-ounce bag). But Hershey's Kisses will work, too. To frost even stripes on the cupcake tops, divide the tops into three even vertical stripes with a ruler and the tip of a sharp knife. Frost the center stripes white, then frost the left of the center green, and the right of the center red.

knife around the edges of the cupcake liners, lift the cupcakes up from the bottoms of the cups using the end of the knife, and pick them out of the cups carefully with your fingertips. Place them on a wire rack to cool for 15 minutes before frosting.

4. Meanwhile, prepare the Buttercream Frosting and divide it evenly among 3 bowls. Color the frosting in one bowl with red food coloring, another with green food coloring. Start with 2 drops of color and add a third, if desired. Leave the frosting in the last bowl white.

5. Spread 3 vertical stripes of frosting on each cupcake: first green, then white in the center, then red. Use a short metal spatula or a spoon to spread it out smoothly. Place a chocolate melt in the center of the white stripe. The cupcakes are ready to serve.

✿ *Store these cupcakes, in a cake saver or under a glass dome, at room tempera-* *ture for up to 3 days or in the refrigerator for up to 1 week. Or freeze them, wrapped in aluminum foil or in a cake saver, for up to 6 months. Thaw the cupcakes overnight in the refrigerator before serving.*

Using Paper Baking Molds

Should you want to splurge, those brown and gold paper baking molds you see wrapped around muffins and cupcakes at high-quality bakeries are available for baking at home. They cost about 20 to 25 cents apiece, but for special arrangements, especially a tiered stand of cupcakes for a birthday, anniversary, or christening, they just might be worth it.

I tested baking molds that I ordered from Beryl's Cake Decorating & Pastry Supplies in Springfield, Virginia (800-488-2749, or on the Web at www.beryls.com). They are also known as panettone molds and come in two sizes—2¼-inch and 2¾-inch. I found that the smaller size is preferable for cupcakes. (It was eye-opening to find that I had to fill the larger molds with twice as much batter as I normally would use for a muffin or cupcake. In other words, if you eat one of these larger cupcakes or muffins, you are eating two servings!)

The molds are freestanding and do not fit inside a cupcake pan, so to bake, arrange them on a baking sheet and fill them no more than halfway with batter. Cupcakes in the smaller molds baked at 350°F for 20 to 25 minutes, whereas the larger molds needed 28 to 32 minutes to reach doneness. To serve cupcakes in these molds, frost, then let everyone peel off the paper mold and eat. In addition to their beautiful appearance, an added plus is that the cupcakes bake up incredibly moist. My children adored them with no frosting at all.

STARS AND STRIPES CUPCAKES

● ● ● ● ●

A platter filled with these cupcakes looks impressive, but scan the ingredients list and you'll see that this recipe is oh, so simple. Yellow cupcakes, cream cheese frosting, blueberries, and strawberries—that's it. You'll also need a platter or serving board at least 20 by 24 inches to accommodate the 42 cupcakes that make up this flag. It's a delicious, festive dessert, intended for large gatherings on the Fourth of July or Memorial Day, or for school programs and dedications where plenty of people are on hand to share.

48 white paper cupcake liners (2½-inch size)

2 packages (18.25 ounces each) plain yellow cake mix

2 packages (3.4 ounces each) vanilla instant pudding mix

2 cups milk

2 cups vegetable oil

8 large eggs

2 teaspoons pure vanilla extract

2 recipes Cream Cheese Frosting (page 336, see "the Cupcake Doctor says")

50 fresh blueberries

33 medium strawberries, rinsed, drained, patted dry, and stemmed, or 17 large strawberries, cleaned, stemmed, and cut vertically in half

✿ **MAKES 42 CUPCAKES (2½ INCHES EACH)**

✿ **PREPARATION TIME: 10 MINUTES**

✿ **BAKING TIME: 16 TO 20 MINUTES PER BATCH**

✿ **ASSEMBLY TIME: 30 MINUTES**

the Cupcake Doctor says...

Prepare the cake batter in two large bowls, side by side, or dump all the ingredients into an extra-large bowl, but take care that the mixer is able to combine all the ingredients well, even those at the bottom of the bowl. You will probably need to bake these cupcakes in two batches as well. Don't begin frosting until all the cupcakes have cooled.

If you are assembling this dessert within an hour or so of serving, why not frost the cupcakes with Sweetened Whipped Cream (page 349)? In the summertime, there is nothing more delightful than whipped cream and fresh berries.

1. Place a rack in the center of the oven and preheat the oven to 350°F. Line 48 cupcake cups with paper liners. Set the pans aside.

2. Place the cake mixes, pudding mixes, milk, oil, eggs, and vanilla in a very large mixing bowl (see "the Cupcake Doctor says"). Blend with an electric mixer on low speed for 30 seconds. Stop the machine and scrape down the sides of the bowl with a rubber spatula. Increase the mixer speed to medium and beat 2 minutes more, scraping down the sides again if needed. Spoon or scoop a heaping ¼ cup batter into each lined cupcake cup, filling it two thirds of the way full. (You will get between 42 and 48 cupcakes; remove the empty liners, if any.) Place the pans in the oven.

3. Bake the cupcakes until they are golden brown and spring back when lightly pressed with your finger, 16 to 20 minutes. Remove the pans from the oven and place them on wire racks to cool for 5 minutes. (Leave the oven on if baking in batches.) Run a dinner knife around the edges of the cupcake liners, lift the cupcakes up from the bottoms of the cups using the end of the knife, and pick them out of the cups carefully with your fingertips. Place them on a wire rack to cool for 15 minutes before frosting. (If you are baking in batches, refill the cupcake cups with the remaining batter, and bake the second batch. You will use only 42 cupcakes for this presentation; freeze the extras for eating later.)

4. Meanwhile, prepare the frosting.

5. Place a heaping tablespoon of frosting on each cupcake and swirl to spread it out with a short metal spatula or a spoon, taking care to cover the tops completely. Place the blueberries on 9 of the cupcakes, dividing them evenly among the cupcakes and placing at least 5 on each. Place either a large capped strawberry stem-side down or a strawberry half cut-side down in the center of the remaining 33 cupcakes. Arrange the cupcakes on a large flat serving board in the form of the American flag by placing the 9 blueberry-topped cupcakes in the top left-hand corner in 3 rows of 3 cupcakes. Complete the rows by placing 4 strawberry cupcakes next to each row of blueberry cupcakes (each row should total 7 cupcakes across). Finish the flag by placing the remaining cupcakes in 3 rows of seven each. You should have 6 rows total. Make sure that the strawberries are straight so that they resemble the red stripes of the flag. The cupcake flag is ready to serve.

✿ *Store this platter of cupcakes, lightly covered with waxed paper, in the refrigerator for up to 2 days. If you are preparing them in advance, add the fruit 1 hour before serving. The unfrosted cupcakes may be baked ahead and frozen for up to 6 months. Thaw the cupcakes overnight in the refrigerator, then frost and decorate.*

FIREWORKS CONFETTI CUPCAKES

• • • • •

Festive is the word for these fun red, white, and blue cupcakes. From the inside to the outside, they are bursting with colorful sprinkles, and are topped with a glittering American flag. The cake batter is a rich vanilla-scented white, and the frosting is a classic buttercream, the perfect neutral backdrop for fireworks of decorations.

✿ **MAKES 22 TO 24 CUPCAKES (2½ INCHES EACH)**
✿ **PREPARATION TIME: 15 MINUTES**
✿ **BAKING TIME: 16 TO 20 MINUTES**
✿ **ASSEMBLY TIME: 40 MINUTES**

24 paper liners for cupcake pans, preferably printed with patriotic themes (2½-inch size)

CUPCAKES:

1 package (18.25 ounces) sour cream white cake mix with pudding (see "the Cupcake Doctor says")

⅓ cup all-purpose flour

1½ cups whole milk

½ cup vegetable oil

3 large eggs

1 teaspoon pure vanilla extract

1 container (2.5 ounces, ½ cup) mixed red, white, and blue sprinkles

Buttercream Frosting (page 318)

GARNISH:

Red edible glitter

White edible glitter

Blue edible glitter

Miniature paper American flags

1. Place a rack in the center of the oven and preheat the oven to 350°F. Line 24 cupcake cups with paper liners. Set the pans aside.

2. Place the cake mix, flour, milk, oil, eggs, and vanilla extract in a large mixing bowl. Blend with an electric mixer on low speed for 30 seconds. Stop the machine and scrape down the sides of the bowl with a rubber spatula. Increase the mixer speed to medium and beat 2 minutes more, scraping down the sides again if needed. Pour in the sprinkles and blend on medium for 10 seconds more. Spoon or scoop ¼ cup batter into each lined cupcake cup, filling it two thirds of the way full. (You will get between 22 and 24 cupcakes; remove the empty liners, if any.) Place the pans in the oven.

3. Bake the cupcakes until they are lightly golden and spring back when lightly pressed with your finger, 16 to 20 minutes. Remove the pans from the oven and place them on wire racks to cool for 5 minutes. Run a dinner knife around the edges of the cupcake liners, lift the cupcakes up from the bottoms of the cups using the end of the knife, and pick them out of the cups carefully with your fingertips. Place them on a wire rack to cool for 15 minutes before frosting.

> ### the Cupcake Doctor says...
>
> I used a Betty Crocker sour cream white cake mix in this recipe, and I was told by General Mills that it contains some pudding in the mix—although not as much as those Betty Crocker mixes that say "1 cup pudding" on the front of the box. You can use any white cake mix, with or without pudding, in this recipe. You'll find edible glitter wherever cake decorating supplies are sold. Wilton's version is called "Patriotic Cake Sparkles."

4. Meanwhile, prepare the Buttercream Frosting.

5. Place about ¾ cup frosting in a pastry bag fitted with a #8 tip or in a small plastic sandwich bag. If using a plastic bag, cut off a small piece of one of the bottom corners. Pipe various-size spikes of frosting over the tops of the cupcakes. Some spikes should be short and squat, some a little taller and thinner—say 1½ inches high. The idea is to make the frosting look

like a fireworks display. Refill the bag with more frosting as it empties. Garnish each cupcake with red, white, and blue edible glitter and place a flag in the center. The cupcakes are ready to serve.

✿ *You can store these cupcakes at room temperature for up to 3 days, but the glitter garnish will begin to weep into the frosting as the cupcakes sit, so they are really best if eaten the day they are baked and decorated. Without frosting and garnish, you can bake and freeze them, wrapped in aluminum foil or in a cake saver, for up to 6 months. Thaw the cupcakes overnight in the refrigerator before frosting and decorating.*

Cupcake Toting

▼ ▼ ▼

I have learned to hang on to those handy shirt boxes with lids that I get from the local laundry, as they are the perfect size for carrying cupcakes from my kitchen to school or a birthday party. Here are some ways you can tote cupcakes to and fro:

✿ Eight cupcakes will fit in a round 12-inch cake saver. For a batch of 24, count on 3 of these.

✿ Twelve cupcakes fit nicely into a 2-inch-deep pan measuring 13 by 9 inches. Cover the top with waxed paper or plastic wrap.

✿ Eighteen cupcakes fit comfortably in one of those handy oblong plastic cake carriers that measure 16 by 11 inches. Many have a locking lid and handle.

✿ Count on 15 to 18 cupcakes fitting in the cardboard shirt boxes from the laundry that measure nearly 16 by 11 inches. Line them with waxed paper, and either place the lid on the box or, if the cupcakes are too tall, drape the top with plastic wrap or waxed paper.

HALLOWEEN SPIDER CUPCAKES

• • • • •

Favorite cupcake alert! My kids and husband nearly inhaled these cupcakes, which are as adorable to look at as they are scrumptious to eat. Imagine rich devil's food cake, smeared with buttercream frosting, and topped with a crunchy chocolate treat in the shape of a spider. Don't worry, no real creepy-crawlies in this recipe!

☆ **MAKES 24 CUPCAKES (2½ INCHES EACH)**
☆ **PREPARATION TIME: 30 MINUTES**
☆ **SPIDER CHILLING TIME: 30 TO 40 MINUTES**
☆ **BAKING TIME: 16 TO 20 MINUTES**
☆ **ASSEMBLY TIME: 15 MINUTES**

24 silver or foil liners for cupcake pans
    (2½-inch size)

CUPCAKES:

1 package (18.25 ounces) plain devil's food
    cake mix
2 tablespoons Dutch process cocoa powder
1⅓ cups buttermilk
½ cup vegetable oil
3 large eggs
1 teaspoon pure vanilla extract

FROSTING:

Buttercream Frosting (page 318)
6 drops yellow food coloring
2 drops red food coloring

GARNISHES:

24 Chocolate Spiders (recipe follows)
Tiny round decorating candies (optional)
Brown decorating gel (optional)

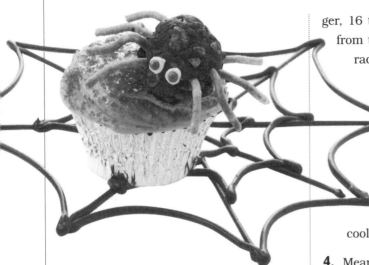

1. Place a rack in the center of the oven and preheat the oven to 350°F. Line 24 cupcake cups with silver paper liners. Set the pans aside.

2. Prepare the cupcake batter: Place the cake mix, cocoa powder, buttermilk, oil, eggs, and vanilla extract in a large mixing bowl. Blend with an electric mixer on low speed for 30 seconds. Stop the machine and scrape down the sides of the bowl with a rubber spatula. Increase the mixer speed to medium and beat 2 minutes more, scraping down the sides again if needed. Spoon or scoop a heaping ¼ cup batter into each lined cupcake cup, filling it two thirds of the way full. (You will get between 22 and 24 cupcakes; remove the empty liners, if any.) Place the pans in the oven.

3. Bake the cupcakes until they spring back when lightly pressed with your fin-

ger, 16 to 20 minutes. Remove the pans from the oven and place them on wire racks to cool for 5 minutes. Run a dinner knife around the edges of the cupcake liners, lift the cupcakes up from the bottoms of the cups using the end of the knife, and pick them out of the cups carefully with your fingertips. Place them on a wire rack to cool completely, 30 minutes.

4. Meanwhile, prepare the Buttercream Frosting. Place ¼ cup of the frosting in a plastic sandwich bag and set aside. Add the yellow and red food coloring to the remaining frosting. Blend well so the frosting is evenly orange. Place a heaping tablespoon of frosting on each cupcake and swirl to spread it out with a short metal spatula or a spoon, taking care to cover the tops completely.

the Cupcake Doctor says...

Here's something to remember when you're making orange-colored frosting: Use drops of yellow and red food coloring in a 3 to 1 ratio, adding for example, 6 drops yellow and 2 drops red.

Spooky Graveyard Cupcakes

▼ ▼ ▼

Bake any cupcake you like and frost with a stiff chocolate frosting. With a pastry bag fitted with a small round tip, pipe the letters "RIP" onto miniature Mint Milano cookies with orange decorating frosting (see the facing page, step 4). Stand a cookie up in each cupcake to resemble a headstone. Arrange the cupcakes on a platter decorated with Chocolate Spiders and an imitation spiderweb, found at party stores (or pipe one using brown decorating gel).

✿ *Store these cupcakes, uncovered or in a cake saver, at room temperature for up to 2 days or in the refrigerator for up to 1 week. Or freeze the unfrosted and undecorated cupcakes in a cake saver for up to 6 months. Thaw the cupcakes overnight in the refrigerator before frosting, decorating, and serving.*

CHOCOLATE SPIDERS

• • • •

You can make these spiders up to two days before you bake the cupcakes. The six extras make wonderful platter decorations or sweet treats by themselves.

1¼ cups chow mein noodles
2½ cups semisweet chocolate chips
⅓ cup milk
½ cup confectioners' sugar
1 cup crispy rice cereal

1. Line a baking sheet with waxed paper and set aside.

5. Garnish the cupcakes: Cut off a small piece from one of the bottom corners of the plastic bag holding the frosting. Pipe 2 eyes on each of the Chocolate Spiders. Place a small round decorating candy in the center of each eye, if desired. Place a spider on top of each cupcake. There will be 6 extra spiders for additional platter garnish or simply to enjoy. If you wish, pipe a web on the platter using brown decorating gel. The cupcakes are ready to serve.

2. Measure out ¾ cup chow mein noodles and break them into small pieces. Break the remaining noodles into 2-inch pieces. These will be the spiders' legs. Set the noodles aside in separate groupings.

3. Combine the chocolate chips and milk in a medium-size saucepan over low heat, stirring frequently, until the chocolate has melted and the mixture is smooth, 3 to 4 minutes. Remove the pan from the heat and stir in the confectioners' sugar, cereal, and the small chow mein noodle pieces until blended. Line a baking sheet with waxed paper. Drop the chocolate mixture by tablespoons in a slightly oblong shape (the body of the spider) onto the prepared baking sheet. You will have about 30 bodies, about 2 inches in size. Immediately insert the noodle legs into

the Cupcake Doctor says...

Once the frosting for the cupcakes is made, reserve a small amount of it to pipe on each spider for its eyes.

the spider bodies, 4 on one side and 4 on the opposite side. Space them evenly apart. Place the baking sheet in the refrigerator and chill the spiders until hardened, 30 to 40 minutes.

4. Once chilled, remove them from the waxed paper by pushing up from the underside of the waxed paper.

✿ *Store the spiders in a plastic storage container at room temperature for up to 2 days.*

LITTLE PUMPKIN CINNAMON CAKES

• • • • •

Seeing these little orange-glazed cakes lined up on a platter gives you the feeling that Halloween must be near! The pumpkin shape comes from baking the cupcakes in 2½-inch Bundt muffin pans and serving them fluted side up. Don't fret if you don't have any; you can still bake the batter as regular cupcakes (see "the Cupcake Doctor says"). Use festive Halloween liners and you're ready for both tricks and treats.

✿ MAKES 34 TO 36 (2-INCH) PUMPKIN CUPCAKES
   (SEE "THE CUPCAKE DOCTOR SAYS")
✿ PREPARATION TIME: 15 MINUTES
✿ BAKING TIME: 12 TO 15 MINUTES PER BATCH
✿ ASSEMBLY TIME: 20 MINUTES

CUPCAKES:

Vegetable oil shortening for greasing the pans

Flour for dusting the pans

*1 package (18.25 ounces) plain yellow
    cake mix*

1 cup canned pumpkin

⅓ cup vegetable oil

½ cup milk

3 large eggs

1 teaspoon pure vanilla extract

1 teaspoon ground cinnamon

½ teaspoon ground nutmeg

GLAZE:

2½ cups confectioners' sugar, sifted

2½ to 3 tablespoons milk

*½ teaspoon pure orange extract
    (see "the Cupcake Doctor says")*

3 drops yellow food coloring

1 drop red food coloring

*24 green gumdrops or Dots candy, cut
    in bite-size pieces for the stem
    (see "the Cupcake Doctor says")*

the Cupcake Doctor says...

This recipe makes more cupcakes than most other recipes in the book because each Bundt mold holds less batter than regular cupcake pan cups. If you bake this recipe in regular cupcake pans with paper Halloween liners (no greasing or flouring is necessary), it will make 24 cupcakes; bake for about 18 minutes.

For the glaze, you can omit the orange extract and opt for a fresher orange taste by adding 1 teaspoon grated orange zest and using orange juice instead of the milk. I found the Summerville Green Apple Candy Bites that I bought at Target really resembled pumpkin stems.

1. Place a rack in the center of the oven and preheat the oven to 350°F. Using a pastry brush, grease the Bundt muffin pans with vegetable oil shortening and dust with flour. Shake out the excess flour and set pans aside.

2. Prepare the cupcake batter: Place the cake mix, canned pumpkin, oil, milk, eggs, vanilla, cinnamon, and nutmeg in a large mixing bowl. Blend with an electric mixer on low speed for 30 seconds. Stop the machine and scrape down the sides of the bowl with a rubber spatula. Increase the mixer speed to medium and beat 2 minutes more, scraping down the sides again if needed. Spoon or scoop 3 tablespoons batter into each prepared pan, filling it two thirds of the way full. (You will get between 34 and 36 pumpkins.) Place the pans in the oven.

3. Bake the cupcakes until they are golden and spring back when lightly pressed with your finger, 12 to 15 minutes. Remove the pans from the oven and place them on wire racks to cool for 5 minutes. (Leave the oven on if baking

in batches.) Run a dinner knife around the edges of the cupcakes, then invert the pan onto the wire rack to unmold the cupcakes. Let them cool for 15 minutes before glazing. (If you are baking in batches, cool the pans, wipe out any stray crumbs, and grease and flour the cups before refilling them with the remaining batter. Then bake the second batch.)

4. Meanwhile, prepare the glaze: Place the confectioners' sugar, milk, orange extract, and yellow and red food colorings in a small mixing bowl and whisk to combine well, making sure that the colors blend evenly.

5. Assemble the pumpkins: Spoon the glaze over the top of the cupcakes. (You may need to restir the glaze between batches.) Immediately place a green gumdrop or other candy piece in the center to resemble a pumpkin stem. Repeat with the remaining cupcakes. The cupcakes are ready to serve.

✿ *Store these cupcakes, in a cake saver or under a glass dome, at room temperature for up to 3 days or in the refrigerator for up to 1 week. Or freeze them, wrapped in aluminum foil or in a cake saver, for up to 6 months. Thaw the cupcakes overnight in the refrigerator before serving.*

PILGRIMS' HATS

• • • • •

One day while shopping for baking supplies at the cookware store, I was thinking about creating a cupcake for Thanksgiving and wondering how to turn one into a Pilgrim's hat. And then I saw it: a crown cupcake pan—a pan with cups like flowerpots so that the tops are pushed up and bake wider and taller than the bottoms. Great for little-girls' parties or Easter, I thought, with flower-shaped lollipops sticking out of green coconut grass, but downright perfect inverted into Pilgrims' hats for Thanksgiving.

I bought two pans and created these special deep-chocolate cupcakes, adding a chocolate glaze, a band of yellow decorating icing, and half a marshmallow for the buckle to complete these simple, moist, delicious autumn Pilgrims' Hats.

CUPCAKES:
Solid vegetable shortening for greasing
    the pans
Flour for dusting the pans
1 package (18.25 ounces) devil's food
    cake mix with pudding
1 cup sour cream
¾ cup water
⅓ cup vegetable oil
3 large eggs
1 teaspoon pure vanilla extract

✿ **MAKES 12 LARGE CUPCAKES (3 INCHES EACH)**
✿ **PREPARATION TIME: 10 MINUTES**
✿ **BAKING TIME: 22 TO 25 MINUTES**
✿ **ASSEMBLY TIME: 30 MINUTES**

GLAZE:

4 tablespoons (½ stick) butter

2 tablespoons unsweetened cocoa powder

3 tablespoons whole milk

2 cups confectioners' sugar, sifted

GARNISH:

1 can (6.4 ounces) yellow decorating icing

6 miniature marshmallows, halved

1. Place a rack in the center of the oven and preheat the oven to 350°F. Grease two 6-cup crown muffin pans and lightly dust with flour. (Or, bake with one pan at a time, in two batches.) Set the pans aside.

2. Prepare the cupcake batter: Place the cake mix, sour cream, water, oil, eggs, and vanilla in a large mixing bowl. Blend with an electric mixer on low speed for 30 seconds. Stop the machine and scrape down the sides of the bowl with a rubber spatula. Increase the mixer speed to medium and beat 2 minutes more, scraping down the sides again if needed. Spoon or scoop a heaping ½ cup batter into each prepared cupcake cup, filling it up to the lower rim of the crown. Place the pans in the oven.

3. Bake the cupcakes until they spring back when lightly pressed with your finger, 22 to 25 minutes. Remove the pans

the Cupcake Doctor says...

If you don't have a crown muffin pan, you can still make Pilgrims' Hats. You'll need a muffin-top pan or a regular cupcake pan, and a miniature cupcake pan. If using a muffin-top pan and a miniature cupcake pan, fill both and bake in a 350°F oven for 15 to 20 minutes. Cool both in the pan for 5 minutes, then on a rack for 15 minutes more. Glaze the muffin tops and minis separately, then place the minis upside down on the tops of the muffin tops. Continue decorating as instructed in step 5 (page 212).

If using a regular-size cupcake pan, fill the cups nearly to the top so they create a large crown or top once baked (22 to 25 minutes). Make at least 12 miniature cupcakes from the remaining batter. When the larger cupcakes have cooled, slice off the tops; save the bottoms for snacking. Place the tops on a platter and glaze. Glaze 12 mini cupcakes and place them on top. Add the band and the buckle and voilà! Pilgrims' Hats.

from the oven and place them on wire racks to cool for 5 minutes. Run a dinner knife around the edges of the cupcakes, invert the pan onto a rack, and lift off the cupcake pan. Let the cupcakes cool for 15 minutes before frosting.

4. Meanwhile, prepare the glaze. Place the butter in a medium-size saucepan and melt over low heat, 3 minutes. Stir in the cocoa powder and milk. Continue stirring and let the mixture come just to a boil, then remove the pan from the heat. Add the confectioners' sugar, whisking until the glaze has thickened and is smooth, 1 to 2 minutes.

5. Pilgrims' Hats are narrower on top than at the bottom, so glaze the cupcakes upside down. Ladle 2 to 3 tablespoons of glaze over each cupcake. Spread the glaze with a

short metal spatula or a spoon, making sure the rims are iced. Let the glaze set for 10 minutes. Pipe a ¼-inch-wide band of yellow decorating icing around each cupcake where the hat meets the brim. Place one half marshmallow on the yellow band as the buckle. The cupcakes are ready to serve.

✿ *Store these cupcakes, in a cake saver or under a glass dome, at room temperature for up to 3 days or in the refrigerator for up to 1 week. Or freeze them, wrapped in aluminum foil or in a cake saver, for up to 6 months. Thaw the cupcakes overnight in the refrigerator before serving.*

SNOWMAN CUPCAKES

• • • • •

Here's another cupcake that's almost too cute to eat. Honestly, with this adorable pudgy white marshmallow snowman perched atop a white cupcake, you might be tempted just to stare at it. But do take a bite, because the cake is moist and the vanilla comes through in the buttercream frosting. These cupcakes are a simple indulgence on snowy days and festive winter occasions. It's an idea I adapted from a marshmallow snowman I saw on the Martha Stewart Web site. Any orange candy that can be shaped will do for the nose, and if you can't find rolled fruit, use ribbon for a scarf.

24 paper liners for cupcake pans
    (2½-inch size)

CUPCAKES AND FROSTING:

1 package (18.25 ounces) plain white
    cake mix
⅓ cup all-purpose flour
1½ cups whole milk
½ cup vegetable oil
3 large eggs
1 teaspoon pure vanilla extract
Buttercream Frosting (page 318)
2 cups sweetened flaked coconut

SNOWMEN:

48 large marshmallows
Chocolate sprinkles
3 orange gumdrops, cut into 24 slivers,
    or 24 pieces of candy corn
Red rolled fruit snack or ribbon for the scarves
72 green gumdrops

❁ **MAKES 22 TO 24 CUPCAKES (2½ INCHES EACH)**
❁ **PREPARATION TIME: 10 MINUTES**
❁ **BAKING TIME: 16 TO 20 MINUTES**
❁ **ASSEMBLY TIME: 30 MINUTES**

the Cupcake Doctor says...

Vary this recipe as you like, baking your favorite cupcake—even if it's chocolate—but always top with a white frosting. And look for white paper liners in the supermarket to complete the all-white look. The coconut can easily be omitted, if your children don't like the texture. In lieu of marshmallows, bake miniature white cupcakes and place a frosted mini cupcake (the head) on top of the frosted regular-size cupcake to look like a snowman. Decorate as you wish.

1. Place a rack in the center of the oven and preheat the oven to 350°F. Line 24 cupcake cups with white paper liners. Set the pans aside.

2. Place the cake mix, flour, milk, oil, eggs, and vanilla in a large mixing bowl. Blend with an electric mixer on low speed for 30 seconds. Stop the machine and scrape down the sides of the bowl with a rubber spatula. Increase the mixer speed to medium and beat 2 minutes more, scraping down the sides again if needed. Spoon or scoop ⅓ cup batter into each lined cupcake cup, filling it three quarters of the way full. (You will get between 22 and 24 cupcakes; remove the empty liners, if any.) Place the pans in the oven.

3. Bake the cupcakes until they are lightly golden and spring back when lightly pressed with your finger, 16 to 20 minutes. Remove the pans from the oven and place them on wire racks to cool for 5 minutes. Run a dinner knife around the edges of the cupcake liners, lift the cupcakes up from the bottoms of the cups using the end of the knife, and pick them out of the cups carefully with your fingertips. Place them on a wire rack to cool for 15 minutes before frosting.

4. Meanwhile, prepare the frosting.

5. Place a heaping tablespoon of frosting on each cupcake and swirl to spread it out with a short metal spatula or a spoon, taking care to cover the tops completely. Sprinkle the tops of the cupcakes with coconut.

6. Make the snowmen: For each body, moisten a toothpick or wooden skewer with water and poke 2 holes, one above the other, into each of 24 marshmallows. Leave about ¼-inch space between the holes. Insert a chocolate sprinkle into each hole to look like buttons.

7. For each head, poke 2 holes for eyes near the top of each of the remaining marshmallows. Poke 1 hole, beneath the eyes and centered, for the nose. And finally, poke 5 holes for the mouth in a smile shape. Insert a sprinkle into each of the eye and mouth holes, and an orange gumdrop sliver into the nose hole.

8. For the hat, cut a strip about 2 inches long and ¼ inch wide from the rolled fruit. Use your thumb to mash together 2 green gumdrops into a flat round shape. Cut a thin slice off the wide end of a gumdrop and press it onto the gumdrop round. Wrap the fruit strip as a hatband, damping the ends to secure it. Repeat with the rolled fruit and remaining gumdrops.

9. For the scarf, cut 48 pieces of rolled fruit about 2 inches long and ½ inch wide. Cut a notch out of one end of each strip about ½ inch deep.

10. To assemble a snowman, place a marshmallow body in the center of each cupcake, pressing it slightly into the frosting to adhere. Place 2 scarf strips on top of the marshmallow, notched ends out, and place a marshmallow head on top of the scarf, pressing down to secure all in place. If the snowman feels wobbly, dampen the scarf ends or dab a bit of frosting on them to help secure all in place. Add another dab of frosting on the top of the snowman's head and place his gumdrop hat. Continue assembling the snowmen until all the cupcakes are used up. The snowmen are ready to be served.

❀ *Store these cupcakes, in a cake saver or under a glass dome, at room temperature for up to 3 days or in the refrigerator for up to 1 week.*

HOLIDAY GIFT CUPCAKES

• • • • •

You may have seen fancy pastries that look like presents, wrapped up in some complicated rolled fondant icing with bows on top that only a professional cake decorator could produce. But this recipe is different. My friend Lucille Osborn, a food stylist, spotted the bow recipe in a *Family Circle* magazine many years ago. We've modified it a bit to simplify the process. You'll need egg white or meringue powder, which is sold at craft and specialty food stores, and a pastry bag, which you can purchase there or at the supermarket. The cupcake is the infamous Red Velvet and it is delicious.

24 gold or silver foil liners for cupcake pans
   (2 ½-inch size)

CUPCAKES:
1 package (18.25 ounces) German chocolate
   cake mix with pudding
1 cup sour cream
½ cup water
¼ cup vegetable oil
3 large eggs
1 bottle (1 ounce) red food coloring
1 teaspoon pure vanilla extract

✿ **MAKES 22 TO 24 CUPCAKES (2½ INCHES EACH)**
✿ **CAKE PREPARATION TIME: 10 MINUTES**
✿ **BAKING TIME: 16 TO 20 MINUTES**
✿ **BOW PREPARATION TIME: 20 MINUTES**
✿ **BOW DRYING TIME: 3 HOURS**
✿ **ASSEMBLY TIME: 20 MINUTES**

FROSTING:

Cream Cheese Frosting (page 36)

Red food coloring or paste

> *(see "the Cake Doctor says")*

Red sugar sprinkles (optional)

24 Meringue Bows and Ribbons

> *(recipe follows)*

1. Place a rack in the center of the oven and preheat the oven to 350°F. Line 24 cupcake cups with foil liners. Set the pans aside.

2. Prepare the cupcake batter: Place the cake mix, sour cream, water, oil, eggs, food coloring, and vanilla extract in a large mixing bowl. Blend with an electric mixer on low speed for 30 seconds. Stop the machine and scrape down the sides of the bowl with a rubber spatula. Increase the mixer speed to medium and beat 2 minutes more, scraping down the sides again if needed. Spoon or scoop ⅓ cup batter into each lined cupcake cup, filling it three quarters of the way full. (You will get between 22 and 24 cupcakes; remove the empty liners, if any.) Place the pans in the oven.

3. Bake the cupcakes until they spring back when lightly pressed with your finger, 16 to 20 minutes. Remove the pans from the oven and place them on wire racks to cool for 5 minutes. Run a dinner

the Cupcake Doctor says...

If you don't want to pipe out 24 bows, you can easily pipe out Christmas trees, Stars of David, or other holiday symbols and sprinkle them with the decorating sugar of your choice. I used Wilton Vivid Red food color paste to get the deep color in the frosting and set it off with red sugar sprinkles. You can also keep the frosting white and sprinkle it with some white sugar sprinkles or Wilton Cake Sparkles (big flakes of edible glitter) to give it a snowy effect.

knife around the edges of the cupcake liners, lift the cupcakes up from the bottoms of the cups using the end of the knife, and pick them out of the cups carefully with your fingertips. Place them on a wire rack to cool for 15 minutes before frosting.

4. Meanwhile, prepare the Cream Cheese Frosting, adding the red food coloring once the frosting is sufficiently beaten. Start with 3 drops and blend them in well. If the color isn't red enough, keep adding more color 1 drop at a time until the frosting is a deep red all over (or to your liking).

5. Place a heaping tablespoon of frosting on each cupcake and swirl to spread it out with a short metal spatula or a spoon, taking care to cover the tops completely. Sprinkle the red sugar sprinkles all over the top, if desired.

6. Remove the meringue bows from the waxed paper, by pushing the bow carefully from underneath the paper to loosen it. Sit a bow straight up on each cupcake and place 2 meringue ribbons coming from the center of the bow to resemble a gift-wrapped present. The cupcakes are ready to serve.

✿ *Store these cupcakes for up to 3 days at room temperature. Don't cover the cupcakes or refrigerate them, as this will cause the bows to weep and wilt.*

MERINGUE BOWS AND RIBBONS

• • • •

On Christmas eve, when everyone is eager to open at least one gift, festive cupcakes with pretty bows just might make the waiting a little easier.

2 cups confectioners' sugar
1½ tablespoons powdered egg whites
3 tablespoons water, plus more for thinning
Gold, silver, or white edible glitter

1. At least 3 hours before baking, prepare the meringue bows: Line two baking sheets with waxed paper, and set them aside. Place the sugar, powdered egg whites, and 3 tablespoons of water in a medium-size mixing bowl and beat with an electric mixer until the mixture is very stiff, about 5 minutes.

2. Spoon 1 cup of the egg white mixture into a pastry bag with a #2 plain tip. Draw outlines of 24 bows in a fancy figure eight, by slowly piping the mixture onto the waxed paper in the desired bow shape. Now pipe the notched ribbon ends that hang off a tied bow separately. Each bow gets 2 ribbon ends. Each bow should measure about 2½ inches wide; each ribbon end about 1½ inches long. Leave 2 inches between bows. To prepare the filling for the bows and ribbon pieces, thin the remaining egg white mixture with water until it has the consistency of white school glue. Use either a toothpick or a small plastic knife to fill in the bow and ribbon outlines with the thinned mixture, taking care to fill the corners. While the icing is still wet, sprinkle gold and silver edible glitter on each bow. Allow the meringue bows to dry for at least 3 hours before using.

How to Make Edible "Plastic Chocolate"

Need big chocolate curls for those extra-special cupcakes? You don't have to be a pastry chef; you just need what is called "plastic chocolate." This edible chocolate putty is rolled out to form curls or leaves or roses, whatever shape you like, to garnish the top of cakes. Here is how it goes:

Melt 2⅔ cups (or 16 ounces) of semisweet chocolate chips in a small heavy saucepan, stirring, over very low heat. (You can also melt them in a medium-size glass bowl in the microwave oven on high power for 30 to 40 seconds total, stirring occasionally.) Then stir in ¾ cup light corn syrup until it is well combined. Scrape this mixture onto a sheet of plastic wrap, shape it into a mound, and seal it tightly. Let it rest at room temperature until it is firm. This might take 3 to 4 hours or overnight, depending on the temperature of your kitchen. Place it in a cool place, but don't refrigerate.

To roll it out, dust the counter with unsweetened cocoa powder, pinch off pieces of the plastic chocolate, and with your hands, a glass, or a small rolling pin, roll it out on a flat surface. With your fingers, roll up the chocolate in a loose cylinder to form a curl. Or stamp out leaves or flower petals, using specialty metal cutters, and place them on cupcakes to decorate. Store leftovers in plastic wrap at room temperature for up to 2 days.

Muffins: Breakfast Cupcakes

❖ ❖ ❖

They're unpretentious, they don't require frosting, sprinkles, or other hoopla (although sometimes it's fun to add them); they're simply muffins—a humble handful. Dessert cupcakes might seem like the main attraction, but muffins are tried-and-true stars. They are a delicious way to start the day.

Muffins and cupcakes are baked in the same pans, but their construction is a tad different. First of all, muffins are best baked in a pan that has been lightly sprayed on the bottom with vegetable oil. Cupcakes, on the other hand, generally need paper liners. (The liners would soften the muffin's crust.) Muffins need a higher heat to rise up quickly and to brown and develop a nice crust, which not only keeps their interior moist but makes them sturdy enough for toting to friends or freezing for later meals.

When you assemble the muffin batter, go easy on it, or the resulting muffins will be tough. Use a wooden spoon if the recipe calls for wet ingredients to be combined with dry. If it calls for an electric mixer to cream the butter and sugar, fine, but when it comes time to add the flour, fold it in with a wooden spoon.

Okay, enough about food science. On to the wonderful recipes you'll find in this chapter. Bake up the Banana Muffins with Big Blackberries and Sugar Crust and the Pineapple Muffins with Coconut Crumble when you're in the mood for a buttery-flavored and moist-textured fruit muffin. There's the Blueberry Yogurt Streusel Muffins and the Double Lemon Poppy Seed Cheesecake Muffins when you want that excellent bake-shop taste.

Want a muffin hearty enough to feel like a meal? Choose the Sweet Potato Casserole Muffin recipe, which combines canned sweet potatoes, a cinnamon muffin mix, pecans, and even marshmallows for the topping if you like. Or, go with the Pumpkin Muffins with Chocolate Chips or the Pumpkin Corn Maple Muffins, perfect for the brown-bag lunch. When I get hungry at 10:00 A.M. and need something to tide me over until lunchtime, I reach for a muffin, and I love the fortifying simplicity of the Raisin and Bran Muffins and the Grated Apple and Ginger Bran Muffins.

Don't forget the Big Bad Chocolate Muffins for an afternoon snack. Or the Green Chile and Corn Muffins, plus the variations, should you need a quick hot nibble with drinks or a basketful of muffins to go with your favorite chili. And I haven't mentioned the Carrot Cake Muffins with a Cream Cheese Surprise, which are treading in dessert territory (yum!), or the Mini Peach Muffins and Fruit Kebabs, a clever way to skewer little muffins and fruit for entertaining or special family meals.

Enjoy every bite!

BLUEBERRY YOGURT STREUSEL MUFFINS

• • • • •

It's hard to resist the flavor of fresh blueberries, especially when they're baked in a moist breakfast muffin. This recipe is doubly good, as fresh berries are folded in along with the drained, canned blueberries that come with the package of mix. Take care when removing these muffins from the pan; you don't want to knock off any of the crunchy streusel topping.

Vegetable oil spray for misting the pan

MUFFINS:
*1 package (18.9 ounces) blueberry
    muffin mix*
*1 container (6 ounces; ¾ cup) yogurt
    of your choice (see "the Cupcake
    Doctor says")*
2 large eggs
1 teaspoon pure vanilla extract
*1 cup fresh blueberries, rinsed and
    patted dry (see "the Cupcake
    Doctor says")*

STREUSEL TOPPING:
¼ cup packed light brown sugar
3 tablespoons all-purpose flour
1 tablespoon butter, at room temperature

✿ **MAKES 12 MUFFINS (2½ INCHES EACH)**
✿ **PREPARATION TIME: 12 MINUTES**
✿ **BAKING TIME: 20 TO 23 MINUTES**

1. Place a rack in the center of the oven and preheat the oven to 400°F. Mist the bottoms of 12 muffin cups with the vegetable oil spray. Set the pans aside.

2. Prepare the muffin batter: Remove the package of blueberries and set it aside. Place the muffin mix in a large mixing bowl. Make a well in the center. Place the yogurt, eggs, and vanilla in a small mixing bowl and stir with a fork to combine and break up the egg yolks. Pour the yogurt mixture into the well of the muffin mix. Stir the wet and dry ingredients together with a wooden spoon just until combined, 20 strokes. Pour the reserved blueberries into a strainer, rinse them under cold running water, and drain well. Fold these blueberries into the batter along with the fresh berries. Stir another 10 strokes just to combine. The batter will still be a little lumpy. Spoon or scoop ⅓ cup batter into each prepared muffin cup, filling it three quarters of the way full. Set the pan aside.

3. Prepare the streusel topping: Place the brown sugar and flour in a small bowl and stir together. Add the butter, mashing it with a fork until the mixture is crumbly. With your hands, sprinkle a heaping teaspoon of this topping on top of each muffin. Place the pan in the oven.

the Cupcake Doctor says...

Yogurt keeps this muffin incredibly moist. I've tried vanilla, blueberry, lemon, and plain yogurt and liked them all. One cup fresh blueberries is about one of the small (half-pint) containers.

4. Bake the muffins until they are lightly golden and just spring back when lightly pressed with your finger, 20 to 23 minutes. Remove the pan from the oven and place it on a wire rack to cool for 5 minutes. Run a dinner knife around the edges of the muffins, lift them up from the bottoms of the cups using the end of the knife, and pick them out of the cups carefully with your fingertips, taking care not to disturb the streusel. Place the muffins on a wire rack to cool for 15 minutes. The muffins are ready to serve.

✿ *Store these muffins, in a cake saver or under a glass dome, at room temperature for up to 5 days or freeze them, wrapped in aluminum foil or in a cake saver, for up to 6 months. Thaw the muffins overnight in the refrigerator before serving.*

BLUEBERRY BANANA MUFFINS

WITH A PECAN CRUNCH

• • • • •

I think that blueberries and bananas are one of those perfect flavor combinations— a match made in heaven, so to speak. Try them together in smoothies, in pancakes, and in these easy muffins with a crunchy pecan topping. I froze the leftover muffins and reheated them a week later for a hurried midweek breakfast. They were delicious.

✿ **MAKES 12 MUFFINS (2½ INCHES EACH)**
✿ **PREPARATION TIME: 10 MINUTES**
✿ **BAKING TIME: 20 TO 23 MINUTES**

Vegetable oil spray for misting the pan

MUFFINS:
1 small ripe banana
1 container (6 ounces; ¾ cup) plain yogurt
1 large egg
½ teaspoon pure vanilla extract
1 package (18.9 ounces) blueberry
    muffin mix

PECAN CRUNCH:
½ cup finely chopped pecans
4 tablespoons packed light brown sugar
3 tablespoons all-purpose flour
1 tablespoon butter, at room temperature

1. Place a rack in the center of the oven and preheat the oven to 400°F. Mist the bottom of 12 muffin cups with the vegetable oil spray. Set the pan aside.

2. Place the banana in a small mixing bowl and mash it with a fork. You should have ½ cup mashed banana. Stir in the yogurt, egg, and vanilla just until combined. Set aside.

3. Place the muffin mix in a large mixing bowl and make a well in the center. Pour the yogurt mixture into the well and stir together with a wooden spoon until the wet and dry ingredients are combined, 20 strokes. Pour the blueberries that come with the muffin mix into a strainer, rinse them under cold running water and drain them well. Fold them into the batter just until combined, another 10 strokes. The batter will still be a little lumpy. Spoon or scoop ⅓ cup batter into each prepared muffin cup, filling it three quarters of the way full. Set the pan aside.

4. Prepare the pecan topping: Place the pecans, brown sugar, and flour in a small bowl and stir together. Add the butter, mashing it with a fork until the mixture is crumbly. With your hands, sprinkle a heaping teaspoon of the topping on top of each muffin. Place the pans in the oven.

the Cupcake Doctor says...

If you're partial to walnuts, use them instead of pecans.

5. Bake the muffins until the pecan topping is deeply golden and the muffins just spring back when lightly pressed with your finger, 20 to 23 minutes. Remove the pan from the oven and place it on a wire rack to cool for 5 minutes. Run a dinner knife around the edges of the muffins, lift them up from the bottom of the cups using the end of the knife, and pick them out of the cups carefully with your fingertips. Place them on a wire rack to cool for 15 minutes. The muffins are ready to serve.

✿ *Store these muffins, in a cake saver or under a glass dome, at room temperature for up to 5 days, or freeze them, wrapped in aluminum foil or in a cake saver, for up to 6 months. Thaw the muffins overnight in the refrigerator before serving.*

BANANA MUFFINS

WITH BIG BLACKBERRIES AND SUGAR CRUST

• • • • •

I first tasted a banana muffin with blackberries mixed in when I was vacationing in San Diego, and the idea stayed with me. Yet I couldn't find a muffin mix suitable for doctoring into a banana muffin. They were too strongly flavored with lemon or they contained blueberries or too much cinnamon. So I relied on my experience as a scratch baker and pulled out a sack of handy self-rising flour. Self-rising flour already has the leavening and salt added, giving you a jump-start when you make this delicious recipe. We love these muffins served warm, split, dabbed with butter, and sprinkled with sugar.

Vegetable oil for misting the pans
8 tablespoons (1 stick) unsalted
    butter, at room temperature
    (see "the Cupcake
    Doctor says")
1 cup packed light
    brown sugar
2 large eggs
1 small banana
3 cups self-rising
    flour
1½ cups buttermilk
¼ teaspoon ground nutmeg
½ cup large fresh blackberries (12),
    rinsed and drained
1 tablespoon coarse sugar for sprinkling
    on top (see the "Sugar, Sugar" box,
    on the facing page)
Unsalted butter, for serving (optional)

✿ **MAKES 15 MUFFINS (2½ INCHES EACH)**
✿ **PREPARATION TIME: 12 MINUTES**
✿ **BAKING TIME: 21 TO 23 MINUTES**

Sugar, Sugar

▼ ▼ ▼

Ever wonder why you like the texture of those bakery muffins so much? It might be because their tops are sprinkled with a coarse or decorating sugar before baking. These sugar granules are four to five times larger than typical granulated sugar, and thus they create a crunchy topping for muffins. Look for them where you buy cake decorating supplies. Look, too, for turbinado sugar for dusting muffin tops. It is a coarse, raw sugar with a pale tan color and is richer in flavor than white sugar.

I. Place a rack in the center of the oven and preheat the oven to 400°F. Mist the bottom of 15 muffin cups with the vegetable oil spray. Set the pans aside.

2. Place the butter and sugar in a large mixing bowl. Beat with an electric mixer on medium speed until the mixture is creamy and light, 1 to 2 minutes. Add the eggs and beat again until the mixture lightens and is lemon colored, 30 seconds. Slice the banana into the bowl. Add 1½ cups of the flour, ¾ cup of the butter-

milk, and the nutmeg. Stir the ingredients with a wooden spoon just until combined, 10 strokes. Add the remaining flour and buttermilk and stir with the spoon to just combine the ingredients, 10 strokes more. The batter will still be a little lumpy. Fold in the blackberries. Spoon or scoop ⅓ cup batter into each prepared muffin cup, filling it three quarters of the way full. Sprinkle the tops with the coarse sugar and place the pans in the oven.

3. Bake the muffins until they are lightly golden and just spring back when lightly pressed with your finger, 21 to 23 minutes. Remove the pans from the oven and place them on a wire rack to cool for 5 minutes. Run a dinner knife around the

the Cupcake Doctor says...

Because self-rising flour contains salt, you must use unsalted butter in this recipe or the muffins will be too salty. Notice that this recipe uses two techniques—an electric mixer for creaming the butter and sugar, and adding eggs, then a wooden spoon for folding in the dry ingredients so the gluten in the flour isn't overworked (which would produce tough muffins).

edges of the muffins, lift them up from the bottom of the pan using the end of the knife, and pick them out of the cups carefully with your fingertips. Serve warm, with butter, if desired.

✿ *Store these muffins, in a cake saver or under a glass dome, at room temperature for up to 5 days or freeze them, wrapped in aluminum foil or in a cake saver, for up to 6 months. Thaw the muffins overnight in the refrigerator before serving.*

What's a Muffin? What's a Cupcake?

The pans for baking muffins and cupcakes may be the same, but what pops out of them can be surprisingly different. Muffins are a quick bread that's sometimes sweet, sometimes savory, and they are usually not frosted. Although muffins contain an egg (sometimes two), the egg is not the sole reason that muffins rise while baking. It is the leavening (baking powder and soda) in the muffin's batter that pushes them upward in the oven. And because muffins contain so few eggs compared to cupcakes, they are less spongy and cakey in texture.

Muffins are known by their pebbly tops and their characteristic bottom and side crust. You achieve this by misting the bottom of a muffin pan with vegetable oil and letting the muffins bake at a high heat (400°F) without paper liners.

Cupcakes, on the other hand, are always sweet. They may be frosted with a creamy buttercream or glazed with a sugar syrup. And because the cupcake batter contains three or four eggs, the texture is soft and spongy and the tops are smooth, all of which is possible because cupcakes bake more slowly and evenly at 350°F. It's up to you whether you place paper liners in a cupcake pan before pouring in the batter. Liners make cleanup easier, and also make transporting the cupcakes less messy.

BUTTER PECAN BANANA MUFFINS

· · · · ·

With pecans on the bottom and pecans on top, these moist, crunchy muffins are a great do-ahead treat for breakfast or brunch. Lined up on a silver platter—or even on a paper plate—they are ready to be enjoyed after a quick dusting of confectioners' sugar.

Vegetable oil spray for misting the pans
1 package (18.25 ounces) plain butterscotch
*   cake mix (see "the Cupcake Doctor says")*
1 package (3.4 ounces) instant
*   butterscotch pudding mix*
1 medium-size banana, mashed (1 cup)

¾ cup buttermilk or water
¼ cup vegetable oil
4 large eggs
1 cup finely chopped pecans
1 tablespoon sifted confectioners' sugar,
*   for sprinkling on top*

1. Place a rack in the center of the oven and preheat the oven to 400°F. Mist the bottom of 16 muffin cups with the vegetable oil spray. Set the pans aside.

2. Place the cake mix and pudding mix in a large mixing bowl and make a well in the center. Place the mashed banana, buttermilk, oil, and eggs in a small mixing bowl and stir with a fork to break up the yolks. Pour the wet and dry banana mixture into the well in the cake mixture. Stir the ingredients together with a wooden spoon until well combined, 30 strokes. Sprinkle a teaspoon of pecans into the bottom of each oiled muffin cup. Spoon or scoop ⅓ cup batter into each cup, filling it three quarters of the way full. Sprinkle the

✿ **MAKES 16 MUFFINS (2½ INCHES EACH)**
✿ **PREPARATION TIME: 12 MINUTES**
✿ **BAKING TIME: 17 TO 20 MINUTES**

the Cupcake Doctor says...

If you have trouble finding a butter-scotch cake mix, you can use a plain yellow cake mix instead. Or omit the pudding mix and substitute a butter pecan cake mix that has pudding in it.

remaining pecans evenly over the tops of the muffins and place the pans in the oven.

3. Bake the muffins until the pecans have browned and the muffins just spring back when lightly pressed with your finger, 17 to 20 minutes. Remove the pans from the oven and place them on a wire rack to cool for 5 minutes. Run a dinner knife around the edges of the muffins, lift them up from the bottom of the cups using the end of the knife, and pick them out of the cups carefully with your fingertips. Place them on a wire rack to cool for 15 minutes. Dust with confectioners' sugar, and the muffins are ready to serve.

✿ *Store these muffins, without the confectioners' sugar garnish, in a cake saver or under a glass dome, at room temperature for up to 5 days or freeze them, wrapped in aluminum foil or in a cake saver, for up to 6 months. Thaw the muffins overnight in the refrigerator. Garnish with confectioners' sugar before serving.*

You're the Tops

▼ ▼ ▼

Love the crunchy top of a muffin? Mist the bottoms of the muffin cups and also the flat top of the pan with oil. Overfill the pan so that the batter reaches nearly to the top. Bake at 350°F so the muffins have a chance to rise slowly and spread. The muffins will bake up tall and spread onto the top of the pan, creating a big-top look. Remove the pan from the oven and let the muffins rest in the pan for 2 to 3 minutes, then with a serrated knife and using the pan as a level, slice off the top of the muffin. Remove it carefully to a rack to cool or to a plate and serve. Serve the muffin bottoms separately.

RAISIN AND BRAN MUFFINS

· · · · ·

A good bran muffin remains one of my favorite snacks. It is the muffin I buy at the airport before a flight. It is the muffin I bake for breakfast Monday through Friday. So I need a recipe that delivers, because nothing is worse than bad bran muffins—horrid, dry creatures no one will go near. I have experimented with countless recipes over the years, and I am delighted to share this simple and good one, which has only five ingredients.

❀ MAKES 6 MUFFINS (2½ INCHES EACH)
❀ PREPARATION TIME: 10 MINUTES
❀ BAKING TIME: 16 TO 19 MINUTES

Vegetable oil spray for misting the pan
1 package (7 ounces) bran muffin mix
  (see "the Cupcake Doctor says")
1 cup sweetened bran flake cereal
  with raisins
1 cup buttermilk
¼ cup vegetable oil
1 large egg

1. Place a rack in the center of the oven and preheat the oven to 400°F. Mist the bottom of 6 muffin cups with the vegetable oil spray. Set the pan aside.

2. Place the muffin mix and cereal in a large mixing bowl and make a well in the center. Place the buttermilk, oil, and egg in the well and stir with a fork to combine and break up the egg yolk. Stir the wet and dry ingredients together with a wooden spoon just until combined, 20 strokes. Let the batter rest in the bowl to soften the bran flakes, 5 minutes.

3. Spoon or scoop ⅓ cup batter into each prepared muffin cup, filling it three quarters of the way full. Place the pan in the oven.

4. Bake the muffins until they are lightly golden and just spring back when lightly pressed with your finger, 16 to 19 minutes. Remove the pan from the oven and place it on a wire rack to cool for 5 minutes. Run a dinner knife around the edges of the muffins, lift them up from the bottom of the pan using

the end of the knife, and pick them out of the cups carefully with your fingertips. Place them on a wire rack to cool for 15 minutes. The muffins are ready to serve.

✿ *Store these muffins, in a cake saver or under a glass dome, at room temperature for up to 5 days or freeze them, wrapped in aluminum foil or in a cake saver, for up to 6 months. Thaw the muffins overnight in the refrigerator before serving.*

5 *Things to Fold into a Bran Muffin Batter:*

▼ ▼ ▼

Add some more pizzazz to a bran muffin without changing the baking time or yield.

1. 1 cup of your favorite granola cereal

2. ½ cup shredded carrots

3. 1 cup grated apple

4. ½ cup shredded zucchini

5. ⅓ cup finely chopped prunes or yellow raisins

GRATED APPLE AND GINGER BRAN MUFFINS

• • • • •

Some of my favorite pies and cakes have grated apple in the mix, and so do these muffins. A cupful adds an easy, homey touch. And a pinch of ginger or cinnamon or nutmeg—whatever suits you—gives a nice hint of spice. These muffins get better after resting on the counter a day before eating. Make them the night before serving, if possible.

✿ **MAKES 6 TO 7 MUFFINS (2½ INCHES EACH)**
✿ **PREPARATION TIME: 10 MINUTES**
✿ **BAKING TIME: 16 TO 19 MINUTES**

Vegetable oil spray for misting the pan
1 package (7 ounces) bran muffin mix
    (see "the Cupcake Doctor says")
1 cup sweetened bran flake cereal
    with raisins
2 tablespoons light brown sugar
½ teaspoon ground cinnamon
¼ teaspoon ground ginger
1 cup buttermilk
¼ cup vegetable oil
1 large egg
1 cup grated fresh apple (see
    "the Cupcake Doctor says")

1. Place a rack in the center of the oven and preheat the oven to 400°F. Mist the bottom of 6 muffin cups with the vegetable oil spray. Set the pan aside.

2. Place the muffin mix, cereal, brown sugar, cinnamon, and ginger in a large mixing bowl and make a well in the center.

the Cupcake Doctor says...

I used a Hodgson Mill bran muffin mix in testing this recipe. Grate a rinsed, unpeeled apple with a coarse shredder. One medium apple will yield about 1 cup grated apple. The recipe can be doubled easily.

Place the buttermilk, oil, and egg in the well and stir with a fork to combine and break up the egg yolk. Add the grated apple and stir the wet and dry ingredients together with a wooden spoon just until combined, 20 strokes. Let the batter rest in the bowl to soften the bran flakes, 5 minutes.

3. Spoon or scoop ⅓ cup batter into each prepared muffin cup, filling it three quarters of the way full. If you have extra batter, mist another muffin cup with vegetable oil spray and spoon in the remaining batter. Place the pan in the oven.

4. Bake the muffins until they are lightly golden and just spring back when lightly pressed with your finger, 16 to 19 minutes. Remove the pan from the oven and place it on a wire rack to cool for 5 minutes. Run a dinner knife around the edges of the muffins, lift them up from the bottoms of the cups using the end of the knife, and pick them out of the cups carefully with your fingertips. Place them on a wire rack to cool for 15 minutes. The muffins are ready to serve, but will taste even better if allowed to rest for at least a few hours more.

✿ *Store these muffins, in a cake saver or under a glass dome, at room temperature for up to 5 days or freeze them, wrapped in aluminum foil or in a cake saver, for up to 6 months. Thaw the muffins overnight in the refrigerator before serving.*

EASY GRANOLA MUFFINS

· · · · ·

You need little more than a package of muffin mix and your favorite granola to make these fast muffins. My children like Quaker granola with coconut in it, but you can suit yourself and add whatever is in your cupboard. Or buy several kinds of granola for sampling and use in baking. When my family gets bored with the same old breakfast cereal, we jazz things up by adding a sprinkling of granola with toasted sunflower seeds and sun-dried cherries, or granola with cinnamon and coconut, or granola with toasted pecans and dried peaches. They are all delicious in this recipe.

Vegetable oil spray for misting the pan
1 package (19.1 ounces) cinnamon swirl
    muffin mix
1¼ cups milk
1 large egg
1½ cups granola cereal

1. Place a rack in the center of the oven and preheat the oven to 400°F. Mist the bottom of 12 muffin cups with the vegetable oil spray. Set the pan aside.

✿ **MAKES 12 MUFFINS (2½ INCHES EACH)**
✿ **PREPARATION TIME: 12 MINUTES**
✿ **BAKING TIME: 20 TO 22 MINUTES**

2. Place the muffin mix in a large mixing bowl and make a well in the center. Place the contents of the cinnamon swirl packet, the milk, egg, and 1 cup of granola in the well of the muffin mix. Save the cinnamon sugar packet (see box, below) to use as a topping, if desired. Stir the wet and dry ingredients together with a fork to break up the egg yolks, then stir just until combined, 20 strokes. The batter will still be a little lumpy. Spoon or scoop ⅓ cup batter into each prepared muffin cup, filling it three quarters of the way full. Sprinkle the remaining granola over the tops of the muffins, patting the granola into the batter lightly with your fingers. If desired, sprinkle the reserved cinnamon sugar packet from the mix over the tops as well. Place the pan in the oven.

3. Bake the muffins until they are lightly golden and just spring back when lightly pressed with your finger, 20 to 22 minutes. Remove the pan from the oven and place it on a wire rack to cool for 5 minutes. Run a dinner knife around the edges of the muffins, lift them up from the bottoms of the cups using the end of the

Nut-Free Topping
▾ ▾ ▾

When reviewing the contents of the cinnamon swirl muffin mix that I use in several recipes in this chapter, I was surprised to read that the cinnamon sugar packet included with the mix contained crushed pecans. It reminded me how important it is to check the ingredient listing on the box to make sure there's nothing unexpected—like those nuts—that may cause problems for people with allergies. If anyone in your family has nut allergies, here's a nut-free topping that makes a great finishing touch on muffins.

Mix together ½ cup granulated sugar, 1 teaspoon cinnamon, ⅓ cup oats, 1 tablespoon flour, and 2 tablespoons room-temperature butter. Sprinkle it over the muffins before baking.

To make plain cinnamon sugar, mix ½ cup sugar and 1 teaspoon cinnamon and measure out the necessary amount (if substituting for the amount in the packet, measure it and use it as a guide). Store any extra in a small storage container.

knife, and pick them out of the cups care-fully with your fingertips. Place them on a wire rack to cool for 15 minutes. The muffins are ready to serve.

✿ *Store these muffins, in a cake saver or under a glass dome, at room temperature for up to 5 days or freeze them, wrapped in aluminum foil or in a cake saver, for up to 6 months. Thaw the muffins overnight in the refrigerator before serving.*

the Cupcake Doctor says...

Granola is plenty sweet, so I don't think you need to sprinkle the cin-namon sugar mixture over the top of these muffins before baking. But should you not want to waste ingre-dients, go ahead! Or save it to use when making cinnamon toast.

GREEN CHILE AND CORN MINI MUFFINS

• • • • •

I love these moist little corn muffins, full of Cheddar cheese and chile peppers. They are perfect with a bowl of chili, and the leftovers hold up well in a plastic bag in the freezer. Once you've tried the basic version, you can shake things up a bit by making one of the variations that follow. Whoever thought you could get so much flavor from a small box of corn muffin mix?

Vegetable oil spray for misting the pans
1 package (8.5 ounces) corn muffin mix
1 can (8.25 ounces) cream-style corn
1 can (4.5 ounces) chopped green chiles
1 large egg
1 cup shredded Cheddar cheese
1 fresh jalapeño pepper, seeded and
*   chopped (about 1 tablespoon)*

1. Place a rack in the center of the oven and preheat the oven to 400°F. Mist the bottom of 30 miniature muffin cups with the vegetable oil spray. Set the pans aside.

2. Place the muffin mix in a large mixing bowl and make a well in the center. Place the corn, chiles, egg, cheese, and pepper in a small mixing bowl. Stir to combine and break up the egg yolk. Pour the corn mixture into the well of the muffin mix. Stir the wet and dry ingredients together with a wooden spoon just until combined, 20 strokes. The batter will still be a little lumpy. Spoon or scoop 2 tablespoons batter into each prepared muffin cup, filling it three quarters of the way full. Place the pans in the oven.

3. Bake the muffins until they are lightly golden and just spring back when lightly

✿ **MAKES 30 MUFFINS (2 INCHES EACH)**
✿ **PREPARATION TIME: 10 MINUTES**
✿ **BAKING TIME: 17 TO 20 MINUTES**

pressed with your finger, 17 to 20 minutes. Remove the pans from the oven and place them on a wire rack to cool for 5 minutes. Run a dinner knife around the edges of the muffins, lift them up from the bottoms of the cups using the end of the knife, and pick them out of the cups carefully with your fingertips. Place them on a wire rack to cool for 15 minutes. The muffins are ready to serve.

✿ *Store these muffins, in a cake saver or under a glass dome, at room temperature for up to 5 days or freeze them, wrapped in aluminum foil or in a cake saver, for up to 6 months. Thaw the muffins overnight in the refrigerator before serving.*

VARIATIONS:

All of these variations use 1 package (8.5 ounces) corn muffin mix and make 30 mini muffins.

✿ **BACON CHEDDAR MINI CORN MUFFINS:** Slowly cook 1 cup chopped onions in 2 tablespoons vegetable oil or bacon grease until soft and golden brown, 8 to 10 minutes. Let cool and fold this into the corn muffin mix along with ½ cup sour cream, 1 large egg, ⅓ cup chopped cooked bacon, and 1 cup shredded sharp Cheddar cheese. Mix and bake as directed.

---

the Cupcake Doctor says...

You can use whatever fresh hot chile pepper you have on hand. And you can also use jack cheese instead of Cheddar, if you like.

✿ **PIMENTO CHEESE MINI CORN MUFFINS:** Add an undrained 2-ounce jar of diced pimento peppers, 1 cup shredded sharp Cheddar cheese, ½ cup sour cream, 1 large egg, ¼ teaspoon coarsely ground black pepper, and ¼ teaspoon dry mustard to the muffin mix. Mix and bake as directed.

✿ **BLUE CHEESE-WALNUT MINI CORN MUFFINS:** Add ½ cup sour cream, 1 large egg, 1 cup crumbled blue cheese, ½ cup chopped walnuts, and ¼ cup water to the corn muffin mix. Mix and bake as directed.

✿ **GARLIC-HERB CREAM CHEESE MINI CORN MUFFINS:** Combine a 6.5-ounce container of garlic- and herb-flavored cream cheese spread, 1 large egg, and ⅓ cup milk. Add to the corn muffin mix, along with 3 tablespoons chopped fresh parsley, oregano, or thyme, and ½ teaspoon black pepper. Mix and bake as directed.

FRESH CHERRY AND CORN MUFFINS

• • • • •

I had no idea that fresh sweet cherries could be such a great partner for cornmeal. Raised in the South, we never added sugar to corn muffins, and my ancestors would have thought it disrespectful to combine something as frivolous as sweet cherries with their revered cornmeal. But I remember seeing a recipe like this in a magazine and thinking "I'm going to try that some-day." What a treat these cherries are when baked up and plump. I also sweetened the muffins with brown sugar and added a little orange juice. They're great for breakfasts on the go.

Vegetable oil spray for misting the pan
2½ cups self-rising cornmeal mix
    (see "the Cupcake Doctor says")
¾ cup packed light brown sugar
½ cup buttermilk or milk
½ cup orange juice
¼ cup vegetable oil
1 large egg
½ cup pitted and chopped fresh sweet
    cherries (about 16 cherries)
    (see "the Cupcake Doctor says")

✿ **MAKES 10 MUFFINS (2½ INCHES EACH)**
✿ **PREPARATION TIME: 10 MINUTES**
✿ **BAKING TIME: 15 TO 18 MINUTES**

1. Place a rack in the center of the oven and preheat the oven to 400°F. Mist the bottom of 10 muffin cups with the vegetable oil spray. Set the pan aside.

2. Place the cornmeal mix and brown sugar in a large mixing bowl and stir to mix. Make a well in the center. Place the buttermilk, orange juice, oil, and egg in a small mixing bowl and stir to combine and break up the egg yolk. Pour the buttermilk mixture into the well of the muffin mix. Stir the wet and dry ingredients with a wooden spoon, just until combined, 10 strokes. Fold the chopped cherries into the batter and stir another 10 strokes, until just combined. Spoon or scoop ⅓ cup batter into each prepared muffin cup, filling it three quarters of the way full. Place the pan in the oven.

3. Bake the muffins until they are lightly golden and just spring back when lightly pressed with your finger, 15 to 18 minutes. Remove the pan from the oven and place it on a wire rack to cool for 5 minutes. Run a dinner knife around the edges

the Cupcake Doctor says...

Self-rising cornmeal mix is a blend of cornmeal, baking powder, salt, and a little flour. It makes a softer muffin than are made from cornmeal. You can substitute 2 cups self-rising cornmeal mixed with ½ cup all-purpose flour. No fresh cherries? Use fresh blueberries instead.

of the muffins, lift them up from the bottoms of the cups using the end of the knife, and pick them out of the cups carefully with your fingertips. Place them on a wire rack to cool for 15 minutes. The muffins are ready to serve.

✿ *Store these muffins, in a cake saver or under a glass dome, at room temperature for up to 5 days or freeze them, wrapped in aluminum foil or in a cake saver, for up to 6 months. Thaw the muffins overnight in the refrigerator before serving.*

PUMPKIN CORN MAPLE MUFFINS

• • • • •

This recipe might sound a bit stodgy, what with the pumpkin and the cornmeal, but let me tell you that the traditional flavors of the Northeast have never been combined to complement each other so well. Pumpkin is a perfect addition to corn muffins—it doesn't overwhelm with strong color or flavor; it just provides a lot of moistness. And the hint of maple makes you wish the muffins would never end. Cornmeal creates muffins sturdy enough to be good travelers, should you want to tote them somewhere. Serve alongside white rolls for a Thanksgiving buffet, or slice and sandwich with ham or turkey for a picnic in the park. The possibilities are endless!

☘ MAKES 12 MUFFINS (2½ INCHES EACH)
☘ PREPARATION TIME: 15 MINUTES
☘ BAKING TIME: 15 TO 18 MINUTES

Vegetable oil spray for misting the pan
2 cups self-rising cornmeal mix
    (see "the Cupcake Doctor says,"
    page 241)
½ cup packed light brown sugar
¼ teaspoon ground ginger
¼ teaspoon ground cinnamon
1 cup canned pumpkin
1 cup milk
¼ cup vegetable oil
1 large egg
1 teaspoon maple flavoring
3 tablespoons coarse sugar
    (see "the Cupcake Doctor says")

1. Place a rack in the center of the oven and preheat the oven to 400°F. Mist the bottom of 12 muffin cups with the vegetable oil spray. Set the pan aside.

2. Place the cornmeal mix, brown sugar, ginger, and cinnamon in a large mixing bowl and stir to mix. Make a well in the center. Place the pumpkin, milk, oil, egg, and maple flavoring in a small mixing bowl and stir to combine and break up the egg yolk. Pour the pumpkin mixture into the well of the muffin mix. Stir the wet and dry ingredients together with a wooden spoon, just until combined, 20 to 25 strokes. Spoon or scoop ⅓ cup batter into each prepared muffin cup, filling it three quarters of the way full. Sprinkle the coarse sugar on top of the muffins. Place the pan in the oven.

3. Bake the muffins until they are lightly golden and just spring back when lightly pressed with your finger, 15 to 18 minutes. Remove the pan from the oven and

the Cupcake Doctor says...

Use coarse decorating sugar or turbinado sugar, which is a coarse, raw, tan-colored sugar, on top of these muffins for a fun, finishing crunch.

place it on a wire rack to cool for 5 minutes. Run a dinner knife around the edges of the muffins, lift them up from the bottoms of the cups using the end of the knife, and pick them out of the cups carefully with your fingertips. Place them on a wire rack to cool for 15 minutes. The muffins are ready to serve.

✿ *Store these muffins, in a cake saver or under a glass dome, at room temperature for up to 5 days or freeze them, wrapped in aluminum foil or in a cake saver, for up to 6 months. Thaw the muffins overnight in the refrigerator before serving.*

DOUBLE LEMON POPPY SEED CHEESECAKE MUFFINS

• • • • •

Many of us have a weakness for cheesecake—I know I do. I adore the creaminess and the way it mellows the sweetness of an accompanying dessert sauce. In this recipe, the creamy cheesecake topping with lemon zest offers the perfect foil to a sweet lemon-scented poppy seed muffin. If you enjoy the cheesecake touch in this recipe, you'll want to try the Carrot Cake Muffins on page 254, too.

✿ **MAKES 12 MUFFINS (2½ INCHES EACH)**
✿ **PREPARATION TIME: 15 MINUTES**
✿ **BAKING TIME: 20 TO 22 MINUTES**

*Vegetable oil spray for misting
   the pan*
*1 package (8 ounces) cream cheese,
   at room temperature*
1 large egg
¼ cup sugar
1 teaspoon grated fresh lemon zest
½ teaspoon pure vanilla extract
*1 package (15.8 ounces) lemon
   poppy seed muffin mix*
1 cup milk
¼ cup vegetable oil
1 large egg

I. Place a rack in the center of the oven and preheat the oven to 400°F. Mist the bottom of 12 muffin cups with the vegetable oil spray. Set the pan aside.

2. Prepare the cheesecake filling: Place the cream cheese, egg, sugar, lemon zest, and vanilla in a large mixing bowl. Blend with an electric mixer on low speed until the mixture is creamy, 1 minute. Set aside.

3. Prepare the muffin batter: Place the muffin mix in a large mixing bowl and make a well in the center. Place the milk, oil, and egg in the well and stir the wet ingredients with a fork to combine and break up the egg yolk. Stir the wet and dry ingredients together with a wooden spoon just until combined, 20 strokes. The batter will still be a little lumpy. Spoon or scoop ⅓ cup batter into each prepared muffin cup, filling it three quarters of the way full. Place a heaping tablespoon of the cream cheese mixture on top of each muffin. Place the pan in the oven.

4. Bake the muffins until they are golden and just spring back when lightly pressed with your finger, 20 to 22 minutes. Remove the pan from the oven and place it on a wire rack to cool for 5 minutes. Run a dinner knife around

the Cupcake Doctor says...

I found that the Betty Crocker lemon poppy seed muffin mix worked well in this recipe.

the edges of the muffins, lift them up from the bottom of the cups using the end of the knife, and pick them out of the cups carefully with your fingertips. Place them on a wire rack to cool for 15 minutes. The muffins are ready to serve.

✿ *Store these muffins, in a cake saver or under a glass dome, at room temperature for up to 2 days or in the refrigerator for up to 5 days, or freeze them, wrapped in aluminum foil or in a cake saver, for up to 6 months. Thaw the muffins overnight in the refrigerator before serving.*

LEMON BUTTER MUFFINS

WITH A LEMON GLAZE

• • • • •

On a spring weekend morning, what could be nicer than a pan of these lemony muffins fresh from the oven? They're delicious with a cup of hot tea. Children love them, too, especially when glazed with milk rather than with lemon juice. However, I prefer the pucker-up quality of a double the dose of lemon.

✿ **MAKES 12 MUFFINS (2½ INCHES EACH)**
✿ **PREPARATION TIME: 20 MINUTES**
✿ **BAKING TIME: 18 TO 20 MINUTES**

Vegetable oil spray for misting the pan

MUFFINS:
6 tablespoons (¾ stick) unsalted butter,
*   at room temperature*
½ cup granulated sugar
1 large egg
1 cup milk
1 large lemon, zested and juiced
*   (see "the Cupcake Doctor says")*
2 cups self-rising flour

GLAZE:
½ cup confectioners' sugar
1 to 2 tablespoons lemon juice or
*   milk (see "the Cupcake*
*   Doctor says")*
1 teaspoon grated fresh
*   lemon zest,*
*   reserved from the*
*   lemon above*

1. Place a rack in the center of the oven and preheat the oven to 400°F. Mist the bottom of 12 muffin cups with the vegetable oil spray. Set the pan aside.

2. Prepare the muffin batter: Place the butter and sugar in a large mixing bowl. Blend with an electric mixer on medium-high speed until the mixture is creamy, 30 seconds. Add the egg, milk, 3 tablespoons lemon juice, and 1 teaspoon lemon zest (reserve the rest for the glaze) and blend on low speed just until combined, 30 seconds. Stop the machine and scrape down the sides of the bowl with a rubber spatula. Fold in the flour with a wooden spoon or the rubber spatula, 25 strokes. The batter will still be a little lumpy. Spoon or scoop ¼ cup batter into each prepared muffin cup, filling it two thirds of the way full. Place the pan in the oven.

3. Bake the muffins until they are lightly golden and just spring back when lightly pressed with your finger, 18 to 20 minutes. Remove the pan from the oven and place it on a wire rack to cool for 5 minutes. Run a dinner knife around the edges of the muffins, lift them up from the bottoms of the cups using the end of the knife, and pick them out of the cups carefully with your fingertips. Place them on a wire rack to cool for 15 minutes before glazing.

4. Meanwhile, prepare the glaze: Place

the Cupcake Doctor says...

A large lemon will yield about 3 tablespoons juice and about 2 teaspoons grated zest. If you add lemon juice to the glaze, you will need to juice an additional lemon. It's easier to zest a scrubbed lemon first, using a handy Microplane zester, then cut it in half and squeeze it over a small strainer, extracting as much juice as possible. If the lemon is hard, roll it firmly against the counter to make juicing easier.

the confectioners' sugar in a small mixing bowl and whisk in 1 tablespoon of either the lemon juice or milk. Add more lemon juice or milk, 1 teaspoon at a time, if needed, to make the mixture pourable from a spoon. Stir in the lemon zest.

5. When the muffins have cooled, spoon a teaspoon of glaze over each muffin and let them rest a few minutes for the glaze to set. The muffins are ready to serve.

❀ *Store these muffins, in a cake saver or under a glass dome, at room temperature for up to 5 days or freeze them, wrapped in aluminum foil or in a cake saver, for up to 6 months. Thaw the muffins overnight in the refrigerator before serving.*

FRESH CRANBERRY ORANGE CINNAMON MUFFINS

• • • • •

Some ideas for recipes just fall together beautifully, and others, well, once you start testing them, they try your patience. This was one of those problem recipes, which I tried a half dozen times before I got it right. I knew I wanted the flavors of orange and cranberry, but what type of cranberry? Dried? Canned sauce? Neither. It turns out that fresh cranberries work best. The cinnamon muffin mix adds just the right background so the cranberries can be front and center. A tablespoon of freshly grated orange zest rounds it all out. Enjoy!

Vegetable oil spray for misting the pan
1 package (15.2 ounces) cinnamon
     streusel muffin mix
     (see "the Cupcake Doctor says")
1 container (6 ounces; ¾ cup) smooth yogurt
     of your choice (without fruit)
1 large egg
2 tablespoons oil or melted butter
1 tablespoon grated fresh orange zest
     (see "the Cupcake Doctor says")
1 cup fresh cranberries, rinsed and
     patted dry (see "the Cupcake
     Doctor says")

❀ **MAKES 12 MUFFINS (2½ INCHES EACH)**
❀ **PREPARATION TIME: 10 MINUTES**
❀ **BAKING TIME: 20 TO 23 MINUTES**

1. Place a rack in the center of the oven and preheat the oven to 400°F. Mist the bottom of 12 muffin cups with the vegetable oil spray. Set the pan aside.

2. Place the muffin mix and the contents of the streusel package in a large mixing bowl and make a well in the center. Place the yogurt, egg, oil, and orange zest in the well and stir the wet ingredients with a fork to combine and break up the yolk. Stir the wet and dry ingredients together with a wooden spoon, just until combined, 10 strokes. Fold in the cranberries and stir another 10 strokes just to combine. The batter will still be a little lumpy. Spoon or scoop ⅓ cup batter into each prepared muffin cup, filling it three quarters of the way full. Place the pan in the oven.

3. Bake the muffins until they are lightly golden and just spring back when lightly pressed with your finger, 20 to 23 minutes. Remove the pan from the oven and place it on a wire rack to cool for 5 minutes. Run a dinner knife around the edges of the muffins, lift them up from the bottoms of the cups using the end of the knife, and pick them out of the cups carefully with your fingertips. Place them on a wire rack to cool for 15 minutes. The muffins are ready to serve.

✿ *Store these muffins, in a cake saver or under a glass dome, at room temperature for up to 5 days or freeze them, wrapped in aluminum foil or in a cake saver, for up to 6 months. Thaw the muffins overnight in the refrigerator before serving.*

---

the Cupcake Doctor says...

Betty Crocker makes a cinnamon streusel muffin mix with cinnamon bits you fold in. I like Microplane zesters for scraping the zest cleanly off an orange or lemon. And remember that cranberries are easily frozen. Buy several bags while they are in season, and pop them in the freezer for future baking. They'll keep frozen for up to six months.

SWEET POTATO CASSEROLE MUFFINS

Why wait until Thanksgiving dinner to enjoy the flavors of sweet potato casserole? In this muffin you'll find sweet potatoes, cinnamon, nutmeg, and pecans. If you like, you can top them with miniature marshmallows. These are hearty muffins, perfect for packing and taking to the mountains or for serving at a cold-weather brunch alongside eggs.

❀ **MAKES 12 TO 15 MUFFINS (2½ INCHES EACH)**
❀ **PREPARATION TIME: 15 MINUTES**
❀ **BAKING TIME: 20 TO 23 MINUTES**

Vegetable oil spray for misting the pans

*1 package (19.1 ounces) cinnamon
    swirl muffin mix (see "the Cupcake
    Doctor says")*

*1 can (15 ounces) canned sweet potatoes
    or yams, drained and mashed*

¾ cup milk

2 tablespoons butter, melted

1 large egg

1 tablespoon grated fresh orange zest

¼ teaspoon ground nutmeg

½ cup chopped pecans

*½ cup miniature marshmallows
    (optional; see "the Cupcake
    Doctor says")*

I. Place a rack in the center of the oven and preheat the oven to 400°F. Mist the bottom of 12 to 15 muffin cups with the vegetable oil spray. Set the pans aside.

2. Place the muffin mix in a large mixing bowl and make a well in the center. Reserve the cinnamon sugar packet (see "the Cupcake Doctor says") to sprinkle on top of the muffins. Place the sweet potatoes, the contents of the cinnamon swirl packet, the milk, melted butter, egg, orange zest, and nutmeg in a medium-size mixing bowl and stir with a fork to combine and break up the egg yolk. Pour the sweet potato mixture into the well of the muffin mix. Stir the wet and dry ingredients together with a wooden spoon until just combined, 20 strokes. The batter will still be a little lumpy. Spoon or scoop ⅓ cup batter into each prepared muffin cup, filling it three quarters of the way full. Sprinkle the pecans and reserved cinnamon and sugar mixture on top. Place the pans in the oven.

3. Bake the muffins until they are lightly golden and just spring back when lightly pressed with your finger, 20 to 23 minutes. Remove the pans from the oven and place them on a wire rack to cool for

the Cupcake Doctor says...

For a totally fun look and a delicious sweet potato casserole flavor, press a few mini marshmallows gently onto the top of each muffin during the last few minutes of baking.

The muffin mix I used comes with both a cinnamon swirl packet and a cinnamon sugar packet inside. It is made by Duncan Hines.

5 minutes. Run a dinner knife around the edges of the muffins, lift them up from the bottoms of the cups using the end of the knife, and pick them out of the cups carefully with your fingertips. Place them on a wire rack to cool for 15 minutes. The muffins are ready to serve.

✿ *Store these muffins, in a cake saver or under a glass dome, at room temperature for up to 2 days or in the refrigerator for up to 5 days. Or freeze them, wrapped in aluminum foil or in a cake saver, for up to 6 months. Thaw the muffins overnight in the refrigerator before serving.*

PUMPKIN MUFFINS

WITH CHOCOLATE CHIPS

• • • • •

Many of you know I'll look for any way to sneak a few chocolate chips into my baking. I am a chocoholic, I admit. But in all fairness, pumpkin and chocolate meld together beautifully. And it is doubly nice that this great-tasting muffin recipe, calling for just five ingredients, is also a snap to prepare. You can dust the tops with a litte confectioners' sugar, but it really isn't necessary.

✿ **MAKES 12 MUFFINS (2½ INCHES EACH)**
✿ **PREPARATION TIME: 10 MINUTES**
✿ **BAKING TIME: 20 TO 22 MINUTES**

the Cupcake Doctor says...

For a dressy appearance, add a sprinkling of powdered sugar mixed with cocoa powder after the muffins have cooled.

I used a Duncan Hines muffin mix in this recipe and a can of pure pumpkin, not pumpkin pie filling.

Vegetable oil spray for misting the pan
1 package (17.8 ounces) chocolate chip muffin mix (see "the Cupcake Doctor says")
1 cup canned pumpkin
½ cup milk
1 large egg
½ teaspoon pumpkin pie spice

1. Place a rack in the center of the oven and preheat the oven to 400°F. Mist the bottom of 12 muffin cups with the vegetable oil spray. Set the pan aside.

Jazzing Up Muffin Mixes

▼ ▼ ▼

Match your mix with some compatible add-ins.

✿ Corn: cherries, blueberries, pumpkin, or cranberries

✿ Blueberry: cinnamon (1/4 to 1/2 teaspoon) and oats

✿ Bran: honey, raisins, and buttermilk

✿ Lemon: other fruit such as blackberries and blueberries

✿ Pumpkin: cinnamon (1/4 to 1/2 teaspoon) and nutmeg (1/4 teaspoon), or chocolate chips

2. Place the muffin mix in a large mixing bowl and make a well in the center. Place the pumpkin, milk, egg, and pumpkin pie spice in the well and stir the wet ingredients with a fork to combine and break up the egg yolk. Stir the wet and dry ingredients together with a wooden spoon just until combined, 20 strokes. The batter will still be a little lumpy. Spoon or scoop 1/3 cup batter into each prepared muffin cup, filling it three quarters of the way full. Place the pan in the oven.

3. Bake the muffins until they just spring back when lightly pressed with your finger, 20 to 22 minutes. Remove the pan from the oven and place it on a wire rack to cool for 5 minutes. Run a dinner knife around the edges of the muffins, lift them up from the bottoms of the cups using the end of the knife, and pick them out of the cups carefully with your fingertips. Place them on a wire rack to cool for 15 minutes. The muffins are ready to serve.

✿ *Store these muffins, in a cake saver or under a glass dome, at room temperature for up to 5 days or freeze them, wrapped in aluminum foil or in a cake saver, for up to 6 months. Thaw the muffins overnight in the refrigerator before serving.*

CARROT CAKE MUFFINS

WITH A CREAM CHEESE SURPRISE

• • • • •

At our house, if you leave these muffins on the kitchen counter they will be gone in minutes. Not only do we love carrot cake, but we also love cheesecake. And those two flavors come together in this stupendous recipe. It is based on a cinnamon swirl muffin mix to which you add shredded carrots and a touch of maple flavoring. A dollop of the cream cheese topping is the nicest surprise, reminiscent of cream cheese frosting.

✿ **MAKES 12 MUFFINS (2½ INCHES EACH)**
✿ **PREPARATION TIME: 20 MINUTES**
✿ **BAKING TIME: 18 TO 20 MINUTES**

Vegetable oil spray for misting the pan

CREAM CHEESE SURPRISE:
4 ounces cream cheese, at room temperature
*   (see "the Cupcake Doctor says")*
1 egg, beaten
1 tablespoon sugar
½ teaspoon pure vanilla extract

MUFFINS:
1 package (19.1 ounces) cinnamon
*   swirl muffin mix*
½ cup milk
¼ cup vegetable oil
1 large egg
1 teaspoon maple flavoring
1 cup shredded carrots (about 3 medium-size;
*   see "the Cupcake Doctor says")*

1. Place a rack in the center of the oven and preheat the oven to 400°F. Mist the bottom of 12 muffin cups with the vegetable oil spray. Set the pan aside.

2. Prepare the creasm cheese surprise: Place the cream cheese in a medium-size mixing bowl. Blend with an electric mixer on medium-high speed until it is fluffy, 30 seconds. Measure out 1 tablespoon of the beaten egg and add this to the cream cheese, along with the sugar and vanilla. Set the remaining beaten egg aside for the muffins. Blend the cream cheese mixture until creamy, 15 seconds more. Set the mixture aside.

3. Prepare the muffin batter: Place the muffin mix in a large mixing bowl and make a well in the center. Reserve the cinnamon sugar packet to sprinkle on top of the muffins. Place the contents of the cinnamon swirl packet, the milk, oil, egg, the remaining beaten egg, and the maple flavoring in the well of the muffin mix. Stir with a fork to combine and break up the egg yolk. Stir the wet and dry ingredients together with a wooden spoon just until combined, 20 strokes. Add the shredded carrots. Stir another 10 strokes just to combine. The bat-ter will still be a little lumpy. Spoon or scoop ⅓ cup batter into each prepared muffin cup, filling it three quarters of the way full. With the back of a teaspoon, make a small well in the center of each muffin, and dollop a teaspoon of cream cheese mixture into this well. Sprinkle the tops of the muffins with the reserved packet of cinnamon sugar (see box, page 236). Place the pan in the oven.

the Cupcake Doctor says...

If you want more Cream Cheese Surprise, simply use 8 ounces soft cream cheese, a whole beaten egg, 2 tablespoons sugar, and 1 teaspoon vanilla. Make a slightly deeper well in the center of each cupcake. Allow a minute or two extra baking time. Although pre-shredded carrots are convenient, they are not the best for this recipe. The pieces are long, tough, and get tangled in the batter. I like to use old-fashioned coarsely shredded carrots, grated by hand or with the help of a food processor.

4. Bake the muffins until they are deeply golden and just spring back when lightly pressed with your finger, 18 to 20 minutes. Remove the pan from the oven and place it on a wire rack to cool for 5 minutes. Run a dinner knife around the edges of the muffins, lift them up from the bottoms of the cups using the end of the knife, and pick them out of the cups carefully with your fingertips.

Place them on a wire rack to cool for 15 minutes. The muffins are ready to serve.

✿ *Store these muffins, in a cake saver or under a glass dome, at room temperature for up to 2 days or in the refrigerator for up to 5 days. Or freeze them, wrapped in aluminum foil or in a cake saver, for up to 6 months. Thaw the muffins overnight in the refrigerator before serving.*

ZUCCHINI SPICE MUFFINS

• • • • •

Shredded zucchini is an abundantly available ingredient in summer, when backyard gardens burst with the green squash. It seems as if you look in the garden one day and don't see any zucchini on the plants, but overnight they appear and swell and by the next morning they are torpedo size. The very large zucchini aren't fit for the sauté pan, but they are perfect for shredding and adding to cakes, cookies, and these cinnamon-scented muffins.

❁ **MAKES 12 MUFFINS (2½ INCHES EACH)**
❁ **PREPARATION TIME: 12 MINUTES**
❁ **BAKING TIME: 18 TO 20 MINUTES**

Vegetable oil spray for misting the pan
1 package (19.1 ounces) cinnamon swirl muffin mix (see "the Cupcake Doctor says")
1 packed cup shredded zucchini (see "the Cupcake Doctor says")
½ cup milk
1 large egg
¼ teaspoon ground nutmeg
½ cup finely chopped walnuts

1. Place a rack in the center of the oven and preheat the oven to 400°F. Mist the bottom of 12 muffin cups with the vegetable oil spray. Set the pan aside.

2. Place the muffin mix in a large mixing bowl and make a well in the center. Reserve the cinnamon sugar packet for sprinkling on top (see box, page 236) of the muffins. Place the contents of the cinnamon swirl packet, the zucchini, milk, egg, and nutmeg in the well and stir the wet ingredients with a fork to combine and

This muffin mix is made by Duncan Hines and it contains both a cinnamon swirl packet and a cinnamon sugar packet. If the shredded zucchini is watery, be sure to drain it well by placing it in a colander and pressing the liquid out with a fork.

break up the egg yolk. Stir the wet and dry ingredients together with a wooden spoon just until combined, 20 strokes. The batter will still be a little lumpy. Spoon or scoop ¼ cup batter into each prepared muffin cup, filling it two thirds of the way full. Sprinkle the reserved cinnamon sugar mixture and the finely chopped walnuts

evenly over the top of each muffin. Place the pan in the oven.

3. Bake the muffins until they just spring back when lightly pressed with your finger and the walnuts have toasted, 18 to 20 minutes. Remove the pan from the oven and place it on a wire rack to cool for 5 minutes. Run a dinner knife around the edges of the muffins, lift them up from the bottoms of the cups using the end of the knife, and pick them out of the cups carefully with your fingertips. Place them on a wire rack to cool for 15 minutes. The muffins are ready to serve.

✿ *Store these muffins, in a cake saver or under a glass dome, at room temperature for up to 5 days or freeze them, wrapped in aluminum foil or in a cake saver, for up to 6 months. Thaw the muffins overnight in the refrigerator before serving.*

CINNAMON APPLESAUCE LUNCHBOX MUFFINS

• • • • •

W hat children don't love a little something sweet packed in their lunchbox? For mine what really works best is a muffin. Cupcakes can be messy banging around in a child's lunchbox, but muffins are sturdy enough to handle the rough ride. They're fun to eat and garner a lot of "oohs" and "aahs" when they emerge from the plastic bag. And this muffin, made with applesauce and topped with

oats, should also meet the approval of moms everywhere.

MUFFINS:
Vegetable oil spray for misting the pan
1 package (19.1 ounces) cinnamon swirl
    muffin mix
1 cup unsweetened applesauce
1 large egg

STREUSEL TOPPING:
Cinnamon sugar packet from the mix
    (see box, page 236)
⅓ cup old-fashioned oats
1 tablespoon all-purpose flour
2 tablespoons butter, at room temperature

✿ **MAKES 12 MUFFINS (2½ INCHES EACH)**
✿ **PREPARATION TIME: 15 MINUTES**
✿ **BAKING TIME: 18 TO 20 MINUTES**

1. Place a rack in the center of the oven and preheat the oven to 400°F. Mist the bottom of 12 muffin cups with the vegetable oil spray. Set the pan aside.

~~~~~~~~~~~~~~~~~~~

the Cupcake Doctor says...

Old-fashioned oats give the topping the most crunch, but you can use quick-cooking or instant oatmeal as well.

~~~~~~~~~~~~~~~~~~~

2. Prepare the muffin batter: Place the muffin mix in a large mixing bowl and make a well in the center. Place the applesauce and egg in the well of the muffin mix. Stir them with a fork to combine and break up the egg yolk. Stir the wet and dry ingredients together with a wooden spoon just until combined, 20 strokes. The batter will still be a little lumpy. Spoon or scoop ¼ cup batter into each prepared muffin cup, filling it two thirds of the way full. Squeeze a small amount from the cinnamon swirl packet on top of each muffin. Using a small knife, gently swirl this into the batter. Set the pan aside.

3. Prepare the streusel topping: Place the contents of the cinnamon sugar packet the oats, flour, and butter in a small bowl and mash the butter into the sugar and flour with a fork until the mixture is crumbly. Sprinkle a heaping teaspoon of this mixture on top of each muffin. Place the pan in the oven.

4. Bake the muffins until they are lightly golden and just spring back when lightly pressed with your finger, 18 to 20 minutes. Remove the pan from the oven and place it on a wire rack to cool for 5 minutes. Run a dinner knife around the edges of the muffins, lift them up from the bottoms of the cups using the end of the knife, and pick them out of the cups carefully with your fingertips. Place them on a wire rack to cool for 15 minutes. The muffins are ready to serve.

✿ *Store these muffins, in a cake saver or under a glass dome, at room temperature for up to 5 days or freeze them, wrapped in aluminum foil or in a cake saver, for up to 6 months. Thaw the muffins overnight in the refrigerator before serving.*

LITTLE CHOCOLATE CHERRY MUFFINS

• • • • •

I bag up these little muffins, six to a sack, for valentine gifts. They're sweet enough, but not too sweet, to be enjoyed with coffee in the morning, and they can relieve that late-afternoon chocolate craving. You can also bake them in regular muffin pans, in which case you'll wind up with 12 muffins that take 18 to 20 minutes to bake.

❀ **MAKES 24 MINIATURE MUFFINS**
   (2 INCHES EACH)
❀ **PREPARATION TIME: 12 MINUTES**
❀ **BAKING TIME: 15 TO 17 MINUTES**

Vegetable oil spray for misting the pans
1 package (3 ounces; scant ½ cup) dried
    tart cherries
¾ cup water
1 package (20 ounces) chocolate muffin mix
    (see "the Cupcake Doctor says")
½ cup vegetable oil
2 large eggs
1 teaspoon pure vanilla or almond extract
½ cup or 1 cup semisweet chocolate chips
    (see "the Cupcake Doctor says")

1. Place a rack in the center of the oven and preheat the oven to 350°F. Mist the bottom of 24 miniature muffin cups with the vegetable oil spray. Set the pans aside.

2. Place the cherries and water in a small glass microwave-safe bowl and microwave on high power to soften, 30 seconds. Remove the bowl and set it aside.

3. Place the muffin mix in a large mixing bowl and make a well in the center. Place the cherries and water, oil, eggs, and

the Cupcake Doctor says...

The intensity of semisweet chocolate chips varies by brand. Nestlé
and Hershey's Chocolate Chips are
mild and sweet. Ghirardelli Double
Chocolate Baking Chips are more
deeply chocolate flavored. And semisweet Callebaut chips (called callets)
are a perfect balance of the two—
plus they are extra creamy and delicious for eating out of hand. If the
muffin mix already contains chocolate chips, as the Ghirardelli mix
does, just add ½ cup chips. If the
muffin mix doesn't contain chocolate
chips, add 1 cup.

vanilla or almond extract in the well. Stir
the wet ingredients with a fork to
combine and break up the egg
yolks. Stir the wet and dry
ingredients together with

a wooden spoon just until combined, 20
strokes. The batter will still be a little
lumpy. Fold in the chocolate chips. Spoon
or scoop 2 tablespoons batter into each
prepared muffin cup, filling it two thirds
of the way full. Place the pans in the oven.

4. Bake the muffins until they just spring
back when lightly pressed with your finger, 15 to 17 minutes. Remove the pans
from the oven and place them on wire
racks to cool for 5 minutes. Run a dinner
knife around the edges of the muffins, lift
them up from the bottoms of the cups
using the end of the knife, and pick them
out of the cups carefully with your fingertips. Place them on a wire rack to cool for
15 minutes. The muffins are ready to
serve.

✿ *Store these muffins, in a cake saver or
under a glass dome, at room temperature
for up to 5 days or freeze them, wrapped in
aluminum foil or in a cake saver, for up to 6
months. Thaw the muffins overnight in the
refrigerator before serving.*

BIG BAD CHOCOLATE MUFFINS

• • • • •

How could anything so good be called bad? Well, when you're talking about chocolate muffins that are this incredibly chocolatey, only the word "wicked"—in its most guilty pleasure usage—comes to mind. They're still muffins, mind you. Sturdy, structured, serious. But don't for a moment compare them to bran muffins. This is what you gobble down after a day on the tennis courts or in the garden. This is the muffin you pack for long car trips. This is one great muffin, big and bad.

Vegetable oil spray for misting the pans
1 package (18.25 ounces) plain devil's food cake mix
1 package (3.9 ounces) instant chocolate pudding mix
1 container (6 ounces; ¾ cup) low-fat vanilla yogurt
¾ cup water
½ cup vegetable oil
3 large eggs
2 cups semisweet chocolate chips

1. Place a rack in the center of the oven and preheat the oven to 400°F. Mist the bottom of 18 muffin cups with the vegetable oil spray. Set the pans aside.

2. Place the cake mix and pudding mix in a large mixing bowl and make a well in the center. Place the yogurt, water, oil, and

✿ **MAKES 18 MUFFINS (2½ INCHES EACH)**
✿ **PREPARATION TIME: 10 MINUTES**
✿ **BAKING TIME: 20 TO 24 MINUTES**

the Cupcake Doctor says...

For a deeper flavor, add 1 tablespoon espresso powder or 1 tablespoon strong brewed coffee to the batter along with the yogurt mixture.

eggs in a small mixing bowl and stir with a fork to break up the egg yolks. Pour the yogurt mixture into the well of the muffin mix. Stir the wet and dry ingredients together with a wooden spoon to just combine, 30 strokes. Fold in the chocolate chips and stir another 10 strokes until just combined. The batter will be smooth. Spoon or scoop ⅓ cup batter into each prepared muffin cup, filling it three quarters of the way full. Place the pans in the oven.

3. Bake the muffins until they just spring back when lightly pressed with your finger, 20 to 24 minutes. Remove the pans from the oven and place them on a wire rack to cool for 5 minutes. Run a dinner knife around the edges of the muffins, lift them up from the bottoms of the cups using the end of the knife, and pick them out of the cups carefully with your fingertips. Place them on a wire rack to cool for 15 minutes. The muffins are ready to serve.

✿ *Store these muffins, in a cake saver or under a glass dome, at room temperature for up to 5 days or freeze them, wrapped in aluminum foil or in a cake saver, for up to 6 months. Thaw the muffins overnight in the refrigerator before serving.*

5 Muffins to Munch at Lunch

▼ ▼ ▼

1. Blueberry Banana Muffins with a Pecan Crunch (page 224)

2. Pumpkin Corn Maple Muffins (page 242)

3. Sweet Potato Casserole Muffins (page 250)

4. Pumpkin Muffins with Chocolate Chips (page 252)

5. Big Bad Chocolate Muffins (page 263)

Muffin Know-how

Once you've been baking muffins for a while, you'll be able to look at the ingredient list of a recipe and tell right away what you need to do to mix up that muffin. If it contains butter, you first need to cream it with the sugar using an electric mixer, then add the egg and other wet ingredients, and fold in the flour at the end. One thing to remember about muffins from scratch: You don't want to overbeat them or they will become tough. Once you add the flour, that wooden spoon is all you need to mix. The batter will still appear lumpy, but it is ready to be spooned into the pan.

If the batter contains either vegetable oil or a fruit puree, you can simply blend that whole batter with a wooden spoon. Place the dry ingredients in a large mixing bowl and stir to combine. Create a well in the center of the ingredients. If you have just an egg and one or two other ingredients, place them in the well and stir to break up the yolk, then stir wet ingredients into the dry ingredients with 20 strokes of the spoon. If the wet ingredients are many, you might want to blend them together first in a smaller bowl, then pour the mixture into the well and use a total of 20 strokes to pull the batter together.

The exception to all this is when you make a muffin using a cake mix (that's a cake mix, *not* a muffin mix). Because these muffins are sweeter and contain more eggs, the flour is tenderized by the sugar, fat, and eggs, and you may use an electric mixer to blend the batter and not worry about tough muffins.

CHUNKY PEANUT BUTTER MUFFINS

• • • • •

What could be more tempting to a peanut fan than a peanut butter muffin, made with chunky peanut butter? These four-ingredient muffins are fast to make, and the addition of chocolate chips is a surprise bonus.

Vegetable oil spray for misting the pan
1 package (17.8 ounces) chocolate chip muffin mix
1 cup milk
½ cup chunky peanut butter
1 large egg

❀ **MAKES 12 MUFFINS (2½ INCHES EACH)**
❀ **PREPARATION TIME: 10 MINUTES**
❀ **BAKING TIME: 20 TO 23 MINUTES**

the Cupcake Doctor says...

If you want less chunky muffins, use smooth peanut butter. And should you want to really cram these with flavor, fold ½ cup butterscotch chips into the chocolate chip muffin mix.

1. Place a rack in the center of the oven and preheat the oven to 400°F. Mist the bottom of 12 muffin cups with the vegetable oil spray. Set the pan aside.

2. Place the muffin mix in a large mixing bowl and make a well in the center. Place the milk, peanut butter, and egg in the center of the well and stir the wet ingredients with a fork to combine and break up the egg yolk. Stir the wet and dry ingredients together with a wooden spoon until just combined, 20 strokes. The batter will still be a little lumpy. Spoon or scoop ⅓ cup batter into each prepared muffin cup, filling it three quarters of the way full. Place the pan in the oven.

3. Bake the muffins until they are lightly golden and just spring back when lightly pressed with your finger, 20 to 23 minutes. Remove the pan from the oven and place it on a wire rack to cool for 5 minutes. Run a dinner knife around the edges of the muffins, lift them up from the bottoms of the cups using the end of the knife, and pick them out of the cups carefully with your fingertips. Place them on a wire rack to cool for 15 minutes. The muffins are ready to serve.

✿ *Store these muffins, in a cake saver or under a glass dome, at room temperature for up to 5 days or freeze them, wrapped in aluminum foil or in a cake saver, for up to 6 months. Thaw the muffins overnight in the refrigerator before serving.*

5 Muffins Your Kids Will Love

▼ ▼ ▼

1. Blueberry Yogurt Streusel Muffins (page 222)

2. Easy Granola Muffins (page 235)

3. Carrot Cake Muffins with a Cream Cheese Surprise (page 254)

4. Chunky Peanut Butter Muffins (page 266)

5. Cinnamon Applesauce Lunchbox Muffins (page 259)

PINEAPPLE MUFFINS

WITH COCONUT CRUMBLE

• • • • •

When eaten warm, these muffins will remind you of your mother's pineapple upside-down cake. They are so nostalgic and buttery and good. And the next day, they will still be amazingly moist—thanks to that canned crushed pineapple. You'll love the tropical flavor the coconut topping lends to this easy recipe.

Vegetable oil spray for misting
*   the pan*

COCONUT CRUMBLE:
½ cup packed light brown sugar
2 tablespoons self-rising flour
1 tablespoon butter, at room
*   temperature*
½ cup sweetened flaked coconut

MUFFINS:
6 tablespoons (¾ stick) unsalted butter,
*   at room temperature*
½ cup granulated sugar
1 large egg
1 can (8 ounces) crushed pineapple,
*   undrained*
½ cup milk
½ teaspoon pure vanilla extract
2 cups self-rising flour

1. Place a rack in the center of the oven and preheat the oven to 400°F. Mist the bottom of 12 muffin cups with the vegetable oil spray. Set the pan aside.

2. Prepare the crumble: Place the sugar, flour, and butter in a small bowl. Work the butter into the mixture using a fork. Stir in the coconut and set the crumble aside.

✿ **MAKES 12 MUFFINS (2½ INCHES EACH)**
✿ **PREPARATION TIME: 15 MINUTES**
✿ **BAKING TIME: 18 TO 20 MINUTES**

the Cupcake Doctor says...

It's important to use unsalted butter in this recipe, because the self-rising flour is salty.

3. Prepare the muffin batter: Place the butter and sugar in a large mixing bowl. Blend with an electric mixer on medium-high speed until the mixture is creamy, 30 seconds. Add the egg, pineapple and juice, milk, and vanilla and blend on low speed until just combined, 30 seconds. Stop the machine and scrape down the sides of the bowl with a rubber spatula. Fold in the flour with a wooden spoon or the rubber spatula, 25 strokes. The batter will still be a little lumpy. Spoon or scoop ¼ cup batter into each prepared muffin cup, filling it two thirds of the way full. Sprinkle a heaping teaspoon of crumble topping on each muffin and gently press the topping into the batter. Place the pan in the oven.

4. Bake the muffins until they are lightly golden and just spring back when lightly pressed with your finger, 18 to 20 minutes. Remove the pan from the oven and place it on a wire rack to cool for 5 minutes. Run a dinner knife around the edges of the muffins, lift them up from the bottoms of the cups using the end of the knife, and pick them out of the cups carefully with your fingertips. Place them on a wire rack to cool for 15 minutes. The muffins are ready to serve.

✿ *Store these muffins, in a cake saver or under a glass dome, at room temperature for up to 5 days or freeze them, wrapped in aluminum foil or in a cake saver, for up to 6 months. Thaw the muffins overnight in the refrigerator before serving.*

MINI PEACH MUFFINS

AND FRUIT KEBABS

• • • • •

Some people just have an eye for presenting food with beautiful style. Food stylist and friend Lucille Osborn suggested creating skewers of miniature muffins and fresh fruit for Mother's Day. Brilliant, I thought, and good for parties, too. Use this or any favorite muffin recipe and place three mini muffins on a long wooden skewer along with fruits of your choice. Alongside a scrambled egg or some strips of bacon, these would be a welcome breakfast for Mom or anyone special.

Vegetable oil spray for misting the pan
4 tablespoons butter, at room
    temperature
½ cup granulated sugar
1 large egg
½ cup peeled, sliced fresh peaches,
    with their juices (3 small)
1½ cups self-rising flour
1 cup assorted fresh fruit,
    such as strawberries,
    melon balls,
    pineapple
    chunks, and
    grapes

✿ **MAKES 12 MUFFINS (2 INCHES EACH) OR**
   4 SERVINGS
✿ **PREPARATION TIME: 15 MINUTES**
✿ **BAKING TIME: 13 TO 15 MINUTES**

the Cupcake Doctor says...

If you place 2 muffins on each skewer, you can serve 6 people. Increase the amount of fruit to nearly 2 cups.

1. Place a rack in the center of the oven and preheat the oven to 400°F. Mist the bottom of 12 miniature muffin cups with the vegetable oil spray. Set the pan aside.

2. Place the butter and sugar in a large mixing bowl. Blend with an electric mixer on medium-high speed until the mixture is creamy, 30 seconds. Add the egg and sliced peaches and juice and blend on low speed just until combined, 30 seconds. Stop the machine and scrape down the sides of the bowl with a rubber spatula. Fold in the flour with a wooden spoon or the rubber spatula, 25 strokes. The batter will still be a little lumpy. Spoon or scoop 2 tablespoons batter into each pre-pared muffin cup, filling each cup two thirds of the way full. Place the pan in the oven.

3. Bake the muffins until they are lightly golden and just spring back when lightly pressed with your finger, 13 to 15 minutes. Remove the pan from the oven and place it on a wire rack to cool for 5 minutes. Run a dinner knife around the edges of the muffins, lift them up from the bottoms of the cups using the end of the knife, and pick them out of the cups carefully with your fingertips. Place them on a wire rack to cool for 15 minutes.

4. To assemble the skewers, alternate pieces of fruit with three muffins on each of 4 wooden skewers. Serve these muffins immediately after assembling.

✿ *Store these muffins, in a cake saver or under a glass dome, at room temperature for up to 5 days or freeze them, wrapped in aluminum foil or in a cake saver, for up to 6 months. Thaw the muffins overnight in the refrigerator before serving.*

Cupcake Cousins

❀ ❀ ❀

This chapter came about by accident. Had I not stored stacks of cupcake pans on my kitchen counter after the recipe testing had concluded, I would not have dreamed I could write another chapter. But I kept looking at those pans, somewhat nostalgically, wondering what I might be doing in the fall with the kids back in school and the cookbook put to bed. Then the light dawned.

Those pans weren't just cupcake and muffin pans. No, they were little molds, vessels for individual portions, and those portions might be custards, frozen layered desserts, or creamy refrigerated confections.

The fancy desserts of my youth came flashing back: my mother's chocolate wafer and whipped cream number. The refrigerated Hershey Bar cake, and those creamy, easy Key lime desserts with sweetened condensed milk and cream cheese. These would be perfect made in a cupcake pan, and there might be others, I thought. What about layered ice cream desserts and trifle-like stacks of pudding and berries? What about a crème brûlée baked in a cupcake pan?

So we made room for another chapter—with recipes for those days and nights when you don't want cake, but you do want something sweet. And these are do-ahead desserts that you can tuck away in the freezer or refrigerator and serve confidently to guests.

❀ ❀ ❀

MINI STRAWBERRY TRIFLES

• • • • •

Who says trifles have to be layered in large glass bowls and feed a crowd? These mini dessert trifles are very English in both taste and appearance. I remember when living in England that we would wait for the first strawberries of the season and serve them with whipped cream, vanilla custard, and cake.

Those flavors come together in these little do-ahead "cupcakes," and they are ready to be served when berries are at their best and your hectic schedule is at its worst!

1 package (3.4 ounces) instant vanilla
    pudding mix
2 cups cold milk
1 teaspoon pure vanilla extract
½ cup heavy (whipping) cream
2 teaspoons confectioners' sugar
8 foil liners for cupcake pans
    (2½-inch size)
1 small (10.75 ounces) loaf frozen
    pound cake
2 tablespoons cream sherry
½ cup chopped fresh ripe strawberries
8 whole medium-size ripe strawberries,
    for garnish

❀ MAKES 8 TRIFLES (2½ INCHES EACH)
❀ PREPARATION TIME: 20 MINUTES
❀ ASSEMBLY TIME: 2 TO 3 MINUTES

1. Prepare the instant pudding according to the package directions, adding the cold milk as directed. Stir in the vanilla. Immediately place the pudding in the refrigerator to chill until it is needed.

2. Meanwhile, place a clean, medium-size mixing bowl and electric mixer beaters in the freezer for 1 minute. Pour the cream into the chilled bowl and beat with the electric mixer on high speed until the cream has thickened, 1½ minutes. Stop the machine and add the sugar. Beat the cream and sugar on high speed until stiff peaks form, 1 to 2 minutes more. Place the whipped cream in the refrigerator to chill.

3. Place the foil liners on a serving platter and set aside.

4. Place the frozen cake on a cutting board. Slice the cake thinly into 16 slices that are about ¼-inch thick. Cut a 2-inch round out of each slice, yielding 16 rounds. Generously brush one side of each round with the sherry.

5. Place 8 rounds, sherry-side up, in the foil liners. Dollop 1 tablespoon of pudding on the top of each cake round. Place 1 tablespoon of chopped strawberries on top of the pudding. Then, dollop with 1 tablespoon more pudding. Place the remaining 8 cake rounds on the top of pudding, sherry-side down. Cover the platter with plastic wrap and chill the cakes until time to serve.

6. Just before serving, slice the whole strawberries. Top each trifle with a heaping tablespoon of whipped cream and garnish with 2 or 3 of the nicest strawberry slices.

✿ *Store these "cupcakes," covered in plastic wrap or in a cake saver, in the refrigerator for up to 3 days.*

the Cupcake Doctor says...

Instant vanilla pudding mix is a good time-saver, but really needs doctoring because it is so bland. At the very least, I add 1 teaspoon of pure vanilla extract or a pinch of grated nutmeg. If I have more time and prepare the cook-and-serve vanilla pudding from the box, I'll add a couple of tablespoons of butter as well, to make it taste richer.

I used Sara Lee pound cake in this trifle. Leftover scraps make a nice dessert-in-a-bowl with a scoop of ice cream or can be turned into cake crumbs, handy for the bottoms and tops of cheesecakes. Of course, scraps go down easily, accompanied by a cup of hot tea.

MINI LEMON BLACKBERRY TRIFLES

• • • • •

The only pans you need to create this easy do-ahead summer dessert are foil cupcake liners. Layer rounds of pound cake smeared with lemon curd and add fresh blackberries or blueberries and plenty of whipped cream, and you have delightful desserts that showcase seasonal fruit.

❀ **MAKES 12 CUPCAKES (2½ INCHES EACH)**
❀ **PREPARATION TIME: 20 MINUTES**
❀ **ASSEMBLY TIME: 2 TO 3 MINUTES**

1 cup heavy (whipping) cream
1 tablespoon confectioners' sugar
12 foil liners for cupcake pans (2½-inch size)
1 large (16 ounces) or 1 small
  (10.75 ounces) frozen pound cake
  (see "the Cupcake Doctor says")
⅓ cup lemon curd
2 cups fresh blackberries or 1½ cups
  fresh blueberries, washed
  and drained

1. Place a large clean mixing bowl and electric mixer beaters in the freezer for 1 minute. Pour the cream into the chilled bowl and beat with the electric mixer on high speed until the cream has thickened, 1½ minutes. Stop the machine and add the sugar. Beat the cream and sugar on high speed until stiff peaks form, 1 to 2 minutes more. Place the whipped cream in the refrigerator to chill.

2. Place the foil liners on a serving platter.

I am normally careful to use all the loaf, can, package—you name it—so there is little waste when preparing a recipe. Yet here I am suggesting that you buy the large loaf of pound cake and then just use half. The reason is that this larger loaf has a larger size slice, which will yield 2 rounds, so you can easily cut out 24 rounds for the 12 cupcakes. You can rewrap the other half and refreeze it for another use, so there really isn't any waste.

3. Remove the frozen pound cake from its container. If using a 16-ounce cake, slice it in half and return one half to the freezer. While the remaining half cake is still frozen, slice it into 12 slices about ¼-inch thick, using a sturdy bread knife. Then, using a 2-inch biscuit cutter, cut 2 rounds from each slice. You will have 24 rounds. If using a small cake, cut it into 24 slices and cut 1 round from each slice. Save the scraps to munch on, or see "the Cupcake Doctor says" on page 274.

4. Carefully spread a thin layer of lemon curd on one side of all 24 rounds. Place half of the rounds in the bottoms of the foil liners, curd-side up. Remove the whipped cream from the refrigerator and dollop about 1 teaspoon of whipped cream on top of the lemon curd. Place about 4 to 5 blackberries (or 6 to 8 blueberries) on top of the whipped cream. Top the fruit with at least 1 tablespoon of whipped cream. Place the remaining 12 cake rounds on top of the whipped cream, curd-side down. Cover the platter with plastic wrap and chill the cakes until time to serve. Return the remaining whipped cream to the refrigerator.

5. Just before serving, dollop 1 heaping tablespoon of whipped cream on top of the cupcakes and garnish them with the remaining berries.

❧ *Store these "cupcakes," covered in plastic wrap or in a cake server, in the refrigerator for up to 3 days.*

5 More Desserts to Build in a Cupcake Pan

1. **Tiramisu.** Cut white cake layers into rounds to fit foil baking cups. Place 1 round in each cup, brush them with a sweet coffee syrup, then spread with mascarpone cheese and dollop with whipped cream. Top with a dusting of cocoa powder.

2. **Summertime berries and cake.** Cut angel food cake into rounds to fit foil baking cups. Place 1 round in each cup. Mash fresh berries of your choice with a little sugar to sweeten and layer with the cake. Chill until firm, then serve with a dollop of whipped cream.

3. **Pecan pie à la mode.** Cut a partially thawed frozen pecan pie into bite-size pieces. Scatter these in the cupcake pan cups, spoon over soft vanilla ice cream, then scatter on a few more small pieces of pie. Cover the pan and freeze until firm. Remove from the freezer 15 minutes before serving.

4. **Brownie pie à la mode.** Cut your favorite brownies into bite-size pieces, scatter them in cupcake pans, spoon over soft vanilla ice cream, add more brownies, and freeze as described in number 3. Yum!

5. **Prunes and Armagnac.** Soak pitted prunes in Armagnac or brandy, covered, at room temperature for a day (about ⅓ cup Armagnac for each cup of prunes). Stir every couple of hours. Place the prunes in a food processor or blender with vanilla ice cream (1 quart ice cream for every 1 cup prunes) and blend until the mixture is not quite smooth—the prunes should still be in pieces. Spoon this into a cupcake pan lined with foil baking cups. Toss graham cracker crumbs with a little melted butter, sugar to taste, and finely chopped pecans. Scatter this mixture on the top, freeze until nearly firm, then serve.

FROZEN PISTACHIO AND CHOCOLATE ICE CREAM CUPCAKES

• • • • •

Around our house we have a weak spot for the flavors of chocolate and pistachio, so chaos broke loose when word got out that I had a pan of chocolate and pistachio ice cream cupcakes in the freezer. My children made a beeline for the kitchen as if they were searching for a pan of gold! Blanket them with Easy Hot Fudge Sauce (page 356) or drizzle with a little chocolate syrup.

✿ **MAKES 12 CUPCAKES (2½ INCHES EACH)**
✿ **PREPARATION TIME: 20 MINUTES**
✿ **FREEZING TIME: 30 MINUTES**
✿ **ASSEMBLY TIME: 2 TO 3 MINUTES**

12 foil liners for cupcake pans (2½-inch size)

CAKES:

1 large (16 ounces) or 1 small (10.75 ounces) loaf frozen pound cake (see "the Cupcake Doctor says," page 276)

1 pint chocolate ice cream or chocolate brownie ice cream

1 pint pistachio ice cream

GARNISHES:

1 cup whipped cream (from ½ cup whipping cream)

1 cup chocolate sauce of your choice

2 tablespoons chopped toasted pistachios (optional)

1. Place the foil liners in a cupcake pan or in a 13- by 9-inch pan. Set them aside.

2. Remove the frozen pound cake from its container. If using a 16-ounce cake, slice it in half; return one half to the freezer. While the remaining cake is still frozen, slice it into 12 slices about ¼-inch thick using a sturdy bread knife. Then, using a 2-inch biscuit cutter, cut 2 rounds from each slice. You will have 24 rounds. If using a small cake, cut it into 24 slices and cut 1 round from each slice (see "the Cupcake Doctor says" on page 274 for tips on using the scraps).

3. Place 12 of the rounds in the bottoms of the 12 foil liners.

4. Remove the chocolate ice cream from the freezer. Place the pint on its side and, using the bread knife, slice through the ice cream carton to make six ½-inch slices. Peel away the carton from 1 slice and, using a 2-inch biscuit cutter, cut out a round of ice cream. Place it on top of a cake round. Using your fingers, reshape the remainder of that ice cream slice and cut a second round from it. Place it on a cake round. Repeat with the remaining slices for a total of 12 ice cream rounds sitting on top of the 12 cake rounds in the foil liners. Return any remaining chocolate ice cream to the freezer.

5. Place the remaining 12 cake rounds on

the Cupcake Doctor says...

Feel free to turn this frozen "cupcake" into almost any combination of flavors—blueberry and strawberry are also nice, and so are raspberry and lemon. Place the brightest color of ice cream or the one with the most interesting appearance on top.

top of the chocolate ice cream. Place the pan of liners in the freezer for 15 minutes.

6. Meanwhile, remove the pistachio ice cream from the freezer and cut out 12 rounds following the method described in step 4 for the chocolate ice cream. Refreeze any remaining pistachio ice cream.

7. Remove the liners from the freezer and place the pistachio ice cream rounds on top of the second cake layer. Cover the pan with plastic wrap and return the liners to the freezer for at least 15 minutes. Remove them from the freezer 5 minutes before serving.

8. To serve, garnish with a dollop of whipped cream and drizzle with chocolate sauce. If desired, sprinkle chopped toasted pistachios over the top.

✿ *Store these "cupcakes," covered in plastic wrap, in the freezer for up to 1 month.*

FRESH RASPBERRY CREAM CAKES

• • • • •

These individual raspberry cakes are both creamy and refreshing at the same time. Not only are they beautifully pink but they are full of fresh raspberry flavor. The reduced-fat cream cheese makes them nice and light. Keep them in the freezer and serve after a casual dinner party or, better yet, on Valentine's Day!

❈ **MAKES 12 CREAM CAKES (2½ INCHES EACH)**
❈ **PREPARATION TIME: 20 MINUTES**
❈ **FREEZING TIME: AT LEAST 3 HOURS**
❈ **ASSEMBLY TIME: 5 MINUTES**

12 foil liners for cupcake
pans (2½-inch size)
¾ cup graham cracker
crumbs
¼ cup finely chopped pecans
3 tablespoons butter, melted
1 cup fresh raspberries, washed and
drained
8 ounces reduced-fat cream cheese,
at room temperature
1 can (14 ounces) sweetened
condensed milk
1 container (8 ounces) frozen whipped
topping, thawed

1. Line 12 cupcake cups with the foil liners and set the pan aside.

2. Place the graham cracker crumbs, pecans, and melted butter in a mixing bowl and stir to combine. Spoon about 1 tablespoon of the mixture into each liner, pressing down on the mixture with your fingers to make the crust.

3. Reserve 12 raspberries for garnish. Place the remaining raspberries in a food processor and pulse the berries until pureed, 10 seconds. Measure out ½ cup for the filling and set aside. Place the remaining puree in a sieve over a small glass bowl to catch the raspberry juices. Push down gently on the puree to extract as much juice as possible. Discard the solids. Cover the raspberry juice with plastic wrap and refrigerate until needed.

4. Place the cream cheese in a large mixing bowl. With an electric mixer on low speed, beat the cream cheese until creamy, 30 seconds. Turn off the machine and add the sweetened condensed milk and the reserved ½ cup pureed raspberries. With the mixer on medium speed, blend until just combined, 20 to 30 seconds. Stop the mixer, add 1 cup of the whipped topping, and blend on low speed to combine, 15 seconds.

5. Top the crusts with the raspberry mixture, dividing it evenly among them. The liners should be very full but not overflowing. Cover the pan with plastic wrap and

the Cupcake Doctor says...

Turn these into strawberry cakes by using ½ cup pureed fresh strawberries (from 1 cup fresh strawberries) in the filling instead of the raspberries. Garnish by drizzling a little strawberry juice over the top and topping with half a strawberry.

place it in the freezer until firm, at least 3 hours.

6. Remove the pan from the freezer 15 minutes before serving. To serve, peel away the foil liners from the cakes and place the cakes on serving plates. Dollop with 1 heaping tablespoon of the remaining whipped topping. Drizzle with the reserved raspberry juice and garnish with a reserved raspberry.

✿ *Store these "cupcakes," ungarnished, covered with plastic wrap, in the freezer for up to 2 weeks.*

KEY LIME CREAM CAKES

• • • • •

If you like the flavor of Key lime, and if you like cool, creamy, and refreshing desserts, and if you have better things to do than spend an afternoon in the kitchen, you're going to love this recipe.

✿ **MAKES 12 CREAM CAKES (2½ INCHES EACH)**

✿ **PREPARATION TIME: 15 MINUTES**

✿ **FREEZING TIME: AT LEAST 3 HOURS**

✿ **ASSEMBLY TIME: 5 MINUTES**

the Cupcake Doctor says...

The sweet graham cookies I used to make the crust in this recipe were Carr's Biscuits for Tea. This is a shortcut, but if you prefer, you can opt for a graham cracker crust using graham cracker crumbs and following the directions for Fresh Raspberry Cream Cakes, step 2 (page 280).

12 foil liners for cupcake pans (2½-inch size)

12 round sweet graham cookies
(see "the Cupcake Doctor says")

8 ounces reduced-fat cream cheese,
at room temperature

1 can (14 ounces) sweetened condensed milk

½ cup Key lime juice

1 container (8 ounces) frozen whipped
topping, thawed

Thin lime twists, for garnish
(see box, facing page)

Lime Twists

▼ ▼ ▼

To make the lime twists, cut a large lime into 12 very thin slices. Cut each slice halfway through from the edge to the center, then twist the lime into a spiral with your fingers.

1. Line 12 cupcake cups with the foil liners. Place the cookies on a cutting board and, using a 2-inch round cutter, cut 1 round from each cookie. Crumble the trimmings and reserve for garnish. Place 1 cookie round on the bottom of each of the 12 liners.

2. Place the cream cheese in a large mixing bowl. With an electric mixer on low speed, beat the cream cheese until creamy, 30 seconds. Turn off the machine and add the sweetened condensed milk and Key lime juice. With the mixer on medium speed, blend until just combined, 20 to 30 seconds. Stop the mixer, add 1 cup of the whipped topping, and blend on low speed to combine, 15 seconds.

3. Spoon the lime mixture on top of the crusts in the foil liners. The liners should be very full, but not overflowing. Cover the pan with plastic wrap and place in the freezer until firm, at least 3 hours.

4. Remove the pans from the freezer about 15 minutes before serving. To serve, peel away the foil liners and place the cakes on serving plates. Dollop with 1 heaping tablespoon of the remaining whipped topping. Sprinkle with the reserved cookie crumbs and garnish with a lime twist.

✿ *Store these cupcakes, covered with plastic wrap, in the freezer for up to 2 weeks.*

LITTLE CHOCOLATE BAR CAKES

• • • • •

This recipe has been in our family for many years, and I'll admit these little frozen cakes are sweet. But if served with unsweetened whipped cream, the outcome is glorious: chocolate, cream, toasted almonds—all my favorite food groups. Keep these in the freezer for unexpected guests— of course, they may start visiting you more often!

✿ MAKES 12 CAKES (2½ INCHES EACH)

✿ PREPARATION TIME: 20 MINUTES

✿ FREEZING TIME: AT LEAST 3 HOURS, PREFERABLY OVERNIGHT

✿ ASSEMBLY TIME: 5 MINUTES

12 foil liners for cupcake pans (2½-inch size)

CRUST:
¾ cup graham cracker crumbs
¼ cup finely chopped almonds
    (see "the Cupcake Doctor says")
3 tablespoons butter, melted

FILLING:
6 small bars (1.45 ounces each) Hershey's
    Milk Chocolate with Almonds
3½ cups miniature marshmallows
    (half a 10.5-ounce bag)
½ cup milk
1 cup heavy (whipping) cream

GARNISHES:
2 to 3 tablespoons toasted almonds
2 tablespoons grated semisweet chocolate
    (see "the Cupcake Doctor says")

1. Line 12 cupcake cups with the foil liners and set the pan aside.

2. Prepare the crusts: Place the graham cracker crumbs, almonds, and melted butter in a mixing bowl and stir the mixture to combine. Spoon about 1 tablespoon of the mixture into each liner, pressing down with your fingers to make the crust.

3. Prepare the filling: Break up the Hershey bars and place them in a large saucepan over low heat with the marshmallows and milk. Heat, stirring frequently with a wooden spoon, until the chocolate and marshmallows melt and the mixture thickens, 10 minutes. Remove the pan from the heat and let the mixture cool slightly, 5 minutes.

4. Place the electric mixer beaters and a large mixing bowl in the freezer for 1 minute. Remove both, pour the cream into the chilled bowl, and beat with the electric mixer on high speed until stiff peaks form, 2 to 3 minutes.

5. Fold 1 cup of the whipped cream into the chocolate mixture until it is well combined. Place the remaining whipped cream, covered, in the refrigerator. Top the crusts with the chocolate mixture, dividing it evenly

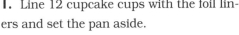

the Cupcake Doctor says...

A 2-ounce bag of blanched and slivered almonds will provide you with enough almonds to use in the crust and as a garnish (toast them briefly in the toaster oven for 3 to 4 minutes at 350°F). To make this a nut-free dessert, use plain Hershey bars and omit the almond garnish.

Run a semisweet chocolate bar down the large holes of a cheese grater to make the grated chocolate for the garnish quickly.

among them. The liners should be very full but not overflowing. Cover the pan with plastic wrap and place it in the freezer until firm, at least 3 hours.

6. Remove the cupcake pan from the freezer 15 minutes before serving. To serve, place a dinner knife underneath the liners and lift out the cakes. Peel away the liners and place the cupcakes on serving plates. Dollop the top of the cupcakes with 1 heaping tablespoon of the reserved whipped cream and garnish with toasted almonds and grated chocolate. The cakes are ready to serve.

❀ *Store these "cupcakes," covered with plastic wrap, in the freezer for up to 2 weeks.*

CARAMEL SUNDAE CUPCAKES

WITH FRESH PEACH SLICES

• • • • •

What a refreshing little frozen dessert this is on summer days. You pull the vanilla-ice-cream-and-caramel-filled granola and graham cracker crusts from the freezer and slice fresh ripe peaches or nectarines over them. They are also delicious later in the fall, when plums are in season, or with sliced ripe bananas year-round.

12 foil liners for cupcake pans
> *(2½-inch size)*

SUNDAES:
½ heaping cup granola
½ heaping cup graham cracker crumbs
3 tablespoons butter, melted
⅓ cup caramel sauce
> *(see "the Cupcake Doctor says")*
2 pints vanilla ice cream or
> *frozen yogurt, softened slightly*

GARNISHES:
4 to 5 medium fresh peaches,
> *peeled and sliced*
½ cup caramel sauce

✿ **MAKES 12 SUNDAES (2½ INCHES EACH)**
✿ **PREPARATION TIME: 20 MINUTES**
✿ **FREEZING TIME: 1 HOUR**
✿ **ASSEMBLY TIME: 2 TO 3 MINUTES**

1. Line 12 cupcake cups with the foil liners, or place them in a 13- by 9-inch pan, and set them aside.

2. Pour the granola onto a cutting board and crush it slightly by rolling a heavy rolling pin back and forth over it. Place the granola in a large mixing bowl and combine with the graham cracker crumbs and melted butter. Spoon about 1 tablespoon into each foil liner, pressing down on the mixture with your fingers to make the crust. Drizzle 1 generous teaspoon of the caramel sauce onto each crust.

3. Spoon the softened vanilla ice cream over the crusts so that the liners are nearly full. Cover the pan lightly with plastic wrap and place in the freezer for at least 1 hour.

the Cupcake Doctor says...

The better the caramel sauce, the better this dessert. If you are serving this to company you might want to spring for a premium caramel sauce from a specialty shop.

4. To serve, peel the liners from the sundaes and place them on serving plates. Cover with peach slices and drizzle with more caramel sauce.

✿ *Store these cupcakes, covered in plastic wrap, in the freezer for up to 1 month.*

PEACH COBBLER CUPCAKES

In truth, my husband is a pie man. He'd rather have a home-baked apple, blackberry, or peach pie than a slice of chocolate cake. However, for years I'd been serving up cakes that I had created for my books. So, when I brought out these mini peach pies masquerading as "cupcakes," John thought he had come home to the wrong house. Forking into sweet fruit and hot pastry, he was one happy guy.

✿ **MAKES 8 CUPCAKES (2½ INCHES EACH)**
✿ **PREPARATION TIME: 25 MINUTES**
✿ **BAKING TIME: 16 TO 18 MINUTES**

1 package (15 ounces) refrigerated pie crusts (2 crusts to a package)
All-purpose flour for dusting a work surface
1 package (16 ounces) frozen sliced peaches, thawed, or 2 heaping cups sliced fresh peaches, well drained
2 tablespoons water, if using frozen peaches
½ cup plus 1 tablespoon granulated sugar
1 tablespoon all-purpose flour
¼ teaspoon ground cinnamon
2 tablespoons cold butter, cut into pieces
Vanilla ice cream, for serving

1. Place a rack in the center of the oven and preheat the oven to 400°F.

2. Unfold the pie crusts onto a lightly floured surface. Cut four 4½-inch circles out of each crust, using a plastic lid or piece of cardboard as a stencil and a sharp paring knife. You will have 8 rounds and plenty of dough scraps. Cut the scraps into strips or small uneven shapes.

3. Place 1 pastry round in the center of a cupcake cup, and gently press the round down to fit the pan. It is fine for the dough to stick up around the edges. Repeat the process with the remaining rounds, and set the pan aside.

4. Chop the peaches coarsely and place them in a medium-size saucepan with ½ cup of water, if they are frozen, or on their own, if they are fresh (see "the Cupcake Doctor says"). Place the pan over medium heat and stir the peaches until they come to a boil. Then reduce the heat to low and stir often while they simmer until softened, 5 to 7 minutes. Drain the peaches.

5. Combine the ½ cup sugar and the flour and cinnamon in a small bowl. Remove the peaches from the heat, and stir in the sugar mixture until it is well combined. Spoon ¼ cup of the peach mixture into each pastry-lined cup. Place 3 or 4 strips of dough over the top of each fruit-filled cup. Use your fingers to press the edges of the dough inward toward the fruit. Distribute the cold bits of butter evenly on top of the pastry strips, and sprinkle them with the remaining 1 tablespoon sugar. Place the pan in the oven.

6. Bake the cobblers until the crust is golden and the filling is bubbly, 16 to 18

the Cupcake Doctor says...

You can make blackberry cobblers using the same method. Substitute the same amount of frozen or fresh blackberries for the peaches. The reason you add a little water to the frozen fruit is that it is often less ripe and harder. In fact, fresh peaches in season are so juicy you must drain them well.

minutes. Remove the pan from the oven and place it on a wire rack to cool for 5 minutes. Run a dinner knife around the edges of the cobblers, lift them up from the bottoms of the cups using the end of the knife, and pick them out of the cups carefully with your fingertips. Serve them warm with vanilla ice cream.

✿ *Store these cupcakes, in a cake saver or under a glass dome, at room temperature for up to 3 days or in the refrigerator for up to 1 week. Or freeze them, wrapped in aluminum foil or in a cake saver, for up to 6 months. Thaw the cupcakes overnight in the refrigerator before serving. To reheat, place them, uncovered, in a 350°F oven until warmed through, 20 minutes.*

CHOCOLATE-CHOCOLATE ICEBOX CUPCAKES

• • • • •

The idea for a miniature version of the well-known refrigerated dessert of whipped cream and dark chocolate wafer cookies had been on my mind since I first looked seriously at a cupcake pan. What better way to house a single serving? Sometimes those legendary wafer cookies are difficult to find, but I came up with a substitute from the health food section—a chocolate graham cracker wafer, not as dark as the Nabisco cookie but chocolate, nevertheless, and just the same size as a cupcake. After a stay in the refrigerator, the cookie absorbs the liquid from the whipped cream and becomes soft and more cakelike in texture.

12 paper liners for cupcake pans
    (2½-inch size)
1 cup heavy (whipping) cream
1 tablespoon confectioners' sugar, or to taste
1 tablespoon unsweetened cocoa powder
1 tablespoon crème de cacao or 1 teaspoon
    pure vanilla extract
48 chocolate wafer cookies, trimmed
    if necessary (see "the Cupcake
    Doctor says")
½ cup chocolate sauce or syrup of your choice

✿ **MAKES 12 CUPCAKES (2½ INCHES EACH)**
✿ **PREPARATION TIME: 20 MINUTES**
✿ **CHILLING TIME: AT LEAST 4 HOURS,**
   PREFERABLY OVERNIGHT

1. Place the cupcake liners in the cupcake cups. Place a clean, medium-size mixing bowl and electric mixer beaters in the freezer for 1 minute.

2. Pour the cream into the chilled bowl and beat with the electric mixer on high speed until the cream has thickened, 1½ minutes. Stop the machine and add the sugar and cocoa powder. Beat the cream on high speed until stiff peaks form, 1 to 2 minutes more. Fold in the crème de cacao or vanilla. Place the bowl in the refrigerator.

3. Place a wafer in each liner, cover with 2 teaspoons chocolate whipped cream, then add another wafer, another 2 teaspoons whipped cream, another wafer, another 2 teaspoons whipped cream, and finally a last wafer, pressing down on the top wafer with your fingertips so that it aligns with the top of the paper liner. Cover the pan with plastic wrap and place it in the refrigerator at least 4 hours, or preferably overnight.

the Cupcake Doctor says...

I used Barbara's Bakery Organic Chocolate Graham Crackers in this recipe. They fit the cupcake pan cups perfectly. If you use Nabisco's Famous Chocolate Wafers, you'll have to break them in half and overlap the halves slightly. Omit the cocoa powder, if desired, and add the liqueur of your choice instead of the crème de cacao. A great do-ahead dessert, this recipe is easy to double for a crowd.

4. To serve, remove the pan from the refrigerator. Place a dinner knife underneath the liners and lift up the cupcakes, placing them on serving plates or a platter. Flip the cupcakes upside down and remove the paper liner so that the bottom wafer cookie is now on top. Spoon a little chocolate sauce or syrup over the cupcakes and serve.

❀ *Store these cupcakes in the pan, covered in plastic wrap, in the refrigerator for up to 3 days.*

BREAD PUDDING "CUPCAKES"

· · · · ·

Bread pudding is, I believe, one of the most tempting desserts around. But each time I order it at a restaurant, I eat two bites and wonder, "How did I ever think I could eat the whole thing?" This hearty dessert, rich with custard, is often too filling after a big meal, especially in those hefty restaurant portions. Here is a lighter alternative. Just as delicious, it is baked in cupcake cups so that each serving is just that— one serving—and a very satisfying

one it is. Omit the brandy if you wish and add ⅓ cup more milk.

1 teaspoon butter, at room temperature
⅓ cup brandy
¼ cup dried currants
6 slices white bread (5 to 6 ounces total;
  see "the Cupcake Doctor says")
2 cups milk
2 large eggs
½ cup sugar
1 teaspoon pure vanilla extract
¼ teaspoon ground cinnamon

1. Preheat the oven to 350°F. Lightly grease an 8-cup cupcake pan (each cup 2½ inches in diameter) with the soft butter and set it aside.

2. Place the brandy and the currants in a small glass bowl in the microwave oven on high power until the brandy has warmed, 20 seconds. Remove and let the currants soak.

❀ **MAKES 8 CUPCAKES (2½ INCHES EACH)**
❀ **PREPARATION TIME: 15 MINUTES**
❀ **BAKING TIME: 20 TO 25 MINUTES**

3. Meanwhile, slice the crusts off the bread slices and discard the crusts or save them for bread crumbs. Cut the bread into small (¼ to ½ inch) cubes. You need 3 cups of bread cubes. Place 1 heaping tablespoon of the bread cubes into each of the cupcake cups and set the pan aside.

4. Place the milk in a small saucepan over medium heat and let it come just to a boil. While the milk is heating, beat the eggs in a medium-size bowl. Whisk in the sugar until the mixture is lemon-colored, 1 minute. When the milk is hot but not boiling, remove the pan from the heat. Measure out ½ cup milk and whisk it into the egg mixture. Slowly whisk the egg mixture back into the hot milk in the pan. Place the pan back over medium heat and whisk the entire mixture until it begins to thicken, about 2 minutes more. Remove the pan from the heat, stirring constantly for another minute.

5. Strain the brandy from the currants and add it, along with the vanilla and cinnamon, to the custard, stirring to combine. Scatter the currants over the top of the bread, about 1 teaspoon for each cupcake. Pour the custard mixture over the bread and currants in each cup, filling it very full.

the Cupcake Doctor says...

I used Pepperidge Farm white bread for the pudding. Any dense, homemade-style sandwich bread will do. Vary the goodies in the pudding by using dried cherries, minced prunes, or dried cranberries in place of the currants.

6. Carefully place the pan in the oven and bake until the cupcakes rise up and the bread cubes are golden brown, 20 to 25 minutes. Remove the pan from the oven and place on a rack to cool for 5 minutes. The mixture will fall slightly. Run a dinner knife around the edges of the cups and lift up the cakes from the bottom. Serve warm.

✿ *Store these "cupcakes" in the pan, lightly covered with plastic wrap, in the refrigerator for up to 3 days. To reheat, place on a microwave-safe plate, uncovered, in the microwave on high power for 45 seconds to 1 minute, or in the pan in a 350°F oven, covered, for 15 minutes.*

MINI CRÈME BRÛLÉES

• • • • •

A cupcake pan is the perfect vehicle for baking velvety crème brûlées with that crunchy sugar topping. They take a little tending—cooling the custard after baking and after melting the sugar on top—but they are worth it. You'll need a kitchen torch, found where good-quality cooking equipment is sold, to melt the sugar to crackly goodness. I know nine crème brûlées is an unusual yield, but the precise measures I devised for the ingredients filled nine cupcake pans perfectly, so nine crème brûlées it is!

✿ **MAKES 9 CREME BRULEES (2½-INCH SIZE)**
✿ **PREPARATION TIME: 10 MINUTES**
✿ **BAKING TIME: 20 TO 25 MINUTES**
✿ **COOLING TIME: 4 HOURS**
✿ **ASSEMBLY TIME: 5 MINUTES**

9 foil liners for cupcake pans
    (2½-inch size)
2 cups heavy (whipping) cream
1 teaspoon pure vanilla
    extract
4 large egg yolks
Pinch of salt
¼ cup plus 3
    tablespoons
    granulated sugar

I. Place a rack in the center of the oven and preheat the oven to 325°F. Line a sheet pan with 1-inch sides with a cotton kitchen towel. Place the liners in the cupcake pan and place the pan on the towel. Set the pan aside. Bring a kettle of water to a boil over high heat.

2. Place the cream in a small saucepan over medium-high heat. Heat, stirring, until the mixture comes to a boil, 4 minutes. Remove the pan from the heat and stir in the vanilla.

3. Place the egg yolks, salt, and ¼ cup sugar in a large mixing bowl and whisk until the mixture is lemon-colored, 1 to 2 minutes. Whisk in the slightly cooled cream, a little at a time, so that the mixture is smooth but the eggs do not curdle. Ladle the custard into 9 cups of the cupcake pan so that they are filled three quarters of the way full. Place the sheet pan on the center oven rack and carefully pour the boiling water into it and around the cupcake pan so that the water comes halfway up the side of the cupcake pan. Cover the sheet pan loosely with aluminum foil.

4. Bake the custards until they have just set around the edges but still are soft in the middle, 20 to 25 minutes. Remove the sheet pan from the oven, remove the cupcake pan from the sheet pan, and let the custards cool for 30 minutes. Cover the cupcake pan with plastic wrap and refrigerate to firm up, 1½ hours.

5. When the custards are firm, sprinkle 1 to 2 teaspoons sugar evenly across the

the Cupcake Doctor says...

For chocolate crème brûlée, place 3 ounces chopped bittersweet chocolate into the hot cream and stir until it melts. Reduce the sugar whisked with the egg yolks to 2 tablespoons. The baking time may increase by 5 minutes.

When using a kitchen blow torch, make sure you tie back your hair and roll up your sleeves. Move all flammable items away from your workspace.

surface of each cupcake. Using a kitchen blow torch, beginning around the edges (but taking care not to burn the liners), melt the sugar evenly until the tops are golden. Let the crème brûlées rest for 15 minutes, then refrigerate until chilled, 1 to 1¼ hours.

6. To serve, run a dinner knife around the edges of each liner, lift up from underneath, and place on a serving plate.

✿ *Store the crème brûlées, covered in plastic wrap, in the refrigerator for up to 3 days.*

✿   ✿   ✿

Cupcake Creations

❁ ❁ ❁

When you have children and grandchildren, you learn that no matter how much you resist, you've got to pull out the pastry bag, the chocolate sprinkles, the candy decorations, and the imagination every now and then, because kids get excited about food that is fun to look at. And you know what? Adults get pretty excited, too. Oh, maybe not about cupcakes in the form of a Saturday-morning cartoon character, but possibly those lemon-scented or almond-filled cupcakes arranged to resemble a bouquet of flowers, a purse, an elegant wreath, or a dazzling wedding cake.

This chapter is all about unconventional presentations you can make once your cupcakes are baked. I've suggested nine projects, but I'm sure you will dream up more.

With each recipe in this chapter you can start with my directions, then let your own creativity take over. Use the candies and supplies already in your kitchen. Choose the colors you prefer. Add another tier to the wedding cake if you're serving a larger group. And most of all—relax, create, have fun.

❁ ❁ ❁

CATERPILLAR CAKE

• • • • •

You can feed a dozen party guests with this cute caterpillar, made of—what else— cupcakes. Be as elaborate or as simple as you like with the decorations, making the caterpillar come alive with bright candy sticks and gummy worms. Thanks to Bradley McDuffie of Knoxville's Bearden High School for this fun idea.

✿ SERVES UP TO 12

Heavy cardboard

Aluminum foil

½ recipe Buttercream Frosting
    (page 318) or Cream Cheese
    Frosting (page 336)

Green food coloring

12 yellow cupcakes
    (see "the Cupcake Doctor says")

24 hard round colorful candies,
    such as Skittles or M&M's

14 candy sticks, each 2 inches long

18 green gummy worms

1. Cut a piece of heavy cardboard to measure 33 by 12 inches. Cover it completely with aluminum foil. Or, set aside a large, flat platter.

2. Tint the frosting starting with 1 or 2 drops of the food coloring. Blend them into the frosting once it is sufficiently beaten. If you'd like a deeper color, add more coloring a drop at a time. Place a heaping tablespoon of frosting on each

cupcake and swirl to spread it out with a short metal spatula or a spoon.

3. Arrange 9 cupcakes on the cardboard so that they form an S shape. Arrange the 3 remaining cupcakes in front of the first cupcake to form a triangle. This is the caterpillar's head.

4. For the caterpillar's eyes, place 2 candies of the same color on the first cupcake of the head triangle, toward the front. Place a candy stick down the center of the cupcake and between the eyes. Stand 2 candy sticks straight up in the frosting toward the back of the cupcake to resemble antennae. Place a candy stick down the center of each of the 2 remaining cupcakes of the caterpillar's head. Place 1 round candy on each side of the candy sticks, varying the colors.

5. Beginning with the first cupcake behind the head, place 1 candy stick down the center of each cupcake, to create a line that follows the curves of the S shape. On each cupcake, center 2 round candies of different colors, one on each side of the candy stick.

the *Cupcake Doctor says...*

Use your favorite yellow or white cupcake from the book for your caterpillar. Some of my favorites include the Butterfly Cupcakes (page 97), White on White Cupcakes (page 166), and Cookies and Cream Cupcakes (page 136).

6. Stick 2 gummy worms on opposite sides of each of the 9 cupcakes that form the S, between the edge of the frosting and the top of the cupcake liner. These will be the caterpillar's legs. The caterpillar is ready to serve.

✿ *Store this cupcake caterpillar, lightly covered with plastic wrap, at room temperature for up to 5 days or in the refrigerator for up to 1 week.*

CUPCAKE PALETTE

· · · · ·

At your next party for budding Michelangelos, provide paints for creating master-pieces and a palette of cupcakes for noshing when the artistic endeavors have been completed. This clever cupcake idea came from Anne Marie Cale of Bearden High in Knoxville. I've described how to create one palette using six cupcakes, but you can make as many as four palettes per batch of cupcakes and frostings. Tint the buttercream as you choose, and for added fun, set up the palettes with unfrosted cupcakes and let the partygoers "paint" them with their own color choices.

Heavy cardboard
Aluminum foil
1 cup Buttercream Frosting,
    (about ⅓ recipe, page 318)
Red, orange, yellow, green, blue,
    and purple food coloring
    (see "the Cupcake Doctor says")
6 yellow or white cupcakes
    (see "the Cupcake Doctor says")
Clean new small paintbrush,
    about ½ inch wide

✿ **SERVES 6**

1. Cut a circle that measures 12 inches in diameter out of the cardboard. Measuring 1 inch in from the edge of the circle, mark 6 circles 3 inches in diameter each around the circumference. In the remaining space, mark a hole large enough to fit your thumb. Using a thin serrated knife or a matte knife, cut out the circles and the thumb hole. Cover the cardboard with aluminum foil, smoothing it out so it lays flat. Take care to cut the foil to fit where the holes have been cut.

2. Divide the frosting among 6 small bowls. Tint each bowl with one of the following colors: red, orange, yellow, green, blue, and purple. Set the frostings aside.

3. Place each color of frosting on a single cupcake and swirl to spread it out with a short metal spatula or a spoon. Place 1 cupcake in each hole in the following order: red, orange, yellow, green, blue, and purple. Place the paintbrush on the palette for a finishing touch.

✿ *Store these cupcakes at room temperature for up to 3 days.*

the Cupcake Doctor says...

Use any of the yellow or white cupcakes in this book—such as The Best Birthday Cupcakes (page 138) or White on White Cupcakes (page 166)—for this recipe. Food coloring in the shades listed is usually found in paste form. Use a toothpick to pick up a small dab of paste and blend it into the frosting. If you use liquid food coloring, mix the specialty colors in a small dish first: 1 drop of red with 2 drops of yellow for orange; 2 drops of blue with 1 drop of red for purple. Since each batch of frosting is so small, it will take very little color to tint it. If you're making more than one palette, adjust the amount of color added to the frosting accordingly.

CUPCAKE WREATH

• • • • •

A wreath may seem like a logical presentation for holiday cupcakes, but I had a hard time figuring out just how the cupcakes should be stacked until I enlisted the math brain of my daughter Kathleen. This wreath of twenty-four cupcakes with green frosting and sugar sprinkles, decorated with red candies to resemble holly berries, is great for the winter holidays (and, in different colors, it's just as pretty any time of the year). Add fresh pine sprigs and pinecones and you'll have a large and glorious wreath.

✿ SERVES APPROXIMATELY 30

Buttercream Frosting (page 318)
Green food coloring
30 cupcakes of your choice
    (see "the Cupcake Doctor says")
Green sugar sprinkles
Round platter at least 15 inches
    in diameter
32 to 48 hard round red
    candies, such as Runts,
    M&M's, or gumdrops
Pine sprigs for greenery
Small pinecones
Fresh cranberries
Silver roping
Red organdy bow

I. Tint the frosting with the food coloring, blending in 3 to 4 drops of liquid food coloring or ¼ teaspoon food coloring paste once the frosting is sufficiently beaten. Place a heaping tablespoon of frosting on each cupcake and swirl to spread it out with a short metal spatula or a spoon, taking care to cover the tops completely. Sprinkle the cupcakes with the sugar sprinkles.

2. Place 9 cupcakes in a circle—¼ inch apart—on the round platter to create the interior circle of the wreath. Make a larger circle of cupcakes surrounding the smaller circle, aligning each cupcake with the ¼-inch space between the cupcakes in the inner circle. The larger circle will take about 12 cupcakes. Top the inner and outer circles with the remaining 9 cupcakes, balancing them over the spaces between the circles.

3. Place the red candies randomly on the cupcakes to resemble berries, pressing them gently into the frosting so they stick.

4. Garnish the outside of the wreath with the pine sprigs, pinecones, cranberries, and silver roping.

the Cupcake Doctor says...

For Christmas, I would choose a dark and chocolatey cupcake, or something fun like Coconut Snowballs (page 66), or Red Velvet Cupcakes (page 36).

Place the bow wherever it looks best to you, and it is ready to serve.

❀ *Store these cupcakes without the sprinkles, lightly covered with plastic wrap, at room temperature for up to a day. Add the sprinkles when you prepare the wreath.*

CUPCAKE BOUQUET

• • • • •

*P*resent this Cupcake Bouquet to a lucky birthday girl, or a soon-to-be mom at a baby shower. Begin with a large half-ball of Styrofoam, attach about two dozen of your favorite cupcakes, fill the gaps with fresh flowers—I like to use a mix of roses and mums or carnations—and greenery, and it's ready. This pretty way to showcase cupcakes is the ingenious idea of Tyler Henry at Knoxville's Bearden High School.

✿ SERVES 24

Buttercream Frosting (page 318)
Yellow and pink food coloring
24 yellow or white cupcakes see
*   "the Cupcake Doctor says")*
10-inch Styrofoam ball, cut in half
8-inch round cake stand, or a mixing bowl, or
*   a new, clean flowerpot, about 8 inches*
*   in diameter, to serve as a pedestal*
Toothpicks
Fresh flowers such as unsprayed red roses,
*   yellow chrysanthemums, and mint*
*   sprigs (see "the Cupcake Doctor says")*

I. Prepare the frosting and place half in a second bowl. Use a smidgen of food coloring paste or a drop of liquid to tint one portion of frosting pale yellow and the other pale pink, blending it in once the frosting is sufficiently beaten. Place a heaping tablespoon of yellow frosting on 12 of the cupcakes and an equal amount of pink frosting on the other 12. Swirl to spread it out with a short metal spatula or a spoon, taking care to cover the cup-

the Cupcake Doctor says...

Any pale, delicate lemon-, almond- or vanilla-flavored cupcake, such as Lemon Chiffon Cupcakes (page 61), Orange Marmalade Ricotta Cupcakes (page 70), or White Russian Cupcakes (page 85), would be delicious in this recipe. Prepare the flowers for the bouquet by trimming the stems to about 3 inches long. You want the flowers to sit slightly higher than the cupcakes. Adjust the stem length as you place the flowers, shortening them more if necessary.

2. Place the foam half-ball flat side down on the cake stand or on top of a bowl or flowerpot. Insert a toothpick halfway into the middle of the bottom of a cupcake. Carefully insert the other half of the toothpick into the top center of the foam ball. Continue inserting the toothpicks, first into a cupcake and then into the foam ball, working your way, in circles, down and around the ball until all the cupcakes are placed. Leave spaces between the cupcakes. Fill in the gaps by tucking in fresh flowers and greenery. The cupcakes are ready to serve.

✿ *Once these cupcakes are placed on the Styrofoam, store in the refrigerator for no longer than 4 hours.*

cakes completely. Set the cupcakes in the refrigerator to chill for 15 minutes.

CUPCAKE CHRISTMAS TREE

• • • • •

With twelve cupcakes you can create a small tree, and with twenty-five you can create a larger one, perfect for winter holiday gatherings. Top the cupcakes of your choice with a green-tinted Buttercream Frosting or the richer Cream Cheese Frosting. Cover the cupcakes that form the tree trunk with chocolate sprinkles. Decorate the tree with candies to make it festive. Yum. Thanks to Gentiana Grajqevci of Knoxville's Bearden High School for helping me to envision cupcake trees.

✿ **SERVES UP TO 25**

Buttercream Frosting (page 318) or
    Cream Cheese Frosting (page 336;
        you'll need ½ recipe for 12 cupcakes)
Green food coloring
12 or 25 cupcakes of your choice
    (see "the Cupcake Doctor says"),
    baked in paper liners
Chocolate sprinkles
18- by 12-inch platter or board
    (for the smaller tree) or 24- by
    18-inch serving platter or board
    (for the larger tree)
Colorful candies, such as gumdrops,
    M&M's, or Skittles
Popcorn strings, for garnish (optional)

I. Prepare the frosting and once it is sufficiently beaten, set aside about 2 heaping tablespoons if making the smaller tree, ¼ cup if making the larger one. Tint the rest with the green food coloring, using 1 to 2 drops for the smaller batch, 2 to 3 drops for the larger.

2. If making the smaller tree, place a heaping tablespoon of the untinted frosting on 2 cupcakes and swirl to spread it out with a short metal spatula or a spoon, taking care to cover the tops completely. If making the larger tree, frost 4 cupcakes with untinted frosting. Cover the untinted frosting heavily with the chocolate sprinkles. Frost the remaining cupcakes with the tinted frosting. Set the cupcakes aside.

3. If making a smaller tree, set the smaller platter on a work surface with the short side closest to you. If making the larger tree, use the larger platter.

4. If making the smaller tree, place 1 cupcake near the top of the platter. Place 2 cupcakes side by side below it. Place 3 cupcakes side by side below the row of 2 cupcakes. And place 4 cupcakes side by side below the row of 3. Make sure the rows form a neat triangular Christmas tree shape. For the trunk, place 1 of the 2 cupcakes with chocolate sprinkles in the center below the 4 cupcakes. Place the last cupcake directly below this cupcake.

If making the larger tree, follow the same method for building the tree, adding a row of 5 cupcakes below the row of 4, and a row of 6 cupcakes below it. Place 2

the Cupcake Doctor says...

For fun, use the green cupcake recipe in the St. Patrick's Pistachio Cupcakes (page 188) or choose any chocolate cupcake recipe you prefer. In order to have enough batter for 25 cupcakes for the larger tree, you will need to slightly underfill the cupcake liners when you bake the cupcakes. You may need to bake them for slightly less time than the recipe says.

sprinkle-covered cupcakes side by side and centered below the row of 6 cupcakes. Place the last 2 cupcakes directly below these cupcakes to create a tree trunk.

5. Decorate the green-tinted cupcakes with the colorful candies to resemble ornaments. Garnish with popcorn strings if desired. The Cupcake Christmas Tree is ready to serve.

✿ *Store the tree without the candies, lightly covered with waxed paper or plastic wrap, in the refrigerator for no longer than 4 hours. Decorate with the candies right before serving.*

BILLIARD BALL CUPCAKES

• • • • •

This clever idea for turning cupcakes into something more is thanks to Alicia Flanery of Knoxville's Bearden High School. You begin with sixteen white cupcakes, but you decorate them with tinted coconut, and write numbers on them with a black food-decorating pen or some black frosting piped through a very thin tip. Voilà! Billiard balls! Arrange 1 through 15 in the shape of a triangle on a platter. Put the last cupcake, which is simply the white cue ball, to the side. This makes a fun conversation piece for parties for all age groups.

✿ SERVES UP TO 16

Buttercream Frosting (page 318)
16 white or yellow cupcakes of
     your choice
2 bags (7 ounces each) sweetened
     flaked coconut
Yellow, orange, red, green, blue, purple,
     brown, and black food colorings
     (or see "the Cupcake Doctor says")
Black food-decorating pen or pastry bag
     fitted with a thin decorating tip
18- by 15-inch serving platter or board

1. Prepare the frosting and place a heaping tablespoon on each of the cupcakes. Swirl to spread it out with a short metal spatula or a spoon, taking care to cover the tops completely. Set aside any leftover frosting.

2. Sprinkle 1 cupcake with the coconut, covering the top completely. Set it aside as the cue ball.

3. Divide the remaining coconut among 8 small plastic bags and add a few drops of a different color of food coloring to each bag. Close the bags and shake to distribute the coloring. Set these aside.

4. Use the food-decorating pen to number the cupcakes 1 through 15, writing the number in the center of each cupcake. Or, tint the remaining frosting with black food coloring. Fit a piping bag with a thin decorating tip and carefully pipe the ball numbers in the center of each cupcake.

5. Using a small spoon, decorate the cupcakes with the tinted coconut, leaving a circle of white around each number. Traditionally, billiard balls are the following colors—1: yellow; 2: blue; 3: red; 4: purple; 5: orange; 6: green; 7: brown; 8: black; 9: yellow stripe down the center, white circle with the number in the center of the stripe, and white on the edges; 10: blue stripe down the center, white circle with the number in the center of the stripe, and white on the edges; 11: red stripe down the center, white circle with the number in the center of the stripe, and white on the edges; 12: purple stripe down the center, white circle with the number in the center of the stripe, and white on the edges; 13: orange stripe down the center, white circle with the number in the center of the stripe, and white on the edges; 14: green stripe down the center, white circle with the number

the Cupcake Doctor says...

Because of the effort that goes into decorating these cupcakes, I start with the simplest white cupcake, such as White on White Cupcakes (page 166). Use food coloring paste, which comes in a wider variety of colors than liquid food coloring, to dye the coconut. Or, use colored sprinkles instead of dying coconut. Or, if you're using the coconut, dye it with all the colors except brown and use chocolate sprinkles for cupcakes number 7 and 15.

in the center of the stripe, and white on the edges; and 15: brown stripe down the center, white circle with the number in the center of the stripe, and white on the edges.

6. Arrange the billiard cupcakes in a triangle on a platter about 18 by 15 inches—row 1: ball 1; row 2: balls 2 and 3; row 3: balls 4, 5, 6; row 4: balls 7, 8, 9, 10; row 5: balls 11, 12, 13, 14, 15. Set the white cupcake (the cue ball), to the side. The Billiard Ball Cupcakes are ready to serve.

✿ *Store these cupcakes, lightly covered in plastic wrap or waxed paper, in the refrigerator for one day.*

CUPCAKE PURSE

· · · · ·

What can you create when you arrange seventeen cupcakes on a platter, then frost and decorate them with M&M's, Tootsie Rolls, and gold dragées? I bet you didn't think of a cupcake purse for your next girls-only party! But that's exactly what comes about if you place the cupcakes just so. For very young little girls, omit the Tootsie Roll (faux leather) trim and the dragées, and opt for a gumdrop clasp and a shower of pink sprinkles. This fun idea came from Melissa Grimes of Knoxville's Bearden High School, and food stylist Karen Tack took it to *haute couture*. I especially thank her for sharing the Tootsie Roll–flattening trick—*très chic!*

Buttercream Frosting (page 318)
1 tablespoon unsweetened cocoa powder
Pink food coloring paste or red liquid
*   food coloring*
17 white or yellow cupcakes, baked in
*   pink cupcake liners*
Pink edible glitter (optional)
17- by 15-inch platter or board
3 small Tootsie Rolls or
*   5 gumdrops all the*
*   same color*
11 brown M&M's
Gold dragées (optional)
White decorating icing or
*   food-decorating pen*
*   for writing (optional)*

❀ **SERVES UP TO 17**

I. Prepare the Buttercream Frosting: Spoon about one third of the frosting into a small bowl and add the cocoa powder. Stir until the cocoa powder is well blended. Tint the remaining frosting a nice pale pink, using about ⅛ teaspoon pink food coloring paste. If you use liquid food coloring to create the pink, start with 1 small drop of red and blend it well into the frosting to create a pale pink.

2. Place a heaping tablespoon of chocolate frosting on 5 cupcakes and spread it out smoothly with a short metal spatula or a spoon, taking care to cover the tops completely. Place any remaining chocolate frosting in a pastry bag fitted with a medium tip. Frost the remaining cupcakes with the pink frosting, again spreading it out smoothly. Sprinkle the pink frosting with pink glitter, if desired.

3. Place a row of 3 pink frosted cupcakes in the center of the platter or board. Create a handle for the purse by placing the 5 cupcakes in a half-circle, beginning above the first pink cupcake in the row and ending above the third cupcake in the row. Below the row of 3 cupcakes, center a row of 4 pink cupcakes, and below this, center a row of 5 pink cupcakes. Set the platter of cupcakes aside.

4. If using Tootsie Rolls, place them on a clean work surface and, using a heavy

the Cupcake Doctor says...

Instead of the Buttercream Frosting, you can also use the Strawberry Cream Cheese Frosting (page 341) for the purse and a half recipe of the Dark Chocolate Buttercream (page 321) for the handle. Another nice decorating trick is to flatten Starburst Fruit Chews with a rolling pin to create the faux leather details, and cut out patches and tags for your purse. For one of those fancy purses with little feet on the bottom, attach a gumdrop to the bottom edges of the first and last cupcake of the bottom row.

rolling pin, roll them out to ¼-inch thickness. Cut 1 flattened Tootsie Roll into an oval to form the purse's nameplate. Place it on the center cupcake in the top row. Cut the remaining 2 flattened Tootsie Rolls into ovals with slightly pointed ends. Place these on the first and last cupcakes in the bottom row so they resemble the leather corners on the purse.

If using gumdrops, line up 3 horizontally across the center cupcake in the top row. Place 2 each on the first and last cupcakes of the bottom row.

5. With the remaining chocolate frosting in the pastry bag, pipe a dot of frosting between the first and last chocolate handle cupcake and their adjoining pink cupcakes. Pipe a dot between each chocolate cupcake and another dot in the center of each chocolate cupcake. Place an M&M on each dot. Surround the M&M's with 5 or 6 gold dragées (optional), pushing them gently into the buttercream so they adhere.

6. If there's any chocolate frosting still left, place a thin tip on the pastry bag and pipe a scalloped border around the outside edges of the purse, starting with the first cupcake in the bottom row and working your way up the rows, across the top and down the last cupcake in each row. Then pipe a border along the outside edge of the bottom row of cupcakes. Pipe a broken border of chocolate frosting around the nameplate and over the top of the corner pieces to resemble stitching. With a tube of white decorating icing, write the name of the birthday girl or party hostess on the Tootsie Roll nameplate, if desired. The Cupcake Purse is ready to serve. (Remove the gold dragées before eating the cupcakes.)

✿ Store these cupcakes, lightly covered in plastic wrap or waxed paper, at room temperature for up to 2 days. If using sugar sprinkles, remember that they will melt into the frosting as the cupcakes are stored, so it's best to serve them right away or do the detail decorating the day of the party.

ICE CREAM CONE CAKES

• • • • •

A chapter on special cupcake creations would not be complete without this recipe, one you will use over and over for birthday parties. You can vary it each time by baking a different type of batter, using different frostings, and topping it with fun candies and other decorations. These cones look great with a large spiral of frosting, so I suggest making an extra batch. But they can also be frosted with a less over-the-top swirl. For an unusual presentation, nestle these cones in a platter of wheat grass, a cloud of cotton candy, or mounds of coconut and candies.

28 flat-bottomed wafer ice cream cones
1 recipe cupcake batter of your choice
(see "the Cupcake Doctor says")
2 recipes Buttercream Frosting
(page 318) or Chocolate
Buttercream (page 319)
Sugar sprinkles or
miniature M&M's

1. Place a rack in the center of the oven and preheat the oven to 350°F. Wrap a small square of aluminum foil around the base of each ice cream cone and stand the cones in ungreased cupcake pan cups.

❀ **SERVES UP TO 28**

the Cupcake Doctor says...

Choose a cupcake batter that contains three eggs and not a lot of other add-ins because you don't want the batter in these cupcakes to be too heavy or to rise too much. The following work well in cones: Monster Monkeys (page 109), Cupcake Zoo (page 150), or White on White Cupcakes (page 166).

2. Prepare the cupcake batter and spoon or scoop about ¼ cup batter into each cone, filling it no more than halfway. Place the pans in the oven; if your oven is not large enough, place two pans on the center rack and place the third pan in the center of the highest rack.

3. Bake the cones until the cake springs back when lightly pressed with your finger, 20 to 25 minutes. Be careful not to overbake the pan on the highest oven rack. Remove the pans from the oven and place them on wire racks to cool for 30 minutes.

4. Meanwhile, prepare the frosting.

5. Remove the foil from the base of each cone. Fill a pastry bag fitted with a large plain tip with frosting and pipe it on the cones in a generous spiral to resemble soft-serve ice cream. Decorate with the sugar sprinkles or M&M's. Carefully place the cones on a platter or back in the cupcake pan and serve.

✿ *Store these ice cream cone cakes at room temperature, lightly covered with plastic wrap, for up to 2 days.*

CUPCAKE WEDDING CAKE

• • • • •

Based on what I've read and the number of e-mails I receive, I know that cupcake wedding cakes are all the rage. People like them because they are unusual and because they can reflect the bride's and groom's personalities. To create the wedding cake, individual cupcakes, beautifully frosted, are stacked attractively on tiers with flowers and greenery cascading down. The recipe that follows serves a party of twenty-four, but you can make as large or as small a wedding cake as you desire, or several cakes. See "the Cupcake Doctor says" for how to expand this recipe to feed more guests.

Buttercream frosting of your choice
24 cupcakes of your choice baked
in gold foil liners
Gold, silver, and pink dragées
3 glass cake stands, 8, 10, and
12 inches in size (see "the
Cupcake Doctor says")
Lace ribbon or paper doilies to
fit the rounds of the stand
Small footed compote dish
to hold top cupcake
Unsprayed flowers,
such as perfect roses
and orchids, and other
greenery, for decoration

✿ **SERVES UP TO 24**

1. Place a heaping tablespoon of frosting on each cupcake and spread it out smoothly with a short metal spatula or a spoon, taking care to cover the tops completely. Decorate the frosting with the dragées, spacing them in an attractive pattern, and set the cupcakes aside.

2. Line each cake stand with lace ribbon or a paper doily. Stack the stands on top of each other to form a tiered stand.

3. Space 10 cupcakes attractively around the bottom tier, 8 cupcakes around the middle tier, and 5 cupcakes around the top tier. Line the compote dish with some of the ribbon or a doily trimmed to fit neatly and nestle 1 cupcake in it. Place the compote dish and cupcake in the center of the top tier.

4. Decorate the top cupcake with small roses or one large beautiful rose, then intersperse roses, other small flowers, and greenery around the remaining cupcakes as desired. Remind guests to remove the dragées before eating the cupcakes.

✿ *A cupcake wedding cake needs to be assembled on site and served as soon as possible.*

the Cupcake Doctor says...

If you are serving more than 24 guests, you have two options: You can create a larger and taller Cupcake Wedding Cake using the cardboard rounds and plastic columns designed for wedding cakes and available at baking supply stores (see Mail-Order Sources, page 19). A frosted cupcake measures about 3 inches across, so you can map out ahead of time what size and how many rounds you will need. Decorate the outside edges of the tiers with grosgrain ribbon adhered with the help of a glue gun. Line them with doilies or lace ribbon. A second option is to make several 24-cupcake wedding cakes and group them attractively together on a central table.

My first choice for a vanilla cupcake is a basic yellow pound cake, such as White Russian Cupcakes (page 85) minus the Kahlúa, then frosted with Buttercream Frosting (page 318) flavored with a teaspoon of pure almond extract. If chocolate is preferred, choose Chocolate Almond Cupcakes (page 41) or Chocolate Cream Cheese Cupcakes (page 34), and frost with Basic Chocolate Ganache (page 332).

Frostings and Glazes

✿ ✿ ✿

My friend Martha arrived in my kitchen exasperated. She had just been offered cupcakes with canned frosting and couldn't understand why anyone would take the time to make cupcakes and not take the time to make frosting from scratch. If you're going to fall back on canned frosting, she declared, you should at least "keep it a secret . . . and don't bring the cupcakes to a potluck and embarrass yourself!"

Strong words, perhaps, but true. I have always felt the same way about making a from-scratch frosting even if you are taking shortcuts and doctoring up a cake mix. There is no substitute for good frosting. You are far better off not frosting—my children love warm cupcakes with nothing on them at all.

But topping the cupcake, whether with a swirl of creamy chocolate buttercream, a slather of vanilla-seasoned cream cheese frosting, a coating of a warm caramel frosting right from the pan, or a drizzle of lemony glaze, is the strand of pearls setting off the classic little black dress. It is the first impression as well as the finishing touch, the opening statement and concluding remarks. Homemade frostings, therefore, should not be taken lightly. Nor should they be difficult to prepare. In this chapter you'll find a variety of frostings, most of which are a snap to assemble. One or two are cooked on the stove, some are glazes that you just whisk together, and most are either based on butter (buttercreams) or a mixture of cream cheese and butter (cream cheese frostings). I know you, too, will find this assortment delicious. You will taste the butter, the sugar, the vanilla, and, in some cases, the chocolate, and you will know in one bite that this is the real thing, not something from a to-be-avoided can.

Cupcake frostings are a little different from frostings used on layer cakes, but only slightly. You need a little less frosting, and that's why these recipes are specially created for cupcakes. The buttercreams and cream cheese frostings will work on a layer cake, but you won't have extra frosting for thick swirls. And it's not so important to make a stiff frosting that will keep the layers lined up straight and tall. Cupcakes can handle a looser, creamier frosting. That's why whipped cream is always a lovely topping for cupcakes.

I suggest frostings to go with many cupcakes, but feel free to mix and match as you choose. Just because I put a white cream cheese frosting on a white cupcake doesn't mean that you couldn't use Caramel Pan Frosting (page 345) or Dark Chocolate Buttercream (page 321). Experiment and enjoy.

BUTTERCREAM FROSTING

• • • • •

This is the basic frosting for many recipes in this book. Yes, it's simple, but the simple, pure flavors combine for a delicious taste. For a slightly lighter color, use unsalted butter and beat it several minutes with the electric mixer to lighten it further before adding the sugar.

8 tablespoons (1 stick) butter, at room temperature (see "the Cupcake Doctor says")

3 cups confectioners' sugar, sifted

3 to 4 tablespoons milk

1 teaspoon pure vanilla extract

✿ **MAKES 2½ CUPS, ENOUGH TO FROST 24 CUPCAKES (2½-INCH SIZE)**

✿ **PREPARATION TIME: 5 MINUTES**

the Cupcake Doctor says...

For almond buttercream, add 1 teaspoon pure almond extract instead of vanilla. For coconut buttercream, add 1 to 2 teaspoons coconut flavoring instead of vanilla. For lower fat, use 4 tablespoons butter and increase the milk by 1 or 2 tablespoons.

1. Place the butter in a large mixing bowl. Blend with an electric mixer on low speed until fluffy, 30 seconds. Stop the machine and add the confectioners' sugar, 3 tablespoons of the milk, and the vanilla. Blend with the mixer on low speed until the sugar is incorporated, 1 minute. Increase the speed to medium and beat until light and fluffy, 1 minute more. Add up to 1 tablespoon more milk if the frosting seems too stiff.

2. Use this frosting to frost the cupcakes of your choice.

CHOCOLATE BUTTERCREAM

· · · · ·

No cupcake book would be complete without a recipe for Chocolate Buttercream frosting. It's the frosting of my childhood, the frosting that we slathered on cupcakes and licked off beaters and spatulas and our fingers. Use this recipe to frost Cookie Dough Cupcakes (page 124), Peanut Butter Surprises (page 161), or just about any cupcake in this book. You'll have plenty of frosting to top the cupcakes generously.

✿ MAKES 3 CUPS, ENOUGH TO FROST
   24 CUPCAKES (2½-INCH SIZE) GENEROUSLY
✿ PREPARATION TIME: 10 MINUTES

5 Tips for Making Buttercream Frosting

▼ ▼ ▼

1. About 3 cups of confectioners' sugar produces the right amount of buttercream frosting for a batch of 24 cupcakes.

2. Use 1 tablespoon liquid to 1 cup sugar to 2 tablespoons plus 2 teaspoons butter.

3. Sift the confectioners' sugar to prevent lumps in the frosting.

4. Begin with soft butter. If needed, soften the butter in the microwave.

5. For a white buttercream frosting, begin with unsalted butter. Beat it on medium-high with an electric mixer to lighten the color. Use milk as the liquid.

the *Cupcake Doctor says...*

For a slightly darker color and more intense chocolate flavor, use warm water instead of milk.

8 tablespoons (1 stick) butter,
    at room temperature
½ cup unsweetened cocoa powder
3 cups confectioners' sugar, sifted
3 to 5 tablespoons milk
1 teaspoon pure vanilla extract

1. Place the butter and cocoa powder in a large mixing bowl. Blend with an electric mixer on low speed until the mixture is soft and well combined, 30 seconds. Stop the machine and add the confectioners' sugar, 3 tablespoons of the milk, and the vanilla. Blend with the mixer on low speed until the sugar is incorporated, 1 minute. Increase the speed to medium and beat until light and fluffy, 1 minute more. Add 1 to 2 tablespoons more milk if the frosting is too stiff.

2. Use this to frost the cupcakes of your choice.

DARK CHOCOLATE BUTTERCREAM

• • • • •

If you want to make a deep, dark chocolate frosting—one that is nearly black—use the darkest cocoa powder of all: Dutch process cocoa powder. I spread it on Buried Treasure Cupcakes (page 141), and it is perfect for spooky Halloween cupcakes. You'll see that the recipe yields a slightly smaller amount because it contains less butter, and yet there is still enough to frost a batch of cupcakes.

4 tablespoons (½ stick) butter,
*   at room temperature*
½ cup Dutch process cocoa powder
2¼ cups confectioners' sugar, sifted
3 to 4 tablespoons hot water

Can You Freeze Frosting?

▼ ▼ ▼

You bet. Buttercream and cream cheese frostings freeze well in plastic containers for up to one month. Let them sit at room temperature to thaw, then place in a bowl and beat with an electric mixer to lighten them before frosting the cupcakes.

❧ MAKES 2 CUPS, ENOUGH TO FROST
20 TO 24 CUPCAKES (2½-INCH SIZE)
❧ PREPARATION TIME: 10 MINUTES

the Cupcake Doctor says...

For a dark mocha frosting, substitute 1 tablespoon of brewed coffee for 1 tablespoon of the water.

1. Place the butter and cocoa powder in a large mixing bowl. Blend with an electric mixer on low speed until the mixture is soft and well combined, 30 seconds. Stop the machine and add the confectioners'

sugar and 3 tablespoons of the water. Blend with the mixer on low speed until the sugar is incorporated, 1 minute. Increase the speed to medium and beat until light and fluffy, 1 minute more. Add up to 1 tablespoon more warm water if the frosting is too stiff.

2. Use to frost the cupcakes of your choice.

MOCHA BUTTERCREAM FROSTING

• • • • •

This tan frosting is a perfect topping for Cappuccino Chip Cupcakes (page 39) and most vanilla or chocolate cupcakes.

¼ cup milk

1 heaping teaspoon instant coffee granules

8 tablespoons (1 stick) butter,
  at room temperature

2 ounces (½ bar) German's sweet chocolate,
  grated

3½ cups confectioners' sugar, sifted

1 tablespoon water, if needed

1. Place the milk and instant coffee in a small glass liquid measuring cup. Place in the microwave oven on high power until the

❀ **MAKES 3 CUPS, ENOUGH TO FROST**
   24 CUPCAKES (2½-INCH SIZE) GENEROUSLY
❀ **PREPARATION TIME: 20 MINUTES**

the Cupcake Doctor says...

For a German chocolate buttercream, just omit the coffee granules.

milk is hot enough to dissolve the instant coffee, 30 to 40 seconds. Remove and stir until the coffee is dissolved. Set aside to cool.

2. Place the butter in a large mixing bowl and add the coffee and grated chocolate. Blend with an electric mixer on low speed until the mixture has softened, 30 seconds. Stop the machine and add the confectioners' sugar. Blend with the mixer on low speed until the sugar is incorporated, 1 minute. Increase the speed to medium and beat until light and fluffy, 1 minute more. Blend in up to 1 tablespoon water if the frosting seems too stiff.

3. Use to frost the cupcakes of your choice.

MALTED MILK BUTTERCREAM

• • • • •

By spooning malted milk powder into a buttercream frosting, you have a frosting that is perfect for Malted Milk Cupcakes (page 129) or any vanilla cupcakes. For a flavor and color contrast, spread this frosting over dark chocolate cupcakes.

8 tablespoons (1 stick) butter,
    at room temperature
3½ cups confectioners' sugar, sifted
5 tablespoons malted milk powder
    (see "the Cupcake Doctor says")
¼ cup milk
1 teaspoon pure vanilla extract

✿ MAKES 3 CUPS, ENOUGH TO FROST
    24 CUPCAKES (2½-INCH SIZE) GENEROUSLY
✿ PREPARATION TIME: 10 MINUTES

the Cupcake Doctor says...

I used Ovaltine malted milk powder in this recipe.

1. Place the butter in a large mixing bowl. Blend with an electric mixer on low speed until fluffy, 30 seconds. Stop the machine and add the confectioners' sugar, malted milk powder, milk, and vanilla. Blend with the mixer on low speed until the sugar is incorporated, 1 minute. Increase the speed to medium and beat until light and fluffy, 1 minute more.

2. Use to frost the cupcakes of your choice.

CREAMY LEMON FROSTING

· · · · ·

Pale yellow in color and vibrantly lemon in taste, this is a nice springtime frosting on yellow cupcakes, or just the right touch for Fresh Pear and Gingerbread Cupcakes (page 59) in the fall. Because the gingerbread recipe makes just fourteen cupcakes, the yield for this recipe is smaller than the others in this book. See "the Cupcake Doctor says" for adapting it for use with larger recipes.

3 tablespoons butter, at room temperature
3 ounces cream cheese, at room temperature
1½ to 2 cups confectioners' sugar, sifted
1 teaspoon grated lemon zest
1 teaspoon fresh lemon juice

1. Place the butter and cream cheese in a large mixing bowl. Blend with an electric mixer on low speed until fluffy, 30 seconds. Stop the machine and add 1½ cups of the confectioners' sugar, the lemon zest, and lemon juice. Blend with the mixer on low speed until the sugar is incorporated, 1 minute. Increase the mixer speed to

✿ MAKES 1½ CUPS, ENOUGH TO FROST
14 CUPCAKES (2½-INCH SIZE)
✿ PREPARATION TIME: 10 MINUTES

medium and beat until light and fluffy, 1 minute longer, adding up to ½ cup more sugar, a tablespoon at a time, if needed to make a spreadable consistency.

2. Use to frost the cupcakes of your choice.

the Cupcake Doctor says...

If you double the ingredients, this will frost 24 cupcakes. A whole lemon is perfect for the doubled recipe. Substitute orange zest and juice to turn this frosting into a Creamy Orange Frosting.

CREAMY LEMONADE FROSTING

• • • • •

You'll love how the tart lemonade concentrate balances the flavor of the sugar and the rich cream cheese and butter. It was created for the light Lemonade Angel Cakes (page 101), but you can use it on any light-colored cupcake.

1 package (8 ounces) cream cheese,
    at room temperature
8 tablespoons (1 stick) butter,
    at room temperature
3 cups sifted confectioners' sugar
3 tablespoons thawed lemonade concentrate
1 teaspoon grated lemon zest

✿ MAKES 3 CUPS, ENOUGH TO FROST
    24 CUPCAKES (2½-INCH SIZE) GENEROUSLY
✿ PREPARATION TIME: 10 MINUTES

the Cupcake Doctor says...

Use pink lemonade concentrate for a frosting that blushes pink.

1. Place the butter and cream cheese in a large mixing bowl. Blend with an electric mixer on low speed until fluffy, 30 seconds. Stop the machine and add the confectioners' sugar, lemonade concentrate, and zest. Blend with the mixer on low speed until the sugar is incorporated, 1 minute. Increase the speed to medium and beat until light and fluffy, 1 minute more.

2. Use to frost the cupcakes of your choice.

MARMALADE BUTTERCREAM FROSTING

• • • • •

If there were frostings just for adults, this might be one. But I know if I say that, some child with a sophisticated palate will tell me how much he or she loves it. So I'll just say that this is a bright, fluffy buttercream with deep, pungent flavor that anyone will enjoy. It is less sweet and more buttery than the other buttercreams in this book. The pieces of orange rind in the marmalade give it texture and interest. It's nice on Orange Marmalade Ricotta Cupcakes (page 70), spice cupcakes, or any plain cupcakes with a pound cake-like texture.

8 tablespoons (1 stick) butter,
    at room temperature
2½ cups confectioners' sugar, sifted
2 to 3 tablespoons fresh or commercial
    orange juice
1 heaping tablespoon orange marmalade

✿ **MAKES 2½ CUPS, ENOUGH TO FROST 24 CUPCAKES (2½-INCH SIZE)**
✿ **PREPARATION TIME: 5 MINUTES**

1. Place the butter in a large mixing bowl. Blend with an electric mixer on low speed until fluffy, 30 seconds. Stop the machine and add the confectioners' sugar and

2 tablespoons of the orange juice. Blend with the mixer on low speed until the sugar is incorporated, 1 minute. Stir in the orange marmalade. Increase the speed to medium and beat until light and fluffy, 1 minute more. Blend in up to 1 tablespoon more orange juice if the frosting seems too stiff.

2. Use to frost the cupcakes of your choice.

the Cupcake Doctor says...

Vary the intensity of the marmalade flavor by using different marmalades. Supermarket marmalade tends to be milder, whereas Scottish marmalade is stronger. Try using lemon or lime marmalade, too.

CHOCOLATE SYRUP FROSTING

• • • • •

This is one of my favorite chocolate frostings, because it is both intense and creamy at the same time. It is as easy to spread onto cupcakes as it is to lick off the tops! I first tasted this frosting when it was submitted, along with a layer cake recipe in my Web site's annual recipe contest, by Maryann Wilkerson of Arkansas. Now I slather it onto cupcakes, both chocolate- and vanilla-flavored.

It is one of the two recommended frostings for the Best Birthday Cupcakes with Two Frostings (page 138).

8 tablespoons (1 stick) butter,
    at room temperature
½ cup unsweetened cocoa powder
½ cup chocolate syrup
3 cups confectioners' sugar, sifted
1 tablespoon milk
1 teaspoon pure vanilla extract

1. Place the butter, cocoa powder, and chocolate syrup in a large mixing bowl. Blend with an electric mixer on low speed until just combined, 30 seconds. Stop the machine and add the sugar, milk, and vanilla. Blend with the mixer on low speed until the sugar is incorporated, 1 minute.

❀ **MAKES 3½ CUPS, ENOUGH TO FROST**
    24 CUPCAKES (2½-INCH SIZE) GENEROUSLY
❀ **PREPARATION TIME: 10 MINUTES**

Increase the speed to medium and beat until light and fluffy, 1 minute more.

2. Use to frost the cupcakes of your choice.

the Cupcake Doctor says...

This recipe has a looser texture than some of the other buttercream frostings, because of the chocolate syrup. Be sure that you measure the confectioners' sugar first, then sift it.

BASIC CHOCOLATE GANACHE

• • • • •

The complex flavor and rich, creamy texture of chocolate ganache make many people think that it is difficult to make. But it is absolutely the easiest frosting there is, with just two ingredients— semisweet chocolate and heavy cream—and possibly an additional flavoring, but fine on its own. What I have learned about making ganache is this: It is best prepared in a stainless steel bowl; semisweet chocolate chips work perfectly; you need to make sure the cream heats long enough to be really hot; you must continue to stir until all the chocolate has melted; and it helps if you allow time for the ganache to rest, uncovered, on the kitchen counter for about an hour before using. It will thicken up a bit to a spreadable consistency. For a stiffer ganache, cover the bowl with plastic wrap and chill it for an hour or two to use, say, for filling Inside-Out Peanut Butter Cupcakes (page 50, and see "the Cupcake Doctor says"). It also fills Warm Chocolate Cupcakes with Molten Centers (page 29).

✿ **MAKES 2 CUPS, ENOUGH TO FROST 24 CUPCAKES (2½-INCH SIZE)**

✿ **PREPARATION TIME: 5 MINUTES**

✿ **SETTING TIME: 1 HOUR**

¾ *cup heavy (whipping) cream*

8 ounces (1⅓ cups) semisweet chocolate
   chips

1 tablespoon liqueur of your choice or
   1 teaspoon pure vanilla extract
   (optional)

1. Place the cream in a small heavy saucepan over medium heat. Bring it to a boil, stirring. Meanwhile, place the chocolate chips in a large stainless steel mixing bowl. Remove the cream from the heat and pour it over the chocolate. Stir with a wooden spoon until the chocolate has melted. Stir in the liqueur, if desired. Let sit at room temperature for 1 hour or

the Cupcake Doctor says...

Double the recipe if you are making Inside-Out Peanut Butter Cupcakes. For a deeper flavor, but with the ease of using chocolate chips, try the Ghirardelli Double Chocolate Baking Chips.

chill for 20 to 30 minutes so it thickens into a spreadable consistency.

2. Use to frost or fill the cupcakes of your choice.

CREAMY CHOCOLATE BLENDER GANACHE

• • • • •

Judy Rosenberg, the Boston baker (Rosie's Bakery) and cookbook author, inspired me to develop this recipe for a glossy ganachelike frosting that thickens in the blender. Starting with Judy's recipe, I came up with a version that thickens more quickly. It is delicious spread on Chocolate Cream Cheese Cupcakes (page 34)

or just about any chocolate cupcake. I use semisweet chocolate chips because they're always on hand in my kitchen!

1 cup semisweet chocolate chips
½ cup (4 ounces) evaporated milk
½ teaspoon pure vanilla extract

1. Place the chocolate chips in a small glass bowl and melt them in the microwave oven on high power for 1 minute. Remove from the microwave and stir with a wooden spoon until all the chips have melted.

2. Place the warm chocolate in a blender along with the evaporated milk and vanilla. Blend on high speed until the frosting is thick and glossy, 2 minutes. Pour the frosting into a clean bowl and let it sit on the

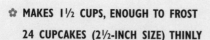

✿ **MAKES 1½ CUPS, ENOUGH TO FROST 24 CUPCAKES (2½-INCH SIZE) THINLY**
✿ **PREPARATION TIME: 5 MINUTES**
✿ **RESTING TIME: 20 MINUTES**

counter for 20 minutes. It should thicken up enough for spreading.

3. Use to frost the cupcakes of your choice.

CREAM CHEESE FROSTING

· · · · ·

This is a perennial favorite frosting for cupcakes, whether they are Red Velvet (page 36)—or any rich chocolate cupcakes—or Plum Good Cupcakes (page 152). Because some people like to frost liberally, while others like just enough frosting, I have included two recipes with different yields. Enjoy every bite.

PLENTY OF FROSTING:

1 package (8 ounces) reduced-fat cream cheese, at room temperature

4 tablespoons (½ stick) butter, at room temperature

3 cups confectioners' sugar, sifted

2 teaspoons pure vanilla extract

✿ **MAKES 3 CUPS, ENOUGH TO FROST 24 CUPCAKES (2½-INCH SIZE) GENEROUSLY**
✿ **PREPARATION TIME: 5 MINUTES**

JUST ENOUGH FROSTING:

2 packages (3 ounces each) reduced-fat cream cheese, at room temperature

4 tablespoons (½ stick) butter, at room temperature

3 cups confectioners' sugar, sifted

1 teaspoon pure vanilla extract

✿ **MAKES 2 CUPS, ENOUGH TO FROST 24 CUPCAKES (2½-INCH SIZE)**
✿ **PREPARATION TIME: 5 MINUTES**

the Cupcake Doctor says...

I prefer to cut calories and fat where I can and find reduced-fat cream cheese works well without sacrificing flavor. If you prefer regular cream cheese, use that. Don't use fat-free cream cheese.

1. Place the cream cheese and butter in a large mixing bowl. Blend with an electric mixer on low speed until combined, 30 seconds for either batch. Stop the machine. Add the confectioners' sugar, a little at a time, blending with the mixer on low speed until the sugar is well incorporated, 1 minute. Add the vanilla, then increase the mixer speed to medium and blend the frosting until fluffy, 1 minute more.

2. Use to frost the cupcakes of your choice.

VARIATION Coconut Cream Cheese Frosting: Add 1 to 2 teaspoons coconut flavoring to the frosting instead of the vanilla extract.

CINNAMON CREAM CHEESE FROSTING

• • • • •

*J*ust try to resist this frosting spread over Cinnamon Toast Cupcakes (page 112) or Monster Monkeys (page 109). It is so good, I've even been known to spread it over regular toast!

1 package (8 ounces) reduced-fat cream
    cheese, at room temperature
4 tablespoons (½ stick) butter,
    at room temperature
3 cups confectioners' sugar,
    sifted
1 teaspoon ground
    cinnamon

✿ **MAKES 3 CUPS, ENOUGH TO FROST**
    24 CUPCAKES (2½-INCH SIZE) GENEROUSLY
✿ **PREPARATION TIME: 5 MINUTES**

the Cupcake Doctor says...

If the cream cheese is too cold, unwrap the package and soften it on a plate in the microwave oven on high power for 20 seconds.

1. Place the cream cheese and butter in a large mixing bowl. Blend with an electric mixer on low speed until combined, 30 seconds. Stop the machine. Add the confectioners' sugar, a little at a time, blending with the mixer on low speed until the sugar is well incorporated, 1 minute. Add the cinnamon, then increase the mixer speed to medium and blend the frosting until fluffy, 1 minute more.

2. Use to frost the cupcakes of your choice.

BUTTERSCOTCH MAPLE FROSTING

• • • • •

This rich and luxurious cream cheese frosting, with maple and butterscotch flavors, is a winning combination that you'll want to try on Triple Butterscotch Cupcakes (page 83) and Prune Spice Cupcakes (page 81), as well as any pound cake–like cupcake.

1 package (8 ounces) reduced-fat cream
    cheese, at room temperature
4 tablespoons (½ stick) butter,
    at room temperature
2 to 2½ cups confectioners' sugar,
    sifted
½ teaspoon maple flavoring
½ cup melted butterscotch chips
½ cup toasted pecans, chopped,
    for garnish (optional)

the Cupcake Doctor says...

Keep a little bottle of maple flavoring on your baking shelf and you'll find it particularly complements butterscotch and vanilla flavors. Add a drop or two to plain frostings or a generous teaspoon to cake batters for a more complex taste.

1. Place the cream cheese and butter in a large mixing bowl. Blend with an electric mixer on low speed until combined, 30 seconds. Stop the machine. Add 2 cups of the confectioners' sugar, a little at a time, blending with the mixer on low speed until the sugar is well incorporated,

✿ MAKES 3 CUPS, ENOUGH TO FROST
    24 CUPCAKES (2½-INCH SIZE) GENEROUSLY
✿ PREPARATION TIME: 5 TO 7 MINUTES

1 minute. Add the maple flavoring and the melted butterscotch chips. Increase the mixer speed to medium and blend the frosting until fluffy, 1 minute longer, adding up to ½ cup more

sugar, 1 tablespoon at a time, if needed to make a spreadable consistency.

2. Use to frost the cupcakes of your choice. Sprinkle toasted pecans on top if desired.

STRAWBERRY CREAM CHEESE FROSTING

• • • • •

I have met people who say they eat this frosting on its own, without a cupcake. And I'll have to admit, it's that good. But I like to pair it with cake and suggest the Pretty in Pink Strawberry Cupcakes (page 106), The Best Birthday Cupcakes with Two Frostings (page 138), or any vanilla cupcake you happen to be baking.

✿ MAKES 3 CUPS, ENOUGH TO FROST
24 CUPCAKES (2½-INCH SIZE) GENEROUSLY
✿ PREPARATION TIME: 10 MINUTES

the Cupcake Doctor says...

It takes about ¾ cup rinsed, well-drained, and hulled strawberries to make ½ cup mashed. Take care to drain out as much juice as you can and reserve it. If you need liquid to pull the frosting together, add a dribble of the fresh reserved juice.

1 package (8 ounces) reduced-fat cream cheese, at room temperature
4 tablespoons (½ stick) butter, at room temperature
3 to 3½ cups confectioners' sugar, sifted
½ cup mashed, drained fresh strawberries (see "the Cupcake Doctor says")

1. Place the cream cheese and butter in a large mixing bowl. Blend with an electric mixer on low speed until combined, 30 seconds. Stop the machine. Add 3 cups of the confectioners' sugar and the drained strawberries. Blend the frosting on low until the sugar is incorporated, 1 minute. Increase the mixer speed to medium and blend the frosting until fluffy, 30 to 45 seconds longer, adding up to ½ cup more sugar if needed to make a spreadable consistency.

2. Use to frost the cupcakes of your choice.

WHITE CHOCOLATE PEPPERMINT CREAM CHEESE FROSTING

• • • • •

I dream about this frosting slathered on Red Velvet cupcakes (page 36), Holiday Gift Cupcakes (page 216), or any dark chocolate cupcakes, because I love the cool creaminess of it. And, as a bonus, it's a breeze to make.

❀ **MAKES 3 CUPS, ENOUGH TO FROST**
   24 CUPCAKES (2½-INCH SIZE) GENEROUSLY
❀ **PREPARATION TIME: 10 MINUTES**

6 ounces white chocolate,
   coarsely chopped
4 ounces (half an 8-ounce package)
   reduced-fat cream cheese,
   at room temperature
4 tablespoons (½ stick) butter,
   at room temperature
1 teaspoon peppermint extract
2 to 2½ cups confectioners' sugar,
   sifted

1. Place the white chocolate in a small glass bowl in the microwave oven on high power for 1 minute. Remove the bowl from the oven and stir with a wooden spoon or rubber spatula until it is smooth. Set the chocolate aside to cool.

2. Place the cream cheese and butter in a large mixing bowl. Beat with an electric mixer on low speed until well combined, 30 seconds. Stop the machine. Add the melted white chocolate and blend on low speed until just combined, 30 seconds. Add the peppermint extract and 2 cups of the confectioners' sugar and blend on low speed until the sugar is incorporated, 30 seconds more. Increase the mixer speed to medium and beat until the frosting is fluffy, 1 minute more, adding up to ½ cup more sugar if needed to make a spreadable consistency.

the Cupcake Doctor says...

Feel free to fold in up to ½ cup crushed peppermint candy for a crunchy and creamy frosting!

3. Use to frost any chocolate cupcakes of your choice.

CARAMEL PAN FROSTING

· · · · ·

Slightly different from my favorite caramel frosting included in previous books, this frosting uses dark brown sugar rather than light, and heavy cream instead of milk (it works nicely with milk, too). Spoon this over A Cupcake Zoo (page 150).

8 tablespoons (1 stick) butter
⅔ cup firmly packed dark brown sugar
½ cup heavy (whipping) cream and
    1 to 2 tablespoons more, if needed
3 cups confectioners' sugar, sifted
1 teaspoon pure vanilla extract

I. Place the butter in a heavy medium-size saucepan over medium heat. Add the brown sugar and stir with a wooden spoon until the butter and sugar melt and the mixture is smooth and bubbly, 2 to 3 minutes. Cook, stirring, for 1 minute. Add the cream and stir another minute as the mixture becomes thickened and shiny. Remove the pan from the heat and stir in the confectioners' sugar and vanilla until smooth. Add a bit more cream if needed to make the frosting spreadable.

2. Spoon immediately over the cupcakes of your choice.

the Cupcake Doctor says...

This frosting is incredible poured warm over vanilla ice cream (it will set as it cools). Add chopped toasted pecans or sliced fresh peaches for a real treat.

❀ **MAKES 3 CUPS, ENOUGH TO FROST**
   24 CUPCAKES (2½-INCH SIZE) GENEROUSLY
❀ **PREPARATION TIME: 10 MINUTES**
❀ **COOKING TIME: 5 MINUTES**

COCONUT PECAN FROSTING

• • • • •

Some frostings you just don't mess with, and this is one of them. It isn't new—in fact, it's the classic frosting for German chocolate cake. But good things bear repeating, and since German Chocolate Cupcakes are in this cookbook (page 27), they should be frosted with this rich frosting.

1 can (12 ounces) evaporated milk

1½ cups granulated sugar

12 tablespoons (1½ sticks)
    unsalted butter

4 large egg yolks, slightly beaten

1½ teaspoons pure vanilla extract

1 package (7 ounces; 2⅓ cups) sweetened
    flaked coconut

1½ cups chopped pecans

I. Place the evaporated milk, sugar, butter, egg yolks, and vanilla in a large saucepan over medium heat. Cook, stirring constantly with a wooden spoon, until thickened and golden brown in color, 10 to 12 minutes. Remove from the heat.

✿ **MAKES 3 CUPS, ENOUGH TO FROST
24 CUPCAKES (2½-INCH SIZE) GENEROUSLY**

✿ **PREPARATION TIME: 5 MINUTES**

✿ **COOKING TIME: 10 TO 12 MINUTES**

✿ **COOLING TIME: 20 MINUTES**

Stir in the coconut and pecans. Cool the frosting to room temperature before spreading, 20 minutes.

2. Use to frost the cupcakes of your choice.

the Cupcake Doctor says...

The pecans and coconut are better if lightly toasted in a 350°F oven for 6 to 7 minutes, but that is up to you. And the cooked frosting really needs to cool down for 20 minutes before you will be able to spread it on the cupcakes. If you need to speed the cooling process a little, place the pan of frosting in a bowl of ice water, stir constantly, and the frosting will cool in 10 to 15 minutes. Or pour the frosting into a shallow pan and stir. The increased surface area will speed cooling.

MARSHMALLOW FROSTING

• • • • •

While I was developing the S'mores Cupcakes (page 121), I knew the frosting had to contain marshmallows. And so it does—marshmallow creme is the main ingredient! This recipe is super easy, just right for those cupcakes you need to bake at 9:00 P.M. the night before the bake sale.

1 jar (13 ounces) marshmallow creme
3 tablespoons regular or
    reduced-fat sour cream
1 teaspoon pure vanilla extract

❀ **MAKES 2 CUPS, ENOUGH TO FROST 24 CUPCAKES (2½-INCH SIZE)**
❀ **PREPARATION TIME: 5 MINUTES**

the Cupcake Doctor says...

It's important to soften the marshmallow creme in the microwave. This makes it easier to remove it from the jar.

1. Remove the lid from glass jar of marshmallow creme and place the jar in the microwave on high power for 45 seconds. With a small rubber spatula, scrape the creme out of the jar and into a mixing bowl. Add the sour cream and vanilla extract. With an electric mixer, beat the mixture on medium speed until the frosting is fluffy and well blended, 1 minute.

2. Use to frost any chocolate cupcakes of your choice.

SWEETENED WHIPPED CREAM

· · · · ·

A versatile topping for cakes, pies, and all sorts of frozen desserts (see Chocolate Almond Cupcakes, page 41), sweetened whipped cream is easy to prepare and so much better tasting than frozen whipped topping. Begin with heavy cream, add confectioners' sugar to sweeten it, and that's it, unless you want to add a little vanilla extract for a fuller flavor.

1 cup heavy (whipping) cream, chilled

¼ cup confectioners' sugar

½ teaspoon vanilla extract (optional)

✿ **MAKES 2 CUPS, ENOUGH TO FROST 24 CUPCAKES (2½-INCH SIZE)**
✿ **PREPARATION TIME: 5 MINUTES**

1. Place a large clean mixing bowl and electric mixer beaters in the freezer for a few minutes while you assemble the ingredients. Pour the cream into the chilled bowl and beat with the electric mixer on high speed until the cream has thickened, 1½ minutes. Stop the machine and add the sugar and vanilla, if desired. Beat the cream and sugar on high speed until stiff peaks form, 1 to 2 minutes more.

2. Use to frost the cupcakes of your choice.

the Cupcake Doctor says...

The nice thing about frosting cupcakes with Sweetened Whipped Cream is that you can just plop a tablespoon onto each cupcake and that's it. Whipped cream doesn't need to be smoothed and fussed with like other frostings.

LEMONY CREAM

• • • • •

Spoon this lemon curd and whipped cream combination on top of the Mini Lemon Curd Cupcakes (page 63) or any lemon or vanilla cupcakes you like. It's also unbelievably good spooned on top of first-of-the-season ripe strawberries.

1 cup heavy (whipping) cream,
    chilled
1 tablespoon confectioners' sugar
⅓ to ½ cup lemon curd

1. Place a large clean mixing bowl and electric mixer beaters in the freezer for a few minutes while you assemble the

✿ **MAKES 2 CUPS, ENOUGH TO FROST 48 MINI (1¾- TO 2-INCH) CUPCAKES OR 24 REGULAR (2½-INCH) CUPCAKES**

✿ **PREPARATION TIME: 5 MINUTES**

the Cupcake Doctor says...

If you want whipped cream that is easier to tote, whip ½ cup whipping cream and combine this with 1 cup of thawed whipped topping. This mixture will not need to be seasoned with the sugar as the whipped topping is already sweetened. Fold in the lemon curd and frost the cupcakes.

ingredients. Pour the cream into the chilled bowl and beat with the electric mixer on high speed until the cream has thickened, 1½ minutes. Stop the machine and add the sugar. Beat the cream and sugar on high speed until stiff peaks form, 1 to 2 minutes more. With a rubber spatula, gently fold in ⅓ cup of the lemon curd. Taste, adding more lemon curd, if desired.

2. Use this right away to frost the cupcakes of your choice, or chill for up to 8 hours before using.

FROSTY LEMON GLAZE

• • • • •

I love this glaze on Lemon Chiffon Cupcakes (page 61), White on White Cupcakes (page 166), or Fresh Pear and Gingerbread Cupcakes (page 59). It's intense and very lemony. The trick is to heat the lemon juice to reduce it by half, and then whisk in the sugar while the lemon juice is warm.

3 large lemons, juiced
    (about 6 tablespoons juice)
1¼ cups confectioners' sugar, sifted

❀ **MAKES 1¼ CUPS, ENOUGH TO GLAZE 24 CUPCAKES (2½-INCH SIZE)**
❀ **PREPARATION TIME: 5 MINUTES**
❀ **COOKING TIME: 5 MINUTES**

the Cupcake Doctor says...

How to get the most juice out of a lemon? Buy juicy lemons in the first place, ones that are heavy for their size, not those big lemons that are all thick skin and little pulp. Press the lemons into the kitchen counter and roll them back and forth to loosen the pulp and release the juice. Or place the lemons in the microwave oven for 10 seconds to warm them slightly. Or do both.

1. Place the lemon juice in a small saucepan over medium-low heat and simmer, uncovered, until the juice has reduced by half, about 5 minutes. Remove the pan from the heat. Whisk in the sugar until all the lumps disappear. Let the pan rest for the glaze to cool, 15 minutes.

2. Spoon over the cupcakes of your choice.

How to Glaze a Cupcake
▼ ▼ ▼

Next to serving a cupcake with a dusting of confectioners' sugar, glazing is the quickest way to frost a cupcake, and it is a relatively lower-fat option. I have found the easiest way to glaze is to line up the cupcakes on a baking rack placed over a sheet of waxed paper to catch the drips. For a blanketed look, use a big serving spoon or ladle and spoon a couple of tablespoons of glaze over each cupcake, letting the glaze drip down the sides of the liners. For a cross-hatch pattern, drizzle the glaze across the cupcake in two or three lines with a soupspoon, then change directions and glaze in two or three lines at right angles to the first lines. If you are garnishing the glaze with citrus peel, finely chopped nuts, or sugar sprinkles, do so before the glaze has set, so the garnish will stick. Let glazed cupcakes rest 10 minutes for the glaze to set before serving.

SIMPLE CHOCOLATE GLAZE

• • • • •

Spoon this glaze over chocolate cupcakes, vanilla ice cream, slices of fresh pound cake—you name it. What I adore about it is that it looks and tastes impressive yet is a breeze to prepare. Four ingredients in a saucepan. What could be simpler?

1 cup semisweet chocolate or
    white chocolate chips
3 tablespoons butter
2 tablespoons light corn syrup
½ teaspoon pure vanilla extract

✿ **MAKES 1 CUP, ENOUGH TO GLAZE
    24 CUPCAKES (2½-INCH SIZE) THINLY**
✿ **PREPARATION TIME: 5 MINUTES**
✿ **COOKING TIME: 2 TO 3 MINUTES**

the Cupcake Doctor says...

You don't have to use semisweet or white chocolate chips for this recipe—a cup of chopped chocolate will do. But chips are easy to measure and ready to go.

1. Place the chocolate chips, butter, and corn syrup in a small saucepan over low heat and stir until the chocolate melts and the glaze comes together, 2 to 3 minutes. Remove the pan from the heat and stir in the vanilla.

2. With a soupspoon, drizzle the warm glaze over the cupcakes of your choice in lines, then switch direction and drizzle in lines again to create a crisscross pattern.

CINNAMON CRÈME ANGLAISE

• • • • •

When the cupcake is elegant and warm, like Warm Chocolate Cupcakes with Molten Centers (page 29), you don't so much need a frosting as you do a sauce. In this case, a custard sauce with a smidgen of cinnamon is just the right touch. It may be made the day ahead of serving. If you want to reheat it, microwave on high power, uncovered, for 1 to 1½ minutes. Stop and stir after 45 seconds.

❀ **MAKES 2 CUPS, ENOUGH TO SPOON ALONGSIDE 24 WARM CUPCAKES (2½-INCH SIZE)**
❀ **PREPARATION TIME: 5 MINUTES**
❀ **COOKING TIME: 5 TO 7 MINUTES**

2 cups whole milk

5 tablespoons sugar

Pinch of salt

4 large egg yolks

1 teaspoon pure vanilla extract

½ teaspoon ground cinnamon

I. Place the milk, sugar, and salt in a heavy-bottomed medium-size saucepan over medium-high heat. Cook, stirring with a wooden spoon, until the sugar dissolves, 2 to 3 minutes. Meanwhile, place the egg yolks in a medium-size mixing bowl and beat with a fork until lemon-colored. Remove the saucepan from the heat and ladle a large spoonful of the hot milk mixture over the egg yolks, stirring the yolks gently. Transfer the yolks to the milk mixture and stir to combine. Place the pan over medium-low heat and cook, stirring constantly, until the sauce thickens, 3 to 4 minutes. Remove the pan from the heat and stir in the vanilla and cinnamon.

2. Spoon a generous tablespoon of the warm sauce onto plates and place Warm Chocolate Cupcakes with Molten Centers on it. Or, chill the sauce and serve cold alongside the cupcake of your choice.

the Cupcake Doctor says...

Omit the cinnamon and you have a plain crème anglaise, a useful sauce for all sorts of desserts. It may also be served warm or cold.

EASY HOT FUDGE SAUCE

• • • • •

This recipe for fudge sauce has been in our family for years. My mother used to make it and keep leftovers in a canning jar in the refrigerator. It would last until we got hungry for vanilla ice cream and hot fudge sauce— sometimes as long as a week. It is nice warmed and spooned over Hot Fudge Spumoni Ice Cream Cakes (page 47).

1½ cups granulated sugar
8 tablespoons unsweetened
    cocoa powder
¼ cup all-purpose flour
Pinch of salt
2 cups milk
2 tablespoons butter
2 teaspoons pure vanilla extract

1. Place the sugar, cocoa powder, flour, and salt in a medium-size saucepan and stir to combine. Whisk in the milk and

✿ **MAKES 3 CUPS, ENOUGH TO SPOON**
    OVER 20 TO 22 CUPCAKES (2½-INCH SIZE)
✿ **PREPARATION TIME: 5 MINUTES**
✿ **COOKING TIME: 5 TO 6 MINUTES**

place over medium heat. Stir and cook until the sauce comes together and begins to thicken, 3 to 4 minutes. Add the butter and vanilla and continue to stir until thickened and smooth, 2 minutes more.

2. Spoon over the cupcakes of your choice.

the Cupcake Doctor says...

Use Dutch process cocoa powder in this recipe instead of regular cocoa powder and the sauce will turn out deeper and darker in color. Whichever cocoa powder you use, the sauce will keep for a week or so, covered, in the refrigerator. Reheat in a saucepan over low heat, stirring frequently.

Approximate Equivalents

1 stick butter = 8 tbs = 4 oz = ½ cup

1 cup all-purpose presifted flour or

dried bread crumbs = 5 oz

1 cup granulated sugar = 8 oz

1 cup (packed) brown sugar = 6 oz

1 cup confectioners' sugar = 4½ oz

1 cup honey or syrup = 12 oz

1 cup grated cheese = 4 oz

1 cup dried beans = 6 oz

1 large egg = about 2 oz = about 3 tbs

1 egg yolk = about 1 tbs

1 egg white = about 2 tbs

Weight Conversions

U.S.	METRIC	U.S.	METRIC
½ oz	15 g	7 oz	200 g
1 oz	30 g	8 oz	250 g
1½ oz	45 g	9 oz	275 g
2 oz	60 g	10 oz	300 g
2½ oz	75 g	11 oz	325 g
3 oz	90 g	12 oz	350 g
3½ oz	100 g	13 oz	375 g
4 oz	125 g	14 oz	400 g
5 oz	150 g	15 oz	450 g
6 oz	175 g	1 lb	500 g

Please note that all conversions are approximate but close enough to be useful when converting from one system to another.

Liquid Conversions

U.S.	IMPERIAL	METRIC
2 tbs	1 fl oz	30 ml
3 tbs	1½ fl oz	45 ml
¼ cup	2 fl oz	60 ml
⅓ cup	2½ fl oz	75 ml
⅓ cup + 1 tbs	3 fl oz	90 ml
⅓ cup + 2 tbs	3½ fl oz	100 ml
½ cup	4 fl oz	125 ml
⅔ cup	5 fl oz	150 ml
¾ cup	6 fl oz	175 ml
¾ cup + 2 tbs	7 fl oz	200 ml
1 cup	8 fl oz	250 ml
1 cup + 2 tbs	9 fl oz	275 ml
1¼ cups	10 fl oz	300 ml
1⅓ cups	11 fl oz	325 ml
1½ cups	12 fl oz	350 ml
1⅔ cups	13 fl oz	375 ml
1¾ cups	14 fl oz	400 ml
1¾ cups + 2 tbs	15 fl oz	450 ml
2 cups (1 pint)	16 fl oz	500 ml
2½ cups	20 fl oz (1 pint)	600 ml
3¾ cups	1½ pints	900 ml
4 cups	1¾ pints	1 liter

Oven Temperatures

°F	Gas	°C	°F	Gas	°C
250	½	120	400	6	200
275	1	140	425	7	220
300	2	150	450	8	230
325	3	160	475	9	240
350	4	180	500	10	260
375	5	190			

Note: Reduce the temperature by 20°C (68°F) for fan-assisted ovens.

Index

✿ ✿ ✿

045326064